Palgrave Histories of Policing, Punishment and Justice

Series Editor
David G. Barrie
University of Western Australia
Crawley, Australia

Since the 1960s, studies of police, punishment and the courts have been an integral and popular part of historical scholarship, and have followed in the historical trajectory of a more expansive criminal justice apparatus around the world. This international book series aims to examine and debate some of the most pressing issues and problems in the field, and to stimulate new directions in research. It will showcase the work of both emerging and leading scholars of the social, cultural and institutional histories of police, punishment and the judicial sphere, and welcomes work grounded in various disciplines including criminology, sociology, history, law, legal history and political science.

More information about this series at
http://www.palgrave.com/gp/series/15080

Alison Adam
Editor

Crime and the Construction of Forensic Objectivity from 1850

palgrave
macmillan

Editor
Alison Adam
Sheffield Hallam University
Sheffield, UK

Palgrave Histories of Policing, Punishment and Justice
ISBN 978-3-030-28839-6   ISBN 978-3-030-28837-2   (eBook)
https://doi.org/10.1007/978-3-030-28837-2

This Palgrave Macmillan imprint is published by the registered company Springer Nature Switzerland AG.
The registered company address is: Gewerbestrasse 11, 6330 Cham, Switzerland

Acknowledgements

I should like to thank the staff at Palgrave, particularly Liam Inscoe-Jones and Josie Taylor for their support in putting together this edited collection. We would also like to thank the series editor, David Barrie. Earlier versions of the ideas in a number of the chapters were presented at the British Crime Historians Symposium in 2016 and 2018 and we would like to thank colleagues for helpful suggestions made at these conferences.

Contents

1   *Crime and the Construction of Forensic Objectivity from 1850*: Introduction   1
Alison Adam

Part I   Forensic Representations: Photographic, Spatial, Dental and Mathematical   15

2   Bodies in the Bed: English Crime Scene Photographs as Documentary Images   17
Amy Helen Bell

3   Murder in Miniature: Reconstructing the Crime Scene in the English Courtroom   43
Alexa Neale

4   The Biggar Murder: 'A Triumph for Forensic Odontology'   69
Alison Adam

5   Making Forensic Evaluations: Forensic Objectivity in the
    Swedish Criminal Justice System   99
    Corinna Kruse

Part II   The Professional Development of Forensic
          Investigation   123

6   The Police Surgeon, Medico-Legal Networks and
    Criminal Investigation in Victorian Scotland   125
    Kelly-Ann Couzens

7   '13 Yards Off the Big Gate and 37 Yards Up the West
    Walls'. Crime Scene Investigation in Mid-nineteenth
    Century Newcastle upon Tyne   161
    Clare Sandford-Couch and Helen Rutherford

8   The Construction of Forensic Knowledge in Victorian
    Yorkshire: Dr Thomas Scattergood and His Casebooks,
    1856–1897   189
    Laura M. Sellers and Katherine D. Watson

9   Reporting Violent Death: Networks of Expertise and the
    Scottish Post-mortem   211
    Nicholas Duvall

Part III   The Media and Ethics in Constructing Forensic
           Objectivity   231

10 Detecting the Murderess: Newspaper Representations of
    Women Convicted of Murder in New York City, London,
    and Ireland, 1880–1914   233
    Rian Sutton and Lynsey Black

11 'Children's Lies': The Weimar Press as Psychological
    Expert in Child Sex Abuse Trials   257
    Heather Wolffram

12 Murder Cases, Trunks and the Entanglement of Ethics:
    The Preservation and Display of Scenes of Crime Material   279
    Angela Sutton-Vane

Index   303

Notes on Contributors

Alison Adam is Professor of Science, Technology and Society at Sheffield Hallam University, UK. Her main research interest is the history of forensic science in twentieth-century Britain, especially Scotland. She is the author of *A History of Forensic Science: British Beginnings in the Twentieth Century* (2016).

Amy Helen Bell is an Associate Professor in the History Department at Huron University College, University of Western Ontario, London ON, Canada. Her research and teaching focuses on the social and cultural history of twentieth-century Britain, and the histories of ordinary people caught up in extraordinary circumstances: bombing raids and violent crimes. She is the author of *Murder Capital: Suspicious Deaths in London* (2014) and *London Was Ours: Diaries and Memoirs of the London Blitz* (2007). Recent work focuses on the intersections between photography, forensics and women's history, ranging from spoof photography by Victorian female students, to the history of abortion crime scene photography in postwar London.

Lynsey Black is a Lecturer in Criminology, in the Department of Law, Maynooth University, Ireland. She researches in the areas of gender and punishment, historical criminology, and the international death penalty. She is an editor of *Law and Gender in Modern Ireland* (2019).

Kelly-Ann Couzens is a doctoral candidate at the University of Western Australia (UWA) and has recently submitted her thesis—*Medicine on Trial: Medical Testimony and Forensic Expertise in the Scottish High Court of Justiciary, c. 1822–1906*—for examination. In 2016 she was awarded the Patricia Crawford Research Award in History and the Frank Broeze Postgraduate Research Award from UWA to further facilitate her PhD research on Scottish criminal justice history. She has published on the links between performance, persuasion and expertise in the space of the nineteenth-century courtroom in *History*. Her research interests include histories and studies of forensic medicine, nineteenth-century criminal justice and the Victorian press.

Nicholas Duvall studied at the Centre for the History of Science, Technology and Medicine at the University of Manchester, obtaining his PhD in 2013, with a thesis entitled 'Forensic Medicine in Scotland 1914–1939.' Since then he has held postdoctoral research posts at the Universities of Manchester and Warwick and University College Dublin.

Corinna Kruse is a Senior Lecturer at the Department of Thematic Studies—Technology and Social Change at Linköping University, Sweden. Her research interests are in knowledge practices—the production as well as the movement of knowledge. This interest has led to an ongoing engagement with forensic evidence in the Swedish criminal justice system. She is the author of *The Social Life of Forensic Evidence* (2016).

Alexa Neale is Leverhulme Trust Early Career Research Fellow in Historical Criminology at the University of Sussex. Her research focuses on capital murder cases in the twentieth century, particularly on forensic narratives and visual representations of crime scenes. She is interested in the extent to which exhibits of evidence and stories about crime influenced perceptions of guilt, feelings of sympathy and decisions to hang or reprieve people sentenced to death in twentieth-century Britain. Her first monograph, *Photographing Crime Scenes in Twentieth Century London: Microhistories of Domestic Murder*, will be published in 2020.

Helen Rutherford is a Solicitor and Senior Lecturer in the Law School at Northumbria University. She is also carrying out PhD research at Newcastle University. She has published on legal history and the English Legal System. Her research interests focus on the life and work of the Victorian Coroner for Newcastle upon Tyne and nineteenth-century crime with a North East England focus.

Clare Sandford-Couch is a Visiting Lecturer in the Law School at Newcastle University. She has published on legal history and the role of the arts and humanities in legal education. Her research interests largely address interactions of law and visual culture, and late medieval Italian art history. Her current research focus includes crime histories in nineteenth-century Newcastle upon Tyne.

Laura M. Sellers holds a PhD from the University of Leeds. Her research focuses on history of medicine, psychiatry, crime and prisons. During her PhD she was the Assistant Curator, and Acting Director, for the Museum of History of Science, Technology and Medicine at the University of Leeds. She now works as a collections access assistant at the Thackray Medical Museum. She is co-editing a volume on integrated history and philosophy of science.

Rian Sutton is completing a PhD in the School of History, Classics and Archaeology at the University of Edinburgh. Her thesis focuses on the agency of women on trial for homicide offences involving an adult victim in New York City and London between 1880 and 1914. The research is conducted using press coverage and court records to consider how the ability of the accused to narrate her own experience was enabled and/or constrained during her encounters with the criminal justice system.

Angela Sutton-Vane is completing an Arts and Humanities Research Council (AHRC)-funded PhD in the History Department at the Open University. She worked for art galleries and museums for over 20 years, nearly 12 of which were spent curating a police museum and archive. It was this experience, along with earlier work as a tape transcriber for the serious crime and child protection units of the Metropolitan Police and as a trained police researcher, which led directly to her current research interests around the materiality of police archives—their transient and vulnerable states, their making and meaning and the trajectories and preservation of both documents and artefacts.

Katherine D. Watson is a Reader in History at Oxford Brookes University. Her research focuses on areas where medicine, crime and the law intersect. She is the author of *Poisoned Lives: English Poisoners and their Victims* (2004) and *Forensic Medicine in Western Society: A History* (2011) and is completing a monograph on medico-legal practice in England and Wales 1700–1914, based on a project funded by the Wellcome Trust; her next book will be about acid attacks in Britain 1790–1975.

Heather Wolffram is a Senior Lecturer in Modern European History at the University of Canterbury, New Zealand. She is the author of *The Stepchildren of Science: Psychical Research and Parapsychology in Germany, c. 1870–1939* (2009) and *Forensic Psychology in Germany Witnessing Crime, 1880–1939* (2018). Her research revolves around two projects on the formation and practice of forensic medicine and forensic science in the late nineteenth and early twentieth centuries. The first is a Marsden-funded project titled 'Criminal Minds: A History of Forensic Psychology' and the second an exploration of medico-legal practice in British colonies such as Egypt and Ceylon.

List of Figures

Fig. 2.1   Untitled bedroom in Stepney, 1934, by Humphrey Spender. (Rights of reproduction given by his widow Rachel Spender in 2018)   23

Fig. 2.2   Untitled crime scene photograph, 1933. (The National Archives, Director of Public Prosecutions. CN 27/8, Photographs extracted from DPP 2/136. Copyright Holder: The National Archives)   26

Fig. 2.3   Untitled crime scene photograph, 1945. (The National Archives, Director of Public Prosecutions. DPP 2/1441. Copyright Holder: The National Archives)   29

Fig. 3.1   © The British Library Board (6496.i.1/3). 'The Model of the Crumbles bungalow' in E. Wallace, *The Trial of Patrick Mahon* (London: Geoffrey Bles, 1928), plate facing page 64   45

Fig. 3.2   © The British Library Board (6496.i.1/3). 'Interior of the bungalow. Model with roof removed' in E. Wallace, *The Trial of Patrick Mahon* (London: Geoffrey Bles, 1928), plate facing page 96   46

Fig. 3.3   Crime scene photograph 'No. 4: Interior of sittingroom' by Detective Inspector William McBride, Metropolitan Police, 3 May 1924. TNA: MEPO 3/1605: Metropolitan Police; Officer of the Commissioner: Correspondence and Papers: Murder of Emily Beilby Kaye by Patrick Herbert Mahon. Used with permission of the Metropolitan Police Service and the Mayor's Office for Policing and Crime   57

Fig. 3.4   Crime scene photograph 'No. 1: The Officer's House, Langney Bungalows' by Detective Inspector William Mcbride, Metropolitan Police, 3 May 1924. TNA: MEPO 3/1605: Metropolitan Police; Officer of the Commissioner: Correspondence and Papers: Murder of Emily Beilby Kaye by Patrick Herbert Mahon. Used with permission of the Metropolitan Police Service and the Mayor's Office for Policing and Crime   58

Fig 6.1   Photograph of Sir Henry Duncan Littlejohn (Credit: Wellcome Collection)   131

Fig. 7.1   Map of Newcastle upon Tyne, copyright © H.J. Rutherford and C. Sandford-Couch, reproduced with kind permission of Newcastle City Library, Local Studies and Family History Centre   162

Fig. 12.1   The Charing Cross trunk at the Crime Museum in 2015   291

1

Crime and the Construction of Forensic Objectivity from 1850: Introduction

Alison Adam

In recent years, the concept of objectivity has been subject to much scrutiny across a spectrum of academic disciplines including philosophy, history of science and historical criminology. Some of this scholarship challenges the traditional approach to epistemology which sees objectivity in terms of uncovering and describing an independent reality, arguing instead that objectivity is temporally and culturally contingent and is created or performed rather than discovered. Notably, the history of objectivity has attracted considerable attention in the history of science (e.g. through the work of Lorraine Daston and Peter Galison) and is a familiar subject for historical enquiry in that field.[1] However, an interest in objectivity is far from confined to the history of the development of scientific knowledge and analyses of crime history show that objectivity in relation to crime and criminals is subject to similar concerns over the culturally contingent nature of its construction.

A. Adam (✉)
Sheffield Hallam University, Sheffield, UK
e-mail: a.adam@shu.ac.uk

© The Author(s) 2020
A. Adam (ed.), *Crime and the Construction of Forensic Objectivity from 1850*, Palgrave
Histories of Policing, Punishment and Justice,
https://doi.org/10.1007/978-3-030-28837-2_1

1

A study of that which is taken to be objective knowledge of crime, scenes of crime, crime materials, criminals and the procedures involved in solving crimes reveals the variety of ways in which what might be termed *forensic objectivity* is constructed and also that many different actors are involved in the construction of forensic objectivity. Forensic objectivity is, therefore, a useful concept for thinking about crime and the ways that knowledge about crime and criminals is created, either explicitly 'scientifically' or otherwise. For historians, it would seem that the best way to understand objectivity is to examine the way it has been created; historical case studies can reveal not only the multifaceted nature of objectivity but can also show that many people, not just experts, are involved in creating it. Of course, there is an important way in which attempts to achieve forensic objectivity can be seen as problematic and this relates to expert witnesses, particularly within the time-span which this book encompasses. In adversarial legal systems, such as those which operate in the UK and USA, an expert witness appears for the prosecution or the defence. There is always a question of impartiality. In the UK, the question of impartiality bedevilled the fortunes of expert witnesses from the nineteenth century onwards when the role began to professionalize, signalling that the relationship between science and law has not always been a happy one.[2] The courtroom is a place where expert witnesses can display their authority and where their analyses can be accepted or rejected.[3] It is a place where forensic objectivity is constructed and challenged (although as we argue in this book it is not the only place where such challenges are made); there may be competing views of forensic objectivity even when juries are presented with the same facts. However, despite a caveat about the role of expert witnesses, and although there are examples of experts disagreeing with one another in this book, the 'warring experts'[4] issue does not feature strongly in what follows, rather the construction of forensic objectivity appears to be more subtle and more complex.

This book approaches crime history through detailed case studies of the ways in which forensic objectivity was constructed in relation to crime (mostly murder), mainly in the UK but with some important international comparisons made possible by the inclusion of chapters set in Germany, USA, Ireland and Sweden. It is notable that three of the

UK-based chapters are set in Scotland which has been subject to much less historical attention than England in terms of the development of forensic sensibilities in relation to criminal justice.[5] The case studies of two of the book's chapters (by Kelly-Ann Couzens and Nicholas Duvall) demonstrate that the development of professional networks in forensic medicine in Scotland through the nineteenth and twentieth centuries was a major element of the development of forensic services and of achieving objective knowledge in relation to crime. There are some demonstrable differences in the legal system, policing and the development of forensic medicine and science in Scotland, when compared to the situation in England, which these chapters analyse. In both England and Scotland, institutional arrangements and indeed state support were to have a substantial impact on epistemological matters. This serves to emphasize a continuing theme in the history of crime, mirrored widely in the academy, which militates against universalist notions of objectivity. Local, contingent arrangements do more than influence the trajectory of knowledge; they make it.

Some of the book's chapters address forensic objectivity directly, others more tangentially suggesting that it may be useful to consider forensic objectivity as a kind of emergent property, developing from professional practices and media commentary, systems of representation of crimes and crime artefacts. The book's time period spans the middle of the nineteenth century to the present day. Around the middle of the nineteenth century important types of representational practices we now take for granted were crystallizing; these had to be worked out and agreed in the making and acceptance of what was taken to be objective knowledge about crime and criminals. Such developments include the beginning of crime photography, the use of diagrams and models specially constructed for and displayed in the courtroom so jurors could be 'virtual witnesses',[6] the professionalization of medical and scientific expert witnesses and their professional networks,[7] ways of measuring, recording and developing criminal records and the role of the media, particularly newspapers in reporting on crime, criminals and legal proceedings and their role in the shaping of public opinion on crime. A number of these developments are considered in the case studies presented here. Hence, the mid-nineteenth century appears to be an appropriate juncture from which to discern the threads of the development of forensic objectivity.

As the project took shape, a cut-off date of somewhere in the middle of the twentieth century began to feel increasingly artificial. Corinna Kruse's chapter set in the present day (in a Swedish forensic laboratory setting) demonstrates, on one hand, the continuity with past approaches to the objective representation of crime, criminals and forensic materials but also shows how newer mathematical, particularly probabilistic approaches to objectivity are created and maintained. This acknowledges the relevance of scholarship on the 'history of the present', particularly as explicated by David Garland in relation to Foucault's writing, '[b]y reconnecting contemporary practices … with the historical struggles and exercises of power that shaped their character'.[8] Including a contemporary case study also serves to reinforce the argument that, in the post-DNA era, the question of forensic objectivity is far from sorted out and, in the paeans to modernity represented by gleaming, new forensic laboratories, truth and objectivity are just as much subject to negotiation, construction and framing even if regulatory regimes have changed and have become sedimented. In addition, forensic technologies and sciences continue to be subject to considerable critical scrutiny, especially in the UK and USA. As a good part of contemporary criticism centres on forensic science's scientific credentials, it is apposite to consider where such scientific credentials have come from and how they have developed historically; this is the very stuff of forensic objectivity.[9] A further reason for extending the temporal period to the present day lies in the potential to make a connection between ethics, in terms of the contemporary ethical treatment of historical material, and forensic objectivity. The ethical treatment of material from past crimes which still exists today is addressed explicitly in Angela Sutton-Vane's chapter. But we must also consider our ethical duty to the victims of past crimes, not only in our descriptions of their lives but also in relation to photographic material, particularly images of victims.

As the case studies make clear, there is no suggestion of a direct progression from 'primitive' approaches to forensic objectivity in the nineteenth century to the present, hence the book is not structured chronologically. By centring the collection mainly on the UK, alongside important international case studies for comparative purposes, over a crucial century and a half for the concepts we explore, we are able to demonstrate some of the ways in which medical, policing and other expert knowledge was changing rapidly, despite always being mediated by public and media understandings of crime and the criminal. It is perhaps obvious to note that crime, especially murder, has received vast amounts of attention in historical, criminological and popular literature. Nevertheless, analysis of the development of management of crime scenes, especially those involving murder or serious assault and how the portrayal and management of crime scenes and crime material contribute to the construction of forensic objectivity, have yet to be subject to the same level of scholarly interest, arguably only receiving detailed historical attention in the last decade or so.[10] Where the crime and crime scene together have received historical treatment, the focus has often been the development of the expertise of forensic pathologists, forensic scientists and the professionalization of policing and detection.[11] In other words, the development of forensic objectivity tends to be framed against the development of professional expertise where the expert is seen as the creator and owner of objective knowledge which is then consumed and possibly reframed by public and press. Acknowledging the significance of such an approach, nevertheless this collection attempts to cast the net wider in describing networks of expertise, the development of professional protocols for achieving objectivity and the creation of new forensic techniques, particularly photography, in the construction of scientific and medical knowledge which included the depiction of victims and their lives. Although the roles of the expert, police and criminal justice officials are acknowledged and are described in detail in a number of the chapters, there is also the question of how far it is possible to decentre the expert and professional expertise to argue that the achievement of forensic objectivity is spread through a web of interests. These are the interests of scientific experts and their formal and informal networks and police and detectives, and also the interests of the victims and their families, the media, politicians and the public and indeed a contemporary audience of academics and others who turn their gaze back to reflect on past murders and serious crimes. Considering the vectors of criminal, victim, class, gender, place, crime scene, experts, media and the public woven together in the performance of forensic objectivity reveals interesting aspects of professional and other networks and the ways in which forensic aspects of crime have been represented over a long period. A further effect of broadening the focus of the historical gaze is to dispel the idea that, historically, there was a linear advance in the successful management and analysis of crime scenes. For instance, Clare Sandford-Couch and Helen Rutherford describe a well-ordered, methodical and even just about 'scientifically' managed crime scene in the mid-nineteenth century, which stands up well if considered against contemporary criteria for the management of crime scenes, and there are many examples of poorly managed crime scenes well into the twentieth century.

The book is structured into three sections which centre on the themes of forensic representation, professional development and media and ethics. However, these themes cut across many of the chapters as almost every chapter deals with forensic representation in one form or another, and the development of professional expertise and challenges to such expertise by the media is evident in a number of chapters. As noted above, ethical considerations in relation to crime scene material and images are increasingly important in our description of past cases. The two sub-themes which have not been made explicit in the book, but are nevertheless important to the discussion are gender and place/space. The victims of murder are so often women, in their domestic space. In terms of place, it has been noted above that three chapters are set in Scotland, with its different legal and policing setting. In addition to this, two chapters are set in the north of England—Newcastle upon Tyne and Yorkshire. Their inclusion serves to emphasize that advanced detection and the development of sophisticated professional networks existed outwith the metropolis in the mid- to late nineteenth century.

Four chapters on forensic representation form the first section. Visual information is a crucial element in the making of forensic objectivity and the use of photography in capturing and creating objectivity became increasingly important over the period covered by this book. The relationship between gender and (male) expertise influences ways in which gendered depictions are enfolded with the 'scientific' and 'objective'. Crime scene photographs can be used to display domestic and other scenes which can be projected onto ideals of women's behaviour set against a domestic ideal. The apparent objectivity of the photograph acts as a classic silent witness. However, as views on class, gender, race and criminality are inscribed in photographs even when no human being is actually present in the depicted scene and where the crime scene has been cleaned up and, sometimes literally, sanitized, it appears that silent witnesses are far from neutral. This is demonstrated in Amy Bell's chapter which considers crime scene photographs from London in the 1930s and 1940s as documentary images, combining new ideals of forensic objectivity with the emotions evoked by signs of violence and disrupted domestic interiors.

When we think of visual representation our thoughts initially turn to forensic photography yet, as Alexa Neale describes in her chapter on the famous 1924 'Crumbles bungalow' murder, the use of scale models and diagrams in courtrooms predates photography and models were more common in nineteenth- and twentieth-century courtrooms than has hitherto been realized. Such models offer the jury the opportunity to understand the crime spatially and to consider how the crime played out in the space of the crime scene. Where photographs survive, tantalizingly, models generally do not and we have to piece together conceptions of models from descriptions and newspaper images. Alison Adam's chapter on a forensic odontology case in 1960s Scotland focuses on protocols which were developed during the representation of an alleged bite-mark in a murder case where casts of suspects' teeth were made, photographs and models of teeth were constructed and an extensive dental research project was undertaken in order to demonstrate a match between the chief suspect's teeth and the bite-mark using transparencies and photos of teeth and mark. Considerable work had to be done, with many steps, to make convincing what was argued to be a match between the suspect's teeth and the putative bite-mark.

Corinna Kruse's chapter, set in contemporary Sweden, demonstrates how forensic objectivity is achieved in a modern, forensically sophisticated laboratory setting where professional roles and laboratory regimes are well defined. This challenges the idea that forensic objectivity is all sewn up in a post-DNA era. In terms of forensic representation, she illustrates the way in which much of contemporary discourse on forensic objectivity is probabilistic. Certainty (or near certainty) is created from materials which are acknowledged to be inherently uncertain. In common with many criminal jurisdictions, the Swedish criminal justice system uses a Bayesian approach to evaluate both forensic laboratory results and findings at the crime scene in the face of such inescapable uncertainty. In short, the Bayesian approach is a mathematical-statistical approach that, in practitioners' words, allows them to formalize laboratory and crime scene practices and experience. This way of evaluating matches and crime scenes is intended to standardize (and also to professionalize) forensic practices and the documents they produce; this is seen both as making practitioners exchangeable thus furthering impartiality and also as making the laboratory's expert statements and the crime scene technicians' crime scene reports more uniform and thus more accessible to their recipients. There are contrasts to be drawn with earlier periods where a probabilistic approach to types of forensic evidence was not available. For instance, detectives and expert witnesses in the murder case in Alison Adam's chapter, set in the 1960s, were asked about the certainty of a bite-mark matching the accused's teeth without a probabilistic estimate being expected or given in the trial. In that case, the experience of key expert witnesses, combined with the rarity of a particular dental feature, demonstrated through examining the teeth of a large sample of individuals, lent weight to the argument that there was a match between the accused's teeth and the bite-mark. It was a kind of probabilistic reasoning but without using a formal probabilistic model of the type that Corinna Kruse describes in use in the twenty-first century.

For many chapters professional organization is a central plank of creating forensic objectivity; indeed all the chapters in this book discuss ways in which detectives and other criminal justice officials interacted with other parts of the criminal justice network to a greater or lesser extent. However, the second section explicitly takes as its focus the professional organization of forensic analyses and investigation. Kelly-Ann Couzens considers the work of the police surgeon in mid-nineteenth century Scotland. The police surgeon occupied a pivotal role working between different professional and public communities, on call at all times, and often the first port of call, in medical terms, for victims and suspects. The police surgeon had to tread a fine line that blurred the professional and practical boundaries between medicine, policing and criminal investigation. Clare Sandford-Couch and Helen Rutherford's chapter is set in

Newcastle upon Tyne in 1863, and their description of the detailed management of the crime scene tends to give the lie to the idea that crime scene management was largely poorly organized in the UK until well into the twentieth century when continental and colonial influences became evident. This chapter analyses the role of the police with an argument which runs counter to the idea that constables were unskilled men whose role was largely crime prevention rather than investigation. Laura Sellers and Katherine Watson focus on the remarkable career of Thomas Scattergood, doctor, lecturer and toxicologist in Yorkshire in the second half of the nineteenth century using his notebooks and media reports to examine the development of forensic techniques and the construction and circulation of forensic knowledge. His growing reputation as an expert toxicologist encompassed deaths and injuries of humans and animals and he undertook a wide range of investigations for coroners, police officers, other doctors, farmers, lawyers and landowners. His notebooks reveal much of the detail of forensic cases, detail which often remains hidden in court proceedings and media reports. While his meticulous forensic practice can be seen as contributing to the making of forensic objectivity, Sellers and Watson note that, as an expert witness, his forensic knowledge can be regarded as being oriented towards his clients. This raises the perennial problem of expert witnessing, namely the impartiality and objectivity of expert witnesses.[12]

Nicholas Duvall's chapter returns to Scotland but some seventy or so years after Couzens' chapter. Aspects of the Scottish legal system continued to influence the way that violent crime was investigated by medicolegal experts. A murder in Dumfries in the south of Scotland in the 1930s forms the case study in this chapter. Although local doctors undertook the original post-mortem they were able to draw upon the expertise of an expert in Edinburgh for an opinion regarding the death of the victim. As written reports from expert witnesses were mandatory in the Scottish legal system they facilitated the ability of other doctors to form a separate opinion, indeed to disagree with the author of the original report. This emphasizes the role of expert witness statements, as written documents in purveying forensic objectivity within professional networks. It was significant that, at this time, there was no legal requirement for expert witnesses to produce a written report in other parts of the UK so the expert witness reports took on a special role in the Scottish system in facilitating other medical and scientific witness and other investigating officers as 'virtual witnesses'.[13]

Although several chapters allude to the role of the media in constructing objectivity, the third section centres on chapters whose main focus is media or ethical considerations. Lynsey Black and Rian Sutton's chapter analyses the intense press interest surrounding women murderers or 'murderesses' where the focus was on physical appearance and the idea of a criminal 'look'. This chapter provides a significant comparison across Ireland, England and the USA showing both distinct differences and similarities in the ways in which women murderers were treated in these countries. It is notable that the press were able to draw upon Lombrosian notions of the 'criminal look' to add emphasis to their reports and this compares to other famous trials such as that of Crippen where the press had a field day in their descriptions of Crippen as having a criminally degenerate appearance.[14] Heather Wolffram's chapter highlights the fact that forensic analysis was better developed in a number of European countries than in the UK in the 1930s. The focus on forensic psychology is welcome as this demonstrates that forensic objectivity should be construed not only in terms of scientific analysis of crime scenes and trace evidence but should also be understood in terms of psychology. As she notes, media involvement can be understood as more than the press reflecting expert views in a digestible form for the public where the question of credibility of juvenile witnesses was seen as crucial. Instead, the press were instrumental in revising and expounding on sensational cases, to the extent that they characterized themselves as experts in their own right to promote a number of political agendas.

Angela Sutton-Vane highlights a number of ethical issues in relation to crimes and crime scenes. By ethics, we do not (just) mean the business of how the individual actors in our historical accounts were treated at the time, we are equally concerned about how posterity treats them. We are often reminded that the dead have no human rights, yet the treatment of images and other materials from past crimes can be disturbing and may invoke mixed emotions in modern readers who are apparently invited to gaze upon the images of those who were murdered long ago. By concentrating on evidentiary material and what happens to it often many years after the crime, she reminds us that objectivity is not just created by the reports and analyses of expert witnesses, detectives and the media but is also created through artefacts, which, with their connection to particular crimes may achieve an almost mythical status. Focusing on trunk murders, we are shown how these objects transmute from domestic objects to forensic evidentiary material. She argues that the preservation of crime scene material and crime records require ethical consideration as they can become 'accidental tourists' when they are preserved in museums.

Such considerations raise ethical questions of how we handle historical images and physical material (including body tissues) of crime victims where no permission has ever been granted for their use and where, at least for visual material, the internet permits access and distribution way beyond the original intention of the published work. Thinking about ethical considerations is important in relation to forensic objectivity as it demands that we confront the uses which we make of photographic imagery of crimes, which was often only intended for a narrow specialist audience but is now widely available digitally. The objects which are left behind in the wake of crimes investigated many years ago also present ethical issues, especially when we discover that some of these are not just the possessions of victims but are actual body parts.[15]

Notes

1. L. Daston, *Objectivity*, New York: Zone Books, 2007; L. Daston and P. Galison, 'The image of objectivity', *Representations*, 1992, 40: 81–128.
2. A. Adam, *A History of Forensic Science: British Beginnings in the Twentieth Century*, Abingdon: Routledge, 2016, p. 25.
3. Ibid., p. 26.
4. Ibid., p. 13.
5. M.A. Crowther and B. White, *On Soul and Conscience. The Medical Expert and Crime. 150 Years of Forensic Medicine in Glasgow*, Aberdeen: Aberdeen University Press, 1988; N. Duvall, *Forensic Medicine in Scotland, 1914–1939*, Unpublished PhD thesis, University of Manchester, 2013.
6. J.L. Mnookin, 'The image of truth: Photographic evidence and the power of analogy', *Yale Journal of Law & the Humanities*, 1998, 10(1),

Article 1: 1–74, Available at: https://digitalcommons.law.yale.edu/yjlh/vol10/iss1/1, Accessed 8 May 2019.

7. For example, see T. Golan, *Laws of Men and Laws of Nature: The History of Scientific Expert Testimony in England and America*, Cambridge, MA and London: Harvard University Press, 2004; Adam, *A History of Forensic Science*.

8. D. Garland. 'What is a "history of the present"? On Foucault's genealogies and their critical preconditions', *Punishment and Society*, 2014, 16(4): 365–384, p. 373.

9. National Research Council, National Academy of Sciences (NRCNAS), *Strengthening Forensic Science in the United States: A Path Forward*, Washington, DC: National Academies Press, 2009; Home Office, APCC, NPCC, *Forensics Review. Review of the Provision of Forensic Science to the Criminal Justice System in England and Wales*, July 2018, Available at: http://www.statewatch.org/news/2019/apr/uk-ho-forensic-science-review-7-18.pdf, July 2018, Accessed 10 June 2019.

10. Adam, *A History of Forensic Science*.

11. I. Burney and N. Pemberton, *Murder and the Making of English CSI*, Baltimore: Johns Hopkins University Press, 2016.

12. Adam, *A History of Forensic Science*, p. 40.

13. The Criminal Justice Act (1967) allowed for written evidence from expert witnesses to be presented in court. See Adam, *A History of Forensic Science*, p. 42.

14. Adam, *A History of Forensic Science*, pp. 91–93.

15. For example, see 'Murdered boys' final remains laid to rest', *The Scotsman*, 9 May 2009. In 1913 the bodies of two young boys were discovered in a well in West Lothian. The cold water and lime present in the well meant that the bodies were uniquely preserved. Medico-legal specialists, Sydney Smith and Henry Littlejohn from the University of Edinburgh kept some of the body parts for further study. A funeral service and cremation was finally held in 2009 at the request of a relative of the boys.

Bibliography

Adam, A., *A History of Forensic Science: British Beginnings in the Twentieth Century*, Abingdon: Routledge, 2016.

Burney, I. and Pemberton, N., *Murder and the Making of English CSI*, Baltimore: Johns Hopkins University Press, 2016.

Crowther, M.A. and White, B., *On Soul and Conscience. The Medical Expert and Crime. 150 Years of Forensic Medicine in Glasgow*, Aberdeen: Aberdeen University Press, 1988.

Daston, L., *Objectivity*, New York: Zone Books, 2007.

Daston, L. and Galison, P., 'The image of objectivity', *Representations*, 1992, 40: 81–128.

Duvall, N., *Forensic Medicine in Scotland, 1914–1939*, Unpublished PhD thesis, University of Manchester, 2013.

Garland, D., 'What is a "history of the present"? On Foucault's genealogies and their critical preconditions', *Punishment and Society*, 2014, 16(4): 365–384, 373.

Golan, T., *Laws of Men and Laws of Nature: The History of Scientific Expert Testimony in England and America*, Cambridge, MA and London: Harvard University Press, 2004.

Home Office, APCC, NPCC, *Forensics Review. Review of the Provision of Forensic Science to the Criminal Justice System in England and Wales*, July 2018, http://www.statewatch.org/news/2019/apr/uk-ho-forensic-science-review-7-18.pdf, Accessed 10 June 2019.

Mnookin, J.L., 'The image of truth: Photographic evidence and the power of analogy', *Yale Journal of Law & the Humanities*, 1998, 10(1), Article 1: 1–74, https://digitalcommons.law.yale.edu/yjlh/vol10/iss1/1, Accessed 8 May 2019.

National Research Council, National Academy of Sciences (NRCNAS), *Strengthening Forensic Science in the United States: A Path Forward*, Washington, DC: National Academies Press, 2009.

Part I

Forensic Representations: Photographic, Spatial, Dental and Mathematical

2

Bodies in the Bed: English Crime Scene Photographs as Documentary Images

Amy Helen Bell

Introduction

This chapter will argue that crime scene photographs from London in the 1930s and 1940s were documentary images, which combined new ideals of forensic objectivity with the emotions evoked by signs of violence and disrupted domestic interiors. In 1926, Scottish filmmaker John Grierson coined the term 'documentary' to describe an image which depicts reality, yet imbues facts with feeling for a social purpose.[1] In the 1930s, documentary press photographers popularized the use of an unobtrusive 35 mm camera to record scenes of street life and urban poverty for *the Daily Mirror*, the Mass Observation social survey organization and the popular photojournalism magazine *Picture Post*.[2] At the same time crime scene photography was developing in England as an objective tool used by the police to record crime scenes for the judge and jury. Although crime scene photographs were presented in court as straightforward

A. H. Bell (✉)
Huron University College, London, ON, Canada
e-mail: abell44@huron.uwo.ca

© The Author(s) 2020
A. Adam (ed.), *Crime and the Construction of Forensic Objectivity from 1850*, Palgrave Histories of Policing, Punishment and Justice,
https://doi.org/10.1007/978-3-030-28837-2_2

reflections of reality, they were framed by the skilled photographers of newly founded police photography departments who were influenced by aesthetic trends and who had some freedom on how to frame, focus and arrange photographs in court exhibition volumes. Crime scene photography shared many of the aesthetic techniques of documentary photography, as well as the desire to evoke an emotional response in the viewer. By comparing crime scene photographs from murders in Lancashire in 1933 and Shropshire in 1946 to one of a set of interior photographs of a flat in Stepney taken in 1934 by photographer Humphrey Spender, we can see how the photographers used emotive photographic techniques such as juxtaposition, oblique lighting and tight framing when representing the rooms in which criminal acts had occurred.[3] Crime scene and documentary photography both sought to use the camera to reveal hidden emotional and forensic clues and to emphasize the contrast between the visible traces of criminality and the ordinariness of their setting.

From its invention in the 1830s, photography was used both as an artistic medium and a tool for scientific documentation in the fields of medicine, botany and the natural sciences: anthropology, archaeology, sociology and astronomy.[4] In the nineteenth century, photography was seen as objectively recording what was placed in front of it, 'innately and inescapably performing a documentary function.'[5] For instance, in England, the late Victorian photographic survey movement sought to create a photographic record of vanishing churches, cottages and folk customs for future generations.[6] This observation and recording, with its epistemic impulse to furnish proof or evidence, was suffused with the emotion of nostalgia, as Val Williams and Susan Bright have observed: 'It was as if the photographers themselves believed that what was disappearing was somehow better, or purer than the present, and that by photographing it, something might be captured for a world so eager to progress that it was casting off what made it great.'[7] Photography's epistemic intent towards truth-telling often outstripped or was at odds with the visual content of the photograph, which relied on explanatory notes or text to explain its significance. Photography's link to specific meanings was complicated further by the ease with which photographs were reproduced, distributed and repurposed across cultural spheres, such as, for example from the family, to the archive, to the tabloid press, to the courtroom.[8]

Crime Scene Photography

As early as the 1850s, those interested in photography discussed its potential for discovering and prosecuting crime. In an 1856 address to the Bengal Photographic Society, the Rev. Joseph Mullins detailed the colonial government's potential use of photography for identifying rioters and 'fixing' 'the scene of a murder and all its attendant circumstances; the position of a body whether hanging up or lying down, the state of its dress, the marks on it, [which] can all be copied with perfect accuracy.'[9] From the 1860s, photographs were routinely admitted into American and British courts as legal evidence in cases of forgery to prove the identities of criminals and, from the 1890s, as pictorial evidence of the scene of the crime. Yet while Anglo-American courts ruled that 'photographs were the product of scientific processes and that they were accurate representations of the world,' at the same time they recognized that photography was an authored and artistic medium and required photographs to be authenticated by a 'knowledgeable witness who could be cross-examined.'[10] In this way, as legal scholar Jenifer Mnookin has argued, photographs could be made to fit existing evidentiary standards for illustrative evidence which had evolved for maps and plans, which defused the novelty of the medium and protected the importance of verbal testimony.[11]

In the 1890s, Alphonse Bertillon at the Parisian Prefecture created a standard methodology for photographing criminals and crime scenes and exhibited examples of these photographs at the 1889 Paris Exhibition and the 1893 World's Columbian Exhibition in Chicago.[12] The photographs of disordered domestic interiors and street scenes, taken from the ground and from above, created a powerful visual methodology for interpreting clues to criminal behaviour and social evidence. Inspired by Bertillon and advancing camera technologies, police crime scene photography developed simultaneously in London, New York, Sydney, Mexico City and other major centres from 1910 onwards. By the 1930s, most major police departments in Britain had access to camera equipment, had begun to develop their own forensic photographic practices and had brought men already skilled in photography into the force. Faster, lighter and less obtrusive cameras, as well as growing audiences for their work, had also influenced the development of a newly named and recognizable 'documentary' movement. These photographic genres shared the desire to tell an objective and clear truth.

Crime scene photographers shared forensic goals but also developed their own local styles. In the London Metropolitan Police, the Photographic Branch developed a separate path of entry and promotion; applicants already had to have a thorough knowledge of photographic equipment, uses and genres and had to pass technical exams to advance in rank.[13] At the same time, budgeting constraints meant they lagged behind commercial photographers in their access to advances in equipment. As late as 1916, the Photographic Branch only had a glass-plate camera with no focusing apparatus—which meant that focus had to be tabulated by estimating distance. As their correspondence shows, they needed faster camera technology to photograph protesting female 'suffragettes' without their knowledge. Not until 1931 did the London Branch buy a Thornton Pickard Ruby Reflex camera, a more lightweight and reliable device that had a Unit focal-plane shutter for various speeds.[14] In 1940, the Photographic Department borrowed a Leica camera and enlarger from the Metropolitan Police Laboratory, which used film instead of glass plates, and noted that 'The rapidity with which the Leica could be manipulated was a great asset.'[15]

Other English photographic departments were also funded in the 1930s. Photographer Harry Martin joined the Manchester City Police Photographic Department in 1937 as a general assistant to Police Surgeon Dr Thomas Blench.[16] Photography was at first a sideline job, but by 1938 he and Sergeant John Easton had become the force's first official photographers. Their equipment included a quarter plate Thornton Pickard Ruby Reflex and a 35 mm Leica Miniature. During the war the Manchester Photographic Department expanded to include special constables, all of whom were enthusiastic amateur photographers. They were responsible for photographing crime scenes and those under arrest, as well as pictures of bomb damage and the identifying marks of blitz victims. One of these special constables, John Fallows Hall, kept prints and albums from his wartime service in a suitcase under his bed. After his death in 1999 they were found and deposited in the Manchester Police Museum and Archive. These examples demonstrate the cross over between amateur and police photographers and the multitude of uses for photography in police departments in these early years, including surveillance, recording fingerprints, criminal identification and documenting crime scenes.

Documentary Modernism

Because of the rich shared international technology and aesthetics of photography, English crime scene photographs have clear visual connections to many other contemporary photographic genres. As art critic Michael Baxandall argues, artists draw on the work of their predecessors in a spectrum of diverse, formal, intentional, reactionary, emulative, adaptive, distortive and coincidental ways.[17] Crime scene photographs emphasized truth-telling and documentary practices, as well as visual clues and cues; they asserted classification and order derived from the sciences and criminalistics of Bertillon and Francis Galton. Their depiction of the human form and of criminality has clear visual links to the erotic New Orleans photographs of E.J. Bellocq and New York press photographer Weegee. The idealized images of the domestic and the family in popular advertising were an invisible foil for cases of family rupture and violence, while cinema and art photography provided examples of how to convey emotional tension. Perhaps most importantly, these visual languages offered a new sense of accessibility to the viewer. Just as cheap Victorian pornographic postcards made pornography accessible to those without the tools of literacy and education, so crime scene photographs allowed jurists to 'read' the photographs in what they saw as a rational and commonsensical way.[18]

Just as police departments were increasingly interested in new photographic tools and techniques, so visual culture was developing quickly in other areas in interwar Britain. Advertising hoardings brought images on to the street, the cinema offered hours of visual entertainment and cheap illustrated publications achieved unprecedentedly large circulation.[19] The vocabulary of visual styles among both professionals and amateurs was expanding rapidly with better photographic technology and more affordable reproduction. The advent of the documentary movement greatly influenced crime scene photography. The documentary genre arose simultaneously and in close relation to cultural modernism in the late 1920s and 1930s Britain. Indeed, many modernist writers and artists were active in the documentary film movement including in the ethnographic organization Mass Observation, to which photographer Humphrey Spender among other prominent figures contributed. Writers, filmmakers and photographers combined Modernist style and realistic subject matter, with the aim of educating the public about the experience of hardship or injustice.[20] Central to the documentary genre was the suggestion that the practitioners were neutral observers, although the aesthetic techniques they used were intended to provoke empathy and compassion for those depicted. As John Grierson defines it, it was 'an anti-aesthetic movement' that nevertheless relied on aesthetics.[21] In Britain, genre spawned a new form—'documentary modernism'—which combined the experimentalism of modernism and the naturalistic explorations of everyday life of the documentary genre.[22]

The 1930s documentary movement sought broadly to 'expose truths,' in the words of Spender, which in Britain and in America often translated as revealing poverty and inequality to a middle-class audience.[23] Other English documentary photographers of the 1930s, including George Davison Reid, Margaret Monck and Bill Brandt, also used their photographs to comment on the vitality and material poverty of working-class life. Brandt, in his 1936 *The English at Home* and 1938 *A Night in London*, used portraiture of both classes juxtaposed on facing pages to portray a nation of social and material extremes. These photographers, like later London documentary photographers Cyril Aropoff and Roger Mayne, worked in black and white, in richly textured prints of streetscapes and domestic interiors. They used the techniques of juxtaposition and either crowded or empty frames to signify deprivation and to evoke compassion in the viewer.[24] In this way early documentary photography worked as a key mechanism, as Thy Phu and Elspeth H. Brown have argued, 'through which the affective and the political are mutually constituted.'[25]

Documenting Crime and Deprivation

In 1934, Spender was asked by probation officer Clemence Paine and Sir William Clarke Hall, barrister and child protection advocate, to take photographs in Stepney to publicize the conditions of the slums.[26] Spender focused on a particularly shabby Stepney bedroom as mitigating evidence in a case of juvenile delinquency, by visually suggesting the unwholesome intimacy that took place in it.[27] He used an early 35 mm film camera, either a Leica or a Zeiss Contax 35, to capture the small, overcrowded room in deep focus and rich detail.[28] The oblique natural lighting from the side windows shows the texture of the worn and rumpled bedclothes and discarded clothing and highlights the only decoration, two tiny framed celebrity photographs of Bing Crosby and Carole Lombard on the mantelpiece (Fig. 2.1). The light from the window, the lines of the bedstead and the broom handle propped against the frame highlight the expanse of an unmade bed and indented pillows, suggesting

Fig. 2.1 Untitled bedroom in Stepney, 1934, by Humphrey Spender. (Rights of reproduction given by his widow Rachel Spender in 2018)

an intimacy at odds with the close proximity of two other beds. The unbuttoned trousers flung over the headboard add another suggestive hint of sexual familiarity. The tightly framed photograph visually evokes overcrowding and suggests feelings of deprivation and hopelessness. Spender himself revealed in a 1997 interview with journalist Miranda Carter that he intended the photograph '... to show overcrowding, yes, but also that incest was a big problem. There were seven people sleeping in that room; a father sharing a bed with his daughter? and it went on.'[29] Both the documentary aesthetic, further developed in Spender's later published work, and the practice of introducing photographs as illustrative background in court influenced how crime scene photographs were framed, focused and understood.[30]

Mass Observation (MO), founded in 1937 by journalist and poet Charles Madge and ornithologist and anthropologist Tom Harrisson, was an important part of the documentary movement. It sought to record the habits of everyday life in Britain, especially among the northern working classes. Working mainly with volunteer observers, MO solicited and collected monthly reports over 13 years by up to 1500 observers, as well as the entries of 500 diarists. One of the most famous projects was to record life in Bolton or 'Worktown,' a northern industrial town. Harrison invited Spender to work on this project with the goal of taking photographs that would 'provide information,' particularly of people who did not know they were being observed on the street or in pubs.[31] Advances in camera technology, including faster film and smaller, lighter cameras, allowed the camera to remain partially hidden to passers-by, which led to a transatlantic genre of street photography from the 1940s. Practitioners included the American Walker Evans and the French Henri Cartier-Bresson.[32] Spender's MO photographs were not published at the time, but have become recognized as an important part of the MO Archive and as of social and artistic significance. As curator Russell Roberts argues, Spender emerged as 'the poet photographer of the group, merging press photography and British documentary realism in a way that often nods to Brassaï and surrealism.'[33]

We can trace visual and affective links between Spender's work and that of other 1930s documentary and crime scene photographs. In particular, the photographs taken of private rooms where domestic murders had taken place showed similar aesthetic qualities. For example, crime scene photographs of a murder and attempted suicide in Blackburn, Lancashire, in 1933 show an intimate bedroom tableau. The deceased was Mary Ann Steen, a forty-year-old woman who lived at 11 Russell Street, Blackburn, Lancashire, with her boyfriend Fred Sanderson, a fifty-two-year-old married lorry driver. She ran a small grocery store out of the downstairs room. Steen and Sanderson had been associating for many years, and had lived together for three, when he became jealous of her suspected association with another man. On a Wednesday morning on March 1, 1933, the neighbours noticed that the shop had not opened and looked through the window to see Sanderson with his head in the oven, in an attempt to commit suicide by coal gas poisoning.[34] They forced the door and found Steen dead in bed upstairs with her head brutally battered and letters of confession from Sanderson on the kitchen table. A hammer with blood and hair on it lay on the bed, near the foot under the eiderdown, suggesting either that Sanderson had covered his victim and the murder weapon with the sheet after killing her or that the police had covered her for the photographs.

The Chief Constable of the Blackburn Constabulary wrote to the Director of Public Prosecutions (DPP) that: 'I have caused photographs of the bedroom in which deceased was found to be taken from various positions and also plans to be prepared of the inside of the house.'[35] He didn't specify whether the photographer was a police officer or a hired freelancer, although the six photographs sent to the DPP suggests an outsider; the in-house photographers at the London Metropolitan Police generally took only two or three photos of a crime scene in this period.[36] The six glass-plate photographs record the bed from various angles, including one photograph in which the bed has been moved to capture another view of Steen's body in the bed and one in which the bed has been moved back to its original position but the body has been removed. The eiderdown is also in different positions around the body in the photographs. These changes show that the photographs were intended not only as proofs of undisturbed forensic evidence as we would understand it but as illustrations of the crime evoking the atmosphere of the room and the objects within in. The fact that the suspect had already confessed makes the photographs also more emotive than explanatory.

Like Spender's photograph, the only light is that coming in from the window, focusing on the bed in the centre of the frame. In this example (Fig. 2.2), the bed is photographed at an oblique angle, in order to show the covered body in the bed but so that the headboard hides the head and face. The light hits the body in the centre of the frame, and the light-coloured sheet and chamber pot draw the eye to the barely visible blood-stained pillow. That and the dark bloodstain under the bed suggest that the inert form in the bed is not sleeping. As in Spender's photograph, the detailed focus in the centre of the frame is on the textures of fabric—the quilted eiderdown rising and falling over the body, the stays and trousers draped over the headboard, the clothing draped over the chair. Both images show bedrooms as repositories of the private; with discarded

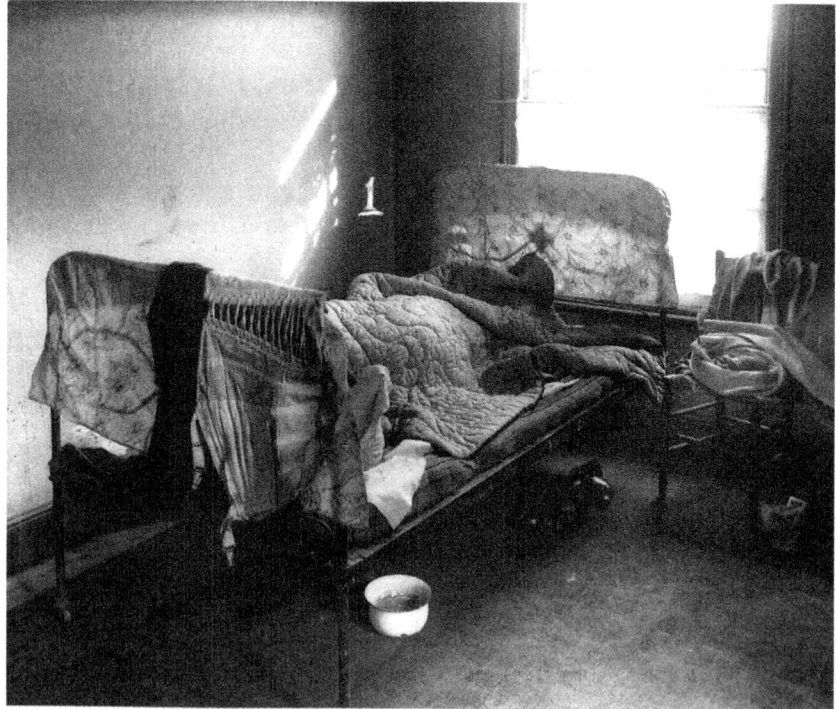

Fig. 2.2 Untitled crime scene photograph, 1933. (The National Archives, Director of Public Prosecutions. CN 27/8, Photographs extracted from DPP 2/136. Copyright Holder: The National Archives)

clothing, personal effects and rumpled beds suggesting the vulnerability of the people who sleep there. Both documentary photographers and crime scene photographers used the technique of juxtaposition to evoke emotion in the viewer. The domestic details in these photographs juxtaposed with the visual hints of the crimes that took place therein evoke emotions of horror, revulsion and, perhaps, compassion. That these photographs were viewed publicly only in the courtroom setting in which crimes were prosecuted also suggests the vulnerability of the people depicted and the loss of privacy the existence of such photographs represents.

Bodies in the Bed

The photographs of Steen were unusual for English crime scene photographs of the 1930s in that one of them shows her face as she lay in the bed. In most crime scene photographs up to the 1960s, the police photographer was careful to angle the camera away from the face when photographing the crime scene itself.[37] The earliest archived interior crime scene photograph, of a farmhouse kitchen in Harrington in 1904, shows no body and a cleaned and rearranged room.[38] A photograph of a back staircase, where a chef was shot by a disgruntled dishwasher in 1933, also shows no body; the man was taken to hospital but later died.[39] Photographs which did show bodies showed them partially covered and with the face hidden from view. In the photographs of a murdered workhouse inmate on Fulham Road, London in 1934, the camera is angled very low to the ground to show the body on the floor without revealing the victim's face.[40] The photographs of the 1941 murder of a rag, coke and wood merchant who lived and worked out of a stable in Kilburn showed him in bed, the covers pulled up to partially conceal his face.[41] The photographs of an elderly woman who died from being bound and gagged during a 1936 robbery in Shepherd's Bush likewise show the bindings covering most of her face.[42] It is likely that the police detectives and perhaps the photographers themselves wanted to keep the faces of murder victims from being photographed, either out of respect for the dead or consideration for members of a potential jury. They did so by rearranging blankets and clothing, as well as by choosing vantage points for the camera shots which obscured the victims' faces. Crime scene photographs were also framed so as not to display nudity, and many early crime scene photographs of female victims appear to show the victim's skirt having been pulled down or a sheet placed over her body.[43]

The reticence of crime scene photographers to show the body *in situ* prevailed for both male and female victims. A photograph taken at a cottage outside Much Wenlock, Shropshire, depicts a rare case of a wife killing her husband. In 1946 Ethel Evans shot Charles Evans twice in the head with a double-barrelled shotgun whilst he was asleep. Since his demobilization he had been erratic, angry, unfaithful and abusive and had spent all his money on cigarettes instead of food and boots for the children. As Ethel told detectives: 'He went like a madman and said the money was his and he could do as he liked with it as we weren't entitled to any of his money. He went up to bed about 8.00 and in a sort of a dream I saw the gun on the wall and I thought we won't get no peace here while he is alive. I loaded the gun and went upstairs and shot him.'[44] Their six sons remained asleep next door. That same night, Detective Inspector (DI) Joseph Taylor of Shropshire Constabulary took three glass-plate photographs of the bed in the room from different angles. The scene is lit by a flash and is consequently less focused and detailed than the first two taken in natural light. In this example, (Fig. 2.3), the photograph is tightly framed on the bedstead heaped with untidy blankets, with the nearest corner out of view and the headboard in the centre of the image. From the headboard, the viewer's eye is drawn down to the bloodstains on the wallpaper to the small rumpled form in the bed, huddled under a darker blanket, and upwards to the peeling and stained wallpaper. As in the other two bedrooms, personal belongings are sparse, in this case a suitcase on a chair with what could be balled-up socks on top, revealing the poverty of the inhabitants. These photographs do not directly show the body which lay underneath the covers, and no close-ups of the bed or body were included in the crime scene photograph album. Only the second set of photographs from the mortuary show the massive damage done by the blast, which removed half of Evans' head. The privacy of the body is inviolate in the crime scene for both female or, as in this case, male victims.

Fig. 2.3   Untitled crime scene photograph, 1945. (The National Archives, Director of Public Prosecutions. DPP 2/1441. Copyright Holder: The National Archives)

The disarranged bed in this photograph, as in the previous two images, stands as a metaphor for domestic breakdown, for the vulnerability of the victim and for the poverty which was an important part of the context in all three cases. These photographs share the two basic aesthetic qualities of the documentary, according to Tyrus Miller: a realism that allows the documentary to be 'true to life' and hence socially functional; and a modernist attention to photographically rendered detail, which emphasizes the effective emotional or aesthetic impact of the image.[45] The reality of the room as a scene of crime, combined with the details of personal lives, sexual intimacy and poverty, evoke the emotions of pity, horror and compassion. These images also point to the ability of the camera to penetrate the boundaries of privacy, for both documentary and crime scene photography to invade and ultimately expose the domestic private world presented in other photographic images in advertising and domestic photograph albums.

Telling a Story with Photographs

The publication conventions of documentary photographs also influenced crime scene photography. Most viewers in the 1930s encountered documentary photographs not as individual prints but as reproductions in books, newspapers and periodicals.[46] Newspapers had been printing photographs since the *Daily Graphic* newspaper in 1880 claimed to be the first to reproduce halftone images directly from a photographic plate on a rotary printing machine.[47] When the *Daily Mirror* relaunched in 1904 as the first illustrated daily newspaper, it used rotogravure illustration, cylinder etchings which could reproduce illustrations at high speed.[48] Photographic reproductions had spread to the staid London *Times* by 1914.[49] As Lynda Nead has argued, photography was central to the new front-page tabloid layout, pioneered by the *Daily Express* in 1933, with larger photographs, more space and bigger headlines to break up the text.[50] Tabloid newspapers used simplified language, pin-ups and greater use of images to appeal to readers. Guy Bartholomew, editor of the *Daily Mirror* in the 1930s and 1940s, helped to perfect the Bartlane method of the radio transmission of photographs which made the air race for foreign photographs obsolete and solidified the new centrality of the photographic image to popular journalism.[51] However, newspapers were constrained by conservative editorial practices, which tended to emphasize the picturesque. Spender, who had been the roving photographer 'Lensman' for the *Daily Mirror* before being recruited to the staff of the radical *Picture Post* in 1938, had been sent to Tyneside by both papers: 'For the *Mirror*, I'd been expected to make the industrial scene picturesque, including unemployment; whereas for *Picture Post* we were able to produce a feature of a realism so harsh that we evoked a strong complaint from the mayor.'[52]

Books and periodicals were less constrained in their use of photographs, which began to appear more regularly in from the mid-1930s. Uncredited photographs were included in George Orwell's *The Road to*

Wigan Pier in order to, as the publisher Victor Gollancz described it, make the book 'fully documentary,' and W.F. Lestrange's book *Wasted Lives* (1936) used photographs to convey the colourlessness and desperation of a generation of unemployed men.[53] New pictorial magazines also began to use photography to illustrate news and human interest stories. Just as the Leica camera used 35 mm film instead of glass plates, magazine editors borrowed ideas from the cinema to create the dramatic picture essay, stories laid out in still photographs. One of the most influential innovators of this new style was Hungarian Stefan Lorant, who left Germany after being imprisoned by Hitler in 1933 and became the first editor of the *Picture Post* in 1938.[54] With a background in progressive magazine editing in Germany, Lorant wanted to appeal to a wide readership that would include 'the common man, the workers and the intelligentsia.'[55] His radical editorial style encouraged a style of photographic reporting that emphasized a common humanity, whether of French soldiers during the Normandy Invasion or of the cosmopolitan poor of Butetown, Cardiff.[56] His then assistant editor, Tom Hopkinson, described how Lorant would let the 'picture stories' he had commissioned accumulate, until late at night shortly before the deadline he would gather them all together, lay them out roughly, then decide what article and captions should be written and by whom.[57] His visual approach and sense of timing were immediately successful, and within six months, the magazine's circulation reached 1.6 million copies a week.[58] The *Picture Post*'s use of photographic layouts to tell a story in turn influenced other photographers to take and display photographs in narrative series. The *Post*'s photographs were always printed in rectangles and regular grids, unlike the irregular cut-outs used by the *Mirror*, to enhance the connotation of realism and the sense of eyewitness.[59]

The popularization and publication of documentary photographs had a profound influence on crime scene photography. It made black and white the definitive format for conveying the truth to the viewer well into the 1980s, and it helped to influence the presentation of crime scene photographs in albums presented in court. From the 1930s the police and Director of Public Prosecutions developed a system of multiple evidentiary albums to be examined first by police detectives, then by the Director of Public Prosecutions. They were then presented at the committal hearings and seen by the defence counsel, defendant and the magistrates. When the case proceeded to trial, they were viewed by the judge and members of the jury.[60] More numerous prints of the crime scene photographs placed in sequence mirrored the narrative construction of the photojournalist essay. Arne Svensson, in *Crime Detection: Modern Methods of Criminal Investigation*, suggested that crime scene photographs should be taken so that they could be arranged in a series which illustrated the events of a crime in a logical sequence. In a homicide, Svensson maintained, the following series might be appropriate: (1) overall view of village, showing murderer's way to the house, (2) exterior of house (scene of the crime and criminal's path), (3) view from different directions of the room in which the crime was committed, including pictures of the body, (4) close-ups of the body, (5) detail of injuries on the body, (6) detail picture of bloodstains, (7) detail showing weapon, (8) view of another room with evidence (such as tool marks on a desk), (9) close-up view of evidence, (11) overall view of house and criminal's fleeing path and (12) exterior view as seen by witness. Svensson notes that the photographs do not have to be taken in this order, but should be arranged this way for the jury to provide a visual illustration of the police's hypothesis of how a crime had been committed.[61]

The association of black and white photography with documentary realism also had a profound effect on crime scene photography. While photographers had been experimenting with colour since the 1890s, the processes were expensive and time-consuming and mostly associated with advertising. So powerful was the association of black and white images with documentary truth that it influenced fine art, such as Picasso's newsreel evocation in *Guernica*, as well as the majority of Second World War propaganda.[62] Black and white also became inextricably associated with documentary photography across the world. In 1935, the American Farm Security Administration (FSA) employed professional photographers to record American life and the ravages of the Depression on the rural population. The resulting black and white photographs have become iconic. In 1978 art historian Sally Stein discovered over 1600 pictures of the FSA that were taken in Kodachrome, a colour slide film introduced by Kodak in 1936. These were not published in contemporary magazines and newspapers with other FSA photographs and continue to be relatively unknown even after their public exhibition in 2004.[63] Such is the association of black and white with documentary photography, as well as the 1930s and 1940s, that these colour images paradoxically seem fake and too highly coloured to evoke historic events. Instead of being seen as missing a fundamental dimension of reality, black and white prints became associated with photography's documentary and truth-telling functions, with dramatic, 'black and white,' clear-cut truths.[64]

Black and white film was also used for crime scene photography well into the 1980s. A Police Research Committee of the Association of Chief Police Officers of England and Wales from December 1962 noted that, although colour film had been available since the 1930s, only a minority of forces were using it because of the concerns about the additional cost, time and staff it required; of the 122 forces surveyed only 47 made any use of colour photography. Other concerns related to colour photography's ability to convey veracity to the viewer and in the courts.[65] While the colour film was better able to show traces of blood, paint or bruises, there were concerns that it had the potential to convey unspecified false information. For instance, barrister J.D. Casswell recalled that in his defence of Mrs Rosina Cornock for the murder of her husband at the Bristol Assizes 1947, he managed to mitigate 'prejudicial' effects of the photographs of Cornock's head by making the photographer admit that the type of film used would make the bruises appear darker than reality.[66] Crime scene photography continued in black and white until the 1980s in open archive files and likely beyond, showing the durability of the belief in black and white film's ability to convey truth and to be intelligible in the courtroom.[67] A 1980 report on the photographic requirements of the London Metropolitan Police noted that the equipment and techniques used police photographers, who were professional civilians by this point, still used black and white film.[68] By the time the transition to colour was complete in the 1990s, another photographic revolution was on the horizon: digital photography.

Conclusion

As the conventions of crime scene photography became established in the 1930s, we can trace the visual vocabularies of other photographic practices. While the genres of crime scene photography and documentary photography may not seem to have anything in common, both kinds of practitioners wanted their images to serve as a factual record; to fix the history of the event and also to evoke a response in the courtroom, the exhibition room or the sitting room. While crime scene photography aimed to convey only intelligible and important forensic information in the courtroom, it absorbed artistic and scientific languages and created its own influential genre. The audiences for these media expanded beyond the judge and jury and newspaper reader to a much wider public. Just as documentary modernism was drained of its social welfare message to become an apolitical visual style, so did crime scene photography expand beyond its judicial use, to become an instantly recognizable aesthetic copied in film, television dramas, advertising and fashion photography. The mutual influences of these genres, as well as their diffusion into other forms, show the permeability of photographic techniques and movements in an increasingly visual culture.

Notes

1. J. Grierson, 'Flaherty's Poetic Moana', *New York Sun*, 8 February 1926, reprinted in Lewis Jacobs (ed.), *The Documentary Tradition*, 2nd ed., New York: Norton, 1979, pp. 5–6.
2. H. Spender, *'Lensman': Photographs 1932–52*, London: Chatto and Windus, 1987.
3. The National Archives, Kew, [TNA], DPP 2/136, DPP 2/1441.
4. See E. Edwards, 'Photographic uncertainties: Between evidence and reassurance', *History and Anthropology* 2006, 25(2): 171–188; P. Prodger, *Darwin's Camera: Art and Photography in the Theory of Evolution*, Oxford: Oxford University Press, 2009; J. Tucker, *Nature Exposed: Photography as Eyewitness in Victorian Science*, Baltimore: John Hopkins University Press, 2013; A. Thomas, *Beauty of Another Order: Photography in Science*, Oxford: Yale University Press, 1997.
5. A. Solomon-Godeau, *Photography at the Dock*, Minneapolis: University of Minnesota Press, 1991, p. 170.
6. E. Edwards, 'Photography and the material performance of the past', *History and Theory*, 2009, 48(4): 130–150.

7. V. Williams and S. Bright, *How We Are: Photographing Britain from the 1840s to the Present*, London: Tate, 2007, p. 15.
8. G. Mitman and K. Wilder (eds.), *Documenting the World: Film, Photography, and the Scientific Record*, Chicago: University of Chicago Press, 2018, pp. 45–64.
9. J. Mullens, 'On the applications of photography in India', *Journal of the Photographic Society of Bengal*, 1857, 2: 33–38, p. 34.
10. R.S. Carter, '"Ocular proof": Photographs as legal evidence', *Archivaria*, 2010, 69: 23–47, p. 24.
11. J. Mnookin, 'The image of truth: Photographic evidence and the power of analogy', *Yale Journal of Law and the Humanities*, 1998, 10(1): 1–74.
12. J. Ellenbogen, *Reasoned and Unreasoned Images: The Photography of Bertillon, Galton, and Marey*, University Park, PA: Pennsylvania State University Press, 2002; S.A. Cole, *Suspect Identities: A History of Fingerprinting and Criminal Identification*, Cambridge, MA: Harvard University Press, 2001.
13. TNA, MEPO 2/5938; J.A. Radley, *Photography in Crime Detection*, London: Chapman and Hall, 1948; W.T. Shore (ed.), *Crime and Its Detection*, London: The Gresham Publishing Company Ltd., 1931.
14. TNA, MEPO 2/2187.
15. TNA, MEPO 3/1997.
16. 'Manchester Police photographer retires', *Manchester Evening News*, 5 August 1980, 8; B. Broady and D. Tetlow, *Law and Order in Manchester*, Stroud: The History Press, 1985.
17. M. Baxandall, *Patterns of Intention: On the Historical Explanation of Pictures*, New Haven, CT: Yale University Press, 1985.
18. L.Z. Sigel, *Governing Pleasures: Pornography and Social Change in England, 1815–1914*, New Brunswick, NJ: Rutgers University Press, 2002.
19. H. Wilkinson, '"The New Heraldry": Stock photography, visual literacy, and advertising in 1930s Britain', *Journal of Design History*, 1997, 10(1): 23–38, p. 27.
20. M.W. Marien, *Photography: A Cultural History*, New York: Harry N. Abrams, 2002, p. 280.
21. Grierson, *Documentary*, p. 179.
22. J.B. Entin, *Sensational Modernism: Experimental Fiction and Photography in Thirties America*, Chapel Hill: University of North Carolina Press, 2007, p. 27; T. Miller, 'Documentary/Modernism: Convergence and

complementarity in the 1930s', *Modernism/Modernity*, 2002, 9(2): 226–241, p. 226.

23. H. Spender, *Worktown People: Photographs from Northern England*, J. Mulford (ed.), Bristol: Falling Wall Press, 1982, p. 16.

24. S. Brooke, 'Revisiting Southam Street: Class, generation, gender, and race in the photography of Roger Mayne', *Journal of British Studies*, 2014, 53(2): 453–496.

25. T. Phu and E.H. Brown (eds.), *Feeling Photography*, Durham and London: Duke University Press, 2014, p. 350.

26. H. Spender, Interview at his home 29th March 2000. The National Life Story Collection, British Library, C466/101/09 F8796B Transcript, p. 13.

27. Spender, 'Interview'; 'Sir William Clarke Hall; An appreciation', *Probation Journal*, January 1933, 211.

28. Spender, *Worktown*, p. 17.

29. M. Carter, 'Unseen Observer', *The Telegraph*, 6 December 1997, http://www.telegraph.co.uk/culture/4711138/Unseen-observer.html, Accessed 14 June 2014.

30. H. Spender, *Humanist Landscapes: Photo-documents 1932–42*, New Haven: Yale University Press, 1997.

31. Spender, *Worktown*, p. 9.

32. C. Scott, *Street Photography: From Atget to Cartier-Bresson*, London: I.B. Tauris, 2007.

33. S. O'Hagan, 'The way we were: Mass observation at the Photographers' Gallery', *The Observer*, 21 July 2013, https://www.theguardian.com/artanddesign/2013/jul/21/mass-observation-photographers-gallery

34. TNA, DPP 2/136.

35. TNA, DPP 2/136.

36. TNA, MEPO series.

37. A. Bell, 'Crime scene photography in England 1903–1980', *Journal of British Studies*, 2018, 57(1): 53–78.

38. TNA, ASSI 6/39.

39. TNA, CB 27/10.

40. TNA, MEPO 3/1696.

41. TNA, CRIM 1/1384.

42. TNA, MEPO 3/1716.

43. TNA, CRIM 1/659, MEPO 3/1691, and CRIM 1/3052.

44. TNA, DPP 2/1441.

45. Miller, *Documentary/Modernism*, p. 228.
46. S. Dell, 'Forward from Wigan Pier': Remaking documentary photography in the 1930s', *Visual Culture in Britain*, 2018, 19(2): 168–188.
47. Martin Conboy, *Journalism in Britain: A Historical Introduction*, London: Sage, 2010, p. 82.
48. Conboy, *Journalism*, p. 83.
49. Ibid.
50. L. Nead, 'Visual cultures of the courtroom: Reflections on history, law and the image', *Visual Culture in Britain*, 2002, 3(2): 119–141, p. 135.
51. H. Cudlipp, *Publish and be Damned: The Astonishing Story of the 'Daily Mirror'*, London: A. Dakers, 1953, p. 51; J. Curran and J. Seaton, *Power Without Responsibility: The Press, Broadcasting, and New Media in Britain*, 6th ed., London: Routledge, 2003, p. 53.
52. Spender, *Lensman*, 14.
53. Dell, *Wigan Pier*, pp. 175, 179.
54. M. Hallett, *The Real Story of Picture Post*, Birmingham: The ARTide Press, 1994, p. 4.
55. Ibid.
56. R. Kee, *The Picture Post Album*, London: Barrie and Jenkins, 1989; C. Gorrara, 'What the liberator saw: British war photography, picture post and the Normandy campaign', *Journal of War & Culture Studies*, 2016, 9(4): 303–318; G. Jordan, *Down the Bay: Picture Post, Humanist Photography and Images of 1950s Cardiff*, Cardiff: Butetown History and Arts Centre, 2001.
57. Hallett, *Picture Post*, p. 11.
58. Williams and Bright, *How We Are*, p. 205.
59. J. Taylor, *War Photography: Realism in the British Press*, London: Routledge, 1991, p. 55.
60. A.K.R. Kiralfy, *The English Legal System*, 4th ed., London: Sweet and Williams, 1967, p. 158.
61. A. Svensson and O. Wendel, *Techniques of Crime Scene Investigation*, 4th ed., London: Elsevier, 1965, pp. 30–31.
62. J. Naremore, *More Than Night: Film Noir in Its Contexts*, Berkeley: University of California Press, 2008, p. 170. See also S. Brooke, 'War and the nude: The photography of Bill Brandt in the 1940s', *Journal of British Studies*, 2006, 45(1): 118–138.
63. P. Hendrickson, 'The color of memory', in D. Aaronson (ed.), *Bound for Glory: America in Color 1939–43*, New York: Harry Abrams, 2004.

64. P. Geimer, 'The colors of evidence: Picturing the past in photography and film', in G. Mitman and K. Wilder (eds.), *Documenting the World: Film, Photography, and the Scientific Record*, Chicago: University of Chicago Press, 2016, pp. 45–64, 45.
65. TNA, HO 287/271.
66. J.D. Casswell, *Only Five Were Hanged*, London, Corgi, 1964, p. 238.
67. TNA, J 299/55.
68. TNA, MEPO 2/10369.

Archives

The National Archives

ASSI 52/2053
ASSI 6/39
CB 27/10
CRIM 1/1384
CRIM 1/3052
CRIM 1/659
DPP 2/136
DPP 2/1441
HO 287/271
J 287/44
J 299/55
MEPO 2/10369
MEPO 2/2187
MEPO 2/5938
MEPO 3/1691
MEPO 3/1696
MEPO 3/1716
MEPO 3/1997

Manchester Police Museum and Archive

Spender, H., Interview at his home, 29 March 2000. The National Life Story Collection, British Library, C466/101/09 F8796B Transcript.

Bibliography

'Manchester Police photographer retires', *Manchester Evening News*, 5 August 1980: 8.

'Sir William Clarke Hall: An appreciation', *Probation Journal*, January 1933, 1: 211.

Baxandall, M., *Patterns of Intention: On the Historical Explanation of Pictures*. New Haven, CT: Yale University Press, 1985.

Bell, A., 'Abortion crime scene photography in London England 1950–1968', *Social History of Medicine*, 2017, 30(3): 661–684.

Bell, A., 'Crime scene photography in England 1903–1980', *Journal of British Studies*, 2018, 57(1): 53–78.

Bendavid-Val, L., *Propaganda and Dreams: Photographing the 1930s in the USSR and US*, Zurich: Edition Stemmle, 1999.

Brandt, B., *The English at Home*. London: Batsford, 1936.

Broady, B. and Tetlow, D., *Law and Order in Manchester*. Stroud: The History Press, 2005.

Brooke, S. 'War and the nude: The photography of Bill Brandt in the 1940s', *Journal of British Studies*, 2006, 45(1): 118–138.

Brooke, S., 'Revisiting Southam Street: Class, generation, gender, and race in the photography of Roger Mayne', *Journal of British Studies*, 2014, 53(2): 453–496.

Carter, M., 'Unseen Observer', *The Telegraph*, 6 December 1997, http://www.telegraph.co.uk/culture/4711138/Unseen-observer.html, Accessed 14 June 2014.

Carter, R.S., '"Ocular Proof": Photographs as legal evidence', *Archivaria*, 2010, 69: 23–47.

Casswell, J.D., *Only Five Were Hanged*, London: Corgi, 1964.

Cole, S.A., *Suspect Identities: A History of Fingerprinting and Criminal Identification*, Cambridge, MA: Harvard University Press, 2001.

Cudlipp, H., *Publish and be Damned: The Astonishing Story of the 'Daily Mirror'*, London: A. Dakers, 1953.

Curran, J. and Seaton, J., *Power Without Responsibility: The Press, Broadcasting, and New Media in Britain*, 6th ed., London: Routledge, 2003.

Dell, S. 'Forward from Wigan Pier': Remaking documentary photography in the 1930s', *Visual Culture in Britain*, 2018, 19(2): 168–188.

Edwards, E., 'Photography and the material performance of the past', *History and Theory*, 2009, 48(4): 130–150.

Edwards, E., 'Photographic uncertainties: Between evidence and reassurance', *History and Anthropology*, 2014, 25(2): 171–188.

Ellenbogen, J., *Reasoned and Unreasoned Images: The Photography of Bertillon, Galton, and Marey*, University Park, PA: Pennsylvania State University Press, 2012.

Entin, J.B., *Sensational Modernism: Experimental Fiction and Photography in Thirties America*, Chapel Hill: University of North Carolina Press, 2007.

Gorrara, C., '"What the liberator saw": British war photography, *Picture Post* and the Normandy campaign', *Journal of War & Culture Studies*, 2016, 9(4): 303–318.

Grierson, J., 'The documentary idea: 1942', in F. Hardy (ed.), *Grierson on Documentary*, London: Collins, 1946.

Grierson, J., 'Flaherty's Poetic Moana', *New York Sun*, 8 February 1926, reprinted in L. Jacobs (ed.), *The Documentary Tradition*, New York: Norton, 1979.

Hallett, M., *The Real Story of Picture Post*, Birmingham: The ARTide Press, 1994.

Hendrickson, P., 'The color of memory', in D. Aaronson (ed.), *Bound for Glory: America in Color 1939–43*, New York: Harry Abrams, 2004.

Jordan, G., *Down the Bay: Picture Post, Humanist Photography and Images of 1950s Cardiff*, Cardiff: Butetown History and Arts Centre, 2001.

Kee, R., *The Picture Post Album*, London: Barrie & Jenkins, 1989.

Kiralfy, A.K.R., *The English Legal System*, 4th ed., London: Sweet and Williams, 1967.

Laybourn, K. and Taylor, D., *Policing in England and Wales: The Fed, Flying Squads and Forensics*, Basingstoke: Palgrave Macmillan, 2011.

Lestrange, W.F., *Wasted Lives*, London: George Routledge and Sons, 1936.

Marien, M.W., *Photography: A Cultural History*, New York: Harry N. Abrams, 2002.

Miller, T., 'Documentary/Modernism: Convergence and complementarity in the 1930s', *Modernism/Modernity*, 2002, 9(2): 226–241.

Mitman, G. and Wilder, K. (eds.), *Documenting the World: Film, Photography, and the Scientific Record*, Chicago: University of Chicago Press, 2016.

Mnookin, J., 'The image of truth: Photographic evidence and the power of analogy', *Yale Journal of Law and the Humanities*, 1998, 10(1): 1–74.

Mullens, J., 'On the applications of photography in India', *Journal of the Photographic Society of Bengal*, 1857, 2: 33–38.

Naremore, J., *More Than Night: Film Noir in Its Contexts*, Berkeley: University of California Press, 2008.

Nead, L., 'Visual cultures of the courtroom: Reflections on history, law and the image', *Visual Culture in Britain*, 2002, 3(2): 119–141.

O'Hagan, S., 'The way we were: Mass observation at the Photographers' Gallery', *The Observer*, 21 July 2013, https://www.theguardian.com/artand-design/2013/jul/21/mass-observation-photographers-gallery.

Phu, T. and Brown, E.H. (eds.), *Feeling Photography*, Durham and London: Duke University Press, 2014.

Prodger, P., *Darwin's Camera: Art and Photography in the Theory of Evolution*, Oxford: Oxford University Press, 2009.

Radley, J.A., *Photography in Crime Detection*, London: Chapman & Hall, 1948.

Scott, C., *Street Photography: From Atget to Cartier-Bresson*, London: I.B. Tauris, 2007.

Shore, W.T. (ed.), *Crime and Its Detection*, London: The Gresham Publishing Company Ltd., 1931.

Sigel, L.Z., *Governing Pleasures: Pornography and Social Change in England, 1815–1914*, New Brunswick, NJ: Rutgers University Press, 2002.

Solomon-Godeau, A., *Photography at the Dock*, Minneapolis: University of Minnesota Press, 1991.

Spender, H., *Worktown People: Photographs from Northern England*, J. Mulford (ed.), Bristol: Falling Wall Press, 1982.

Spender, H., *'Lensman': Photographs 1932–52*, London: Chatto & Windus, 1987.

Spender, H., *Humanist Landscapes: Photo-documents 1932–42*, New Haven: Yale University Press, 1997.

Svensson, A. and Wendel, O., *Techniques of Crime Scene Investigation*, 4th ed., London: Elsevier, 1965.

Taylor, J., *War Photography: Realism in the British Press*, London: Routledge, 1991.

Thomas, A., *Beauty of Another Order: Photography in Science*, Oxford: Yale University Press, 1997.

Tucker, J., *Nature Exposed: Photography as Eyewitness in Victorian Science*, Baltimore: Johns Hopkins Press, 2013.

Wilkinson, H., '"The New Heraldry": Stock photography, visual literacy, and advertising in 1930s Britain', *Journal of Design History*, 1997, 10(1): 23–38.

Williams, V. and Bright, S., *How We Are: Photographing Britain from the 1840s to the Present*, London: Tate, 2007.

3

Murder in Miniature: Reconstructing the Crime Scene in the English Courtroom

Alexa Neale

Introduction

'INCIDENTS IN THE CRUMBLES TRIAL' announced the *Daily Mirror* newspaper on 17 July 1924. 'The Bungalow Murder,' as it was also known, had already illustrated local and national press front pages for more than two months, but the *Mirror* was arguably the most persistent in picturing every unfolding detail. This edition showed jurors striding towards Lewes Assize Court and portraits of two witnesses. Beside them, two photographs of a strangely bare, white, single-storey house on a perfectly square island surrounded by giant hexagonal flagstones. Look again and the scale is betrayed by the dado-rail frame: the plot is only a yard wide, the chimneys no higher than a bystander's mid-calf. The garden walls with little gates are a few inches high, the coal shed by the back door might be two matchboxes, and the paths, grass and soil must be rendered

A. Neale (✉)
University of Sussex, Brighton, UK
e-mail: a.neale@sussex.ac.uk

© The Author(s) 2020
A. Adam (ed.), *Crime and the Construction of Forensic Objectivity from 1850*, Palgrave Histories of Policing, Punishment and Justice,
https://doi.org/10.1007/978-3-030-28837-2_3

in felt or sandpaper. The building walls are whitewashed bare, devoid of detail, but every tile on the hipped roof is carefully outlined. The chimney stacks stand proud, individual bricks painted with mortar, topped with tiny pipes. The other photograph sees the roof removed, revealing its function as a lid. Inside walls and floors are blank, like an unoccupied dolls' house, except for the richly furnished sitting-room. This, the caption declares, is where 'the tragedy is alleged to have taken place.'[1]

Crime scene miniatures were not unknown to newspaper readers and consumers of criminal trials in interwar England and Wales. These three-dimensional scale models were mentioned frequently by the press from about the mid-nineteenth century,[2] though rarely described in detail. Transcripts and published accounts of trials also mention miniatures, showing they were regularly used in courtrooms up to and including the 1920s and 1930s, then steeply declined, disappearing around 1950. Lack of detail about models in the press is echoed by lack of scholarship, likely also because only two are known to have survived to the present, other than in a handful of photographs. However, this chapter argues that crime scene miniatures deserve to be restored to their significant role in English trials, particularly because they provide a useful way of thinking about a variety of sources for crimes past. Highlighting issues around meanings of evidence including visual representations, material and forensic exhibits compared to textual documents and oral testimony, murders in miniature can illuminate many methodological challenges posed by crime sources. This chapter uses crime scene miniatures to demonstrate the importance of spatialized understandings of crimes in court, arguing that evidence was mapped onto visual representations of crime scenes to imagine the competing narratives of events presented to them. This included statements, depositions and reports by 'expert' and lay witnesses, investigating police and defendants. This unsettles some of the literature that posits early crime photography as depicting objective 'truth,'[3] and particularly highlights the potential for the lens of the forensic present to distort evidence from the past. The unique medium of the crime scene miniature is therefore used here to argue for prioritizing the courtroom context in readings of sources designed to be viewed there.

Picturing Miniatures in the Past

The images (including Figs. 3.1 and 3.2) published in the *Daily Mirror* on 17 July 1924 were few of many taken by press photographers outside Lewes Court during the trial of Patrick Mahon for the murder of Emily Kaye.[4] Ever-eager to highlight public interest, they pictured queuing crowds sweating in the stifling summer heatwave. Those lucky enough to gain a seat inside found no relief from the temperature, though there were fewer cameras. Taller than it was wide, the vast courtroom was divided vertically by a balustraded balcony forming a packed public viewing gallery on three sides. From there, observers peered down into the well of the court with the defendant in the dock at the centre, an actor on stage or a specimen on display. High above them all, the curved glass-panelled roof, designed to maximize and focus the sun's light, made the courtroom a hothouse. Every surface besides was wood-panelled, groaning and creaking in the heat with every slight movement of the many occupants. Rows of benches like church pews faced the business end of

Fig. 3.1 © The British Library Board (6496.i.1/3). 'The Model of the Crumbles bungalow' in E. Wallace, *The Trial of Patrick Mahon* (London: Geoffrey Bles, 1928), plate facing page 64

Fig. 3.2 © The British Library Board (6496.i.1/3). 'Interior of the bungalow. Model with roof removed' in E. Wallace, *The Trial of Patrick Mahon* (London: Geoffrey Bles, 1928), plate facing page 96

the courtroom where wigged and gowned legal men spread their papers on desks, their backs to the man whose life they argued over. On their right, the stepped wooden witness box and press benches, on their left, the pews for the jury. In the centre, a raised desk for the clerk and high, grand dais for the Judge. There, the throne-like chair was framed by wood panelling covering the entire wall, curving up and overhead in an imposing ornamental porch leaving no doubt whose authority prevailed here.[5] At the Mahon trial in July 1924 this seat was filled by Justice Horace Avory, who had already exercized his prerogative powers by banning women from the jury.[6]

Avory's position allowed him to look down onto the table between himself and legal counsel. On this surface and under it an unlikely assortment of artefacts was arranged, each tagged or marked with a number from 1 to 100. They included a tortoiseshell brush, mirror and comb; axe head and broken handle; women's clothing, fur coat, hats, shoes and jewellery; a ten-inch cook's knife and meat saw; a pile of French francs; a bundle of bloody rags; part of a door; leather luggage including trunk, Gladstone bag and hat box; two pieces of floorboard; an album of photographs and a few loose portraits; hotel register book; small black cauldron with bent leg; glass sample bottles containing tiny hairs; banknotes totalling 500 British pounds; biscuit tin; pieces of carpet; fragments of bone; receipt books and notebooks; many piles of papers; and the scale model of a bungalow.[7] Though dwarfed by the vast space of the courtroom, the model occupied the most important position at the literal and figurative centre of the trial. As the *Taunton Courier* described:

> A conspicuous object situated immediately below the Judge's desk was an elaborate model of the Officer's House. The open spaces of the Crumbles surrounding it, the approaches, and the big garden (imitated in green baize), surrounded by a wall, were all faithfully shown, while the little slate roof, with its tiny red chimney pots, could be lifted off, revealing a bird's-eye view of the interior.[8]

The *Daily Mirror* pictures were likely the first time a crime scene model had been seen in print and even descriptions like the above were unusual. Much more frequent were brief mentions of models which show they had regularly featured in criminal trials for about a century by 1924, though they had a much longer pedigree. At the 1754 trial of Elizabeth Canning for perjury, for example, a carpenter and surveyor produced a model of the hayloft in which Canning alleged she was held captive. This was a key exhibit because the conditions Canning claimed to have been kept in were disputed.[9] In the first few decades of the nineteenth century, models were most frequently entered into evidence at trials for arson. Constructed in wood by surveyors, architects and carpenters, these miniatures allowed witnesses to indicate to the court where they had seen a fire started, or how the accused might have entered or escaped.[10] From around the middle of the nineteenth century, models were increasingly mentioned in cases of murder or manslaughter in the *Old Bailey Proceedings*, usually described as depicting a house or room where a death occurred.[11] The account of Francois Courvoisier's trial for the murder of Lord William Russell in 1840 is illustrative of the ways models helped courts and juries establish a spatialized narrative of the crime. Witnesses pointed to a miniature interpretation of part of the house when describing evidence and events, using it as a visual aid to determine whether it was Courvoisier the valet or an intruder that had killed Lord Russell.[12] The use of models for these purposes was not confined to the Old Bailey, though the digitisation of the *Proceedings* makes them easier to discover there. Cases tried at other courts in England and Wales also mention miniature crime scenes, suggesting they were used in the same ways; to describe movement between rooms and objects, giving spatial context to different types of evidence including material, verbal and what we might now call forensic exhibits.[13]

By the 1880s and 1890s, surveyors were still constructing models but police officers were increasingly taking over the task, testifying they were qualified because they 'understood surveying' or were 'skilled at making models.'[14] No advice for making crime scene miniatures was published in the *Police Journal*, however, unlike photographs and plans.[15] More likely officers learned their skills as hobbyists and craftsmen in model railway building or dollhouse collecting, where the most popular scales match those of crime scene models. It may be in these leisure pursuits, clubs and specialist shops that officers learned to construct, decorate and furnish their models, working with wood, card, plaster, papier-mâché, wallpaper, paints, textiles and pre-produced miniature furniture. Newspapers suggest the transition to police makers coincided with the growing popularity of scale models which peaked in the 1920s and 1930s, including model villages, railways and buildings for entertainment, play and display, as well as architectural design and urban planning. Susan Stewart places model railways, dolls and dollhouses, miniatures all, in a centuries-long history of both adults and children collecting objects of scale. Whether playthings, collectors' items or status symbols, the miniatures she describes allow a larger whole to be possessed, viewed and transported more cheaply and conveniently than the full-size equivalents.[16] The same can be said of crime scene miniatures, which allowed places outside the courtroom to be seen inside it. However, despite the vast cultural proliferation and relatively small size of models, only two representing crime scene in England and Wales has survived the centuries.

At the trial of George Parker in 1901 for the murder of William Pearson, 'a perfectly appointed scale model' of South Western Railway carriage No. 269 was produced by the prosecution who 'remarked that references to it would make the evidence clearer.'[17] Newspapers and *Old Bailey Proceedings* disagree as to the maker, but whether constructed by a police superintendent or draughtsman, or re-purposed from a manufactured model train-set, the miniature is on display at York Railway Museum and on their website.[18] Prosecution counsel's comment underscores the purpose of the crime scene miniature; to set the (crime) scene in the courtroom, to situate the evidence in three-dimensional space without actually going there. Constructed by men with recognized specialist skills, qualifications or experience, used by both prosecution and defence, English crime scene miniatures possessed a uniquely objective position in court. However, models did not go so far as to claim to be exact copies of crime scenes or evidence in themselves. As the following section will show, miniature crime scenes in more recent contexts risk a kind of '*CSI* effect,'[19] distorting understandings of models in the past.

Miniatures in the Present

Museum of London, 9 October 2015, enthusiastic early visitors poured into the Linbury Gallery for the opening of the 'Crime Museum Uncovered' exhibition. Here, it was promised, were displayed to the public for the first time some of Scotland Yard's most famous artefacts, selected from the collection known as the 'Black Museum.' Row upon row of cabinets showed deadly relics from crimes past accompanied by text describing foul deeds and clever captures; discarded balaclavas, failed bombs, shoe-print plaster-casts, firearms bearing fingerprints and spittle-marked cigarette ends, all items that once helped identify and convict. Among them, tiny articles of dolls' house furniture, each no more than two inches tall; a settee and armchairs covered in oversized floral chintz, stained with dust and age; coarse wooden chairs no thicker than match-sticks, glue showing at the joins, somewhat wonky; a covered table, cloth loose and frayed at the edges; and a cauldron no bigger than a cotton reel. Interpretation boards and exhibition guidebook described the objects as 'all that remains of the model reconstruction of the bungalow made by PC Edward Shelah of Brixton police station for use in the [Mahon] trial...'[20]

In many ways it is unsurprising that, excepting these few pieces of furniture and Carriage No. 269, no miniatures made for use in court have survived. Objects that were entered into evidence as exhibits were stored and transported in different ways than flat documents, the latter under the jurisdiction of civil servants, legal secretaries and court clerks. Depositions, photographs, floorplans, letters, newspaper clippings, cheques, ticket stubs, receipts and even books, all fitted, literally, within established bureaucratic systems designed for paper. They moved freely between departments, signed and stamped in and out under a practised system of degrees of secrecy and access, noted and indexed, prepared for storage in standard sized and shaped folders, echoed today by their uniform cardboard containers at The National Archives. Objects, however, took a different journey to and from courtrooms, usually cared for, transported and later retained by police.[21] In high-profile cases many exhibits ended their evidentiary journeys in personal collections, taken home and kept as career mementoes, preserved as family heirlooms or sold.[22] Alternatively, they might be proudly displayed to other officers at the 'Black Museum' where the entire miniature Crumbles bungalow and at least one other were once housed. Sadly, they seem not to have survived to be selected for display at the Museum of London in 2015.

Recent publications describing the Mahon investigation and trial in 1924 have situated it as 'a pivotal moment in the making of English CSI [crime scene investigation],' though they make no mention of the model crime scene.[23] In her study of the 'afterlives' of evidence, Katherine Biber discusses the tiny furniture at the Crime Museum exhibition and makes the link between the bungalow model and the miniature crime scenes imagined in the US by Frances Glessner Lee in the 1940s and by the writers of *CSI: Crime Scene Investigation* in the early 2000s.[24] Biber is the exception to the rule that English crime models, and specifically the miniature Crumbles bungalow, have been overlooked, though not without good reason, considering the furniture is all that remains. Images of the model were printed in *The Mirror* and in the inter-pages of *The Trial of Patrick Mahon* (published as a book shortly after the event), but the above press quote is the fullest published description. Only the archived trial transcript, which describes courtroom action with little editorial intervention, can show how the miniature was used, why it was commissioned and what knowledge claims it made. Shani D'Cruze's article, titled with an extract from *The Trial of Patrick Mahon*, describes the Victorian melodrama it and other published accounts of trials evoked, but not the miniature stage set upon which the murder of Emily Kaye was rehearsed in the courtroom.[25] This is because the central role the model played was all but written out of the script, contributing to arguments regarding the specific and heavily edited format of published trials in the 'Notable' and 'Famous' series and the *Old Bailey Proceedings*, which implied accuracy but failed to capture all courtroom words and actions.[26]

Notable and Famous Trials published only a few selected cases and the *Old Bailey Proceedings* ceased in 1913. Historians and criminologists interested in the twentieth century have instead prioritized depositions, statements, reports and newspapers, in part because they survive in far greater numbers than transcripts for this period. However, as Katherine Watson has observed of the nineteenth century, transcripts of trials can offer particular insights, including the ways narratives of crime were deployed and argued over, performed and evidenced, as well as experiences of criminal justice.[27] They also illustrate how depositions, statements and reports, relied upon by scholars, as well as less frequently used material objects (including miniatures, visual representations and forensic 'traces') had particular meanings and contexts as evidence in the courtroom. Paying attention to the meanings of exhibits of evidence, asking 'what did it *do*, in court, *then?*' recognises not only their specificities in the historical moment but also the context of the smaller world they were made for: the courtroom. Focusing attention on the possibilities and limitations of evidence, narrative and imagined space, English crime scene miniatures and transcripts showing them in use demonstrate the previously underestimated significance of crime scene representations. They show that plans, models and photographs were repeatedly referenced in court, but not because contemporaries understood them as 'proof' of what they showed. It was not until at least the post-war decades, when the crime scene miniature had shrunk from view, that visual representations of crime scenes constituted investigative tools, or were privileged as scientific evidence with claims to 'truth' or accuracy.[28]

This argument differs sharply from more recent iterations of crime scene miniatures. *CSI*'s Miniature Killer (2006) rendered every perfectly copied object a meaningful clue that could be read by investigators, who need not select from superfluous detail.[29] Indeed the criticism that television CSIs seemed never to be distracted by abundant domestic detritus as possible evidence was also levelled at life-size storylines across many series.[30] In Lee's Nutshells too (1940s), investigators in training read clues from the miniature scenes by following tiny footprints and interpreting pinprick blood-spatter.[31] They were used this way until as recently as 2017 when the entire collection was displayed publicly for the first time at the Smithsonian American Art Museum where visitors were invited to play the roles of trainee investigators, taking up torches, looking for clues, 'solving' cases and comparing them with 'solutions.'[32] Both the *CSI* and Nutshell miniatures contained tiny doll dead bodies, marked by their manner of death in alarming detail, but these were fictional people and places that never existed at the macro level. As the following section shows by focusing on the model of the Crumbles bungalow in the Mahon trial, English crime scene miniatures were quite different than more recent iterations of crime models, or crime investigation in popular culture more generally, suggest. This highlights a kind of miniature '*CSI* effect'[33] that risks influencing understandings of visual and spatial evidence for crimes past.

The Bungalow Murder in Miniature

On 2 May 1924, a respectable-looking well-dressed man of middle-class appearance collected a Gladstone bag from the cloakroom at Waterloo Station where Scotland Yard detectives were waiting. They arrested him, demanding an explanation of the contents including a ten-inch cook's knife and pieces of blood-soaked silk, strong evidence he recently dissected a human body. 'Rubbish,' snorted Patrick Mahon, he had been carrying meat for his dogs, he said. But Chief Inspector Percy Savage had already examined the bag and determined the blood was human.[34] Mahon back-pedalled. His lover died by accident, he claimed, in the sitting-room of the holiday home he had rented. He panicked and tried to dispose of her body. Savage rushed to the address; The Officer's House, Langney Bungalows, one of ten single-storey homes on the edge of a long, lonely shingle beach known as The Crumbles, between the Sussex seaside towns of Eastbourne and Pevensey. The next few days, Savage and colleagues travelled back and forth between capital and coast, responding to Mahon's statements, looking for evidence to corroborate or contradict his story.[35] Mahon showed a degree of forensic, or at least investigative awareness by altering his narrative, offering a revised statement each time Savage visited the scene.[36] His adaptations can be explained by common police interview tactics in which officers told accused, even if only ambiguously, that they 'knew everything,' even if they knew little. Allowing the accused, waiting in custody, to imagine police reading the crime scene encouraged him to reveal information that could assist investigations.[37] Finally, with enough evidence to secure a conviction, Savage wrote a lengthy report summarizing his investigations, evidence found, tests and interviews conducted, which formed the basis of the pre-trial brief for the Director of Public Prosecutions. In a key passage Savage reported:

> It would be most unlikely that the coal cauldron would have been left in this spot [so close to the door and so far from the fireplace]. The account of the prisoner of this struggle with the woman [in the sitting-room] is not borne out by anything that we have found.[38]

Next, the Director of Public Prosecutions commissioned a miniature of the bungalow sitting-room. Sir Archibald Bodkin must have been familiar with the medium, and known who to ask to make one, because there was no other reason to call on Police Constable Edward Shelah. His Division, based at Brixton Police Station, was not involved in the Mahon investigation. Yet Shelah was asked to visit the bungalow on 7 June with Scotland Yard detectives who focused his attention on the sitting-room and two coal receptacles.[39] These Shelah scaled down and reproduced in miniature, based on measurements he took himself,[40] following a tradition that, as described above, had existed for well over a century. Though parts of Kaye's body and traces of its destruction had been found in many rooms at the bungalow, it was the walls of the sitting-room that formed the primary boundary of the crime scene. Mahon himself had identified it as the place where Kaye died, and his own life depended on what exactly happened there. The prosecution's case was that Mahon had planned Kaye's death and killed her deliberately, motive and 'malice aforethought' defining murder as a capital offence for most of the twentieth century.[41] To escape the noose, Mahon would have to convince the jury that Kaye's death in the sitting-room was caused by accident, self-defence, or provocation. As they were unable to view the bungalow sitting-room in person, the miniature was a life-or-death exhibit.

Savage's report and the prosecution's case alleged that Mahon and Kaye had been having an affair and he promised to divorce his wife and marry her. Kaye's pregnancy may have expedited their plans. She gave up her rooms in London, bought some French francs and withdrew her savings, packed her trousseau and went away with her fiancé to spend a few weeks in a holiday cottage by the seaside before they travelled to Paris then South Africa. Kaye had related this plan to her sister and friends, but Mahon secretly had another. He told his wife he was going away on business, as usual, rented the bungalow in a false name and purchased a chef's knife and meat saw to dispose of Kaye's body. One evening she was writing goodbye letters in the sitting-room when he called her to the bedroom. As she reached the door he stepped out from behind it with an axe which he broke on her skull. There was a lot of blood. Kaye's goodbyes to her friends would help Mahon get away with her murder and her money.[42]

At the pre-trial police court hearing, Mahon had an opportunity to see and hear all the evidence that would be presented against him, allowing him to adapt a counter-narrative that accounted for the most incriminating exhibits. A simplified version begins with his declaration to Kaye that he was returning to his wife. The lovers argued, she threw the coal-axe at him, it broke against the doorframe. In a rage, she attacked him with her hands and they struggled, falling together. Kaye's head hit the coal cauldron, causing a fatal wound that bled profusely onto the carpet, underfelt and wooden floor. Horrified, Mahon panicked and blindly attempted to clean up and hide her body in her travelling trunk in a bedroom, but it would not fit so, using a chef's knife and meat saw he had purchased for innocent purposes, he dissected her body.[43] He burned randomly selected parts in the bungalow fireplaces, including her head, uterus and hands (not deliberately chosen, he insisted, to conceal her cause of death, early pregnancy or identity). He boiled other parts in pots and pans around the place in attempts to destroy them and what remained he wrapped in shreds of her clothes, placed in hatboxes, biscuit tins and his Gladstone bag. He took the latter away with him, intending to scatter the contents, including the knife, by throwing them from train windows on his journeys, but left the bag in the cloakroom at Waterloo rather than taking it home to his wife.[44]

These two competing narratives required different interpretations of the same exhibits of evidence, including statements, documents and objects, discussed by witnesses and counsel at the trial in a non-chronological order that would have been difficult to follow without the visual aid of a model or photograph. Kaye's murder in particular required three-dimensional visual interpretation because the case hinged on the way events played out in the sitting-room. The key significance of the space of the crime scene in the courtroom is underscored by the order in which witnesses were called at the trial. Shelah, the model-maker, was the first to take the oath, although his testimony over four pages in the trial transcript is reduced to a single sentence in the published account.[45] By the twentieth century, model-makers, plan-makers and crime scene photographers were consistently the earliest witnesses called, sworn and questioned in front of the jury, 'proving' or 'producing' (in the parlance of the court) a representation of the relevant spaces to set the scene for all verbal, written and physical evidence that followed. Unlike many other police, expert, or lay witnesses, cross-examination was rarely hostile and challenging, because neither prosecution nor defence treated visual representations of crime scenes as direct 'evidence' of anything themselves. Rather they were objects both sides of the adversarial exchange used to situate their own narratives. In answer to closed, yes or no questions from the prosecution, Shelah confirmed his name and occupation, that yes, he had made this model according to his own measurements and the scale was two inches to one foot. 'As regards the sitting room, is that correct according to scale and detail?' Havers (prosecuting) asked. 'Yes' replied Shelah.[46]

Cross-examined by Cassels for the defence: 'The bed-rooms you have not put any articles in at all? A. No.'[47] In contrast to the twenty-first-century treatment of visual representations of crime scenes in which the law seeks to find or 'prove' facts such as location, identity and corroboration,[48] court transcripts show that crime scene photographs in the first half of the twentieth century were not used in this way. At the Mahon trial the photographs were referred to only rarely, far less frequently than the model, and significantly neither was used to 'prove' the locations of any objects in the rooms. Visual representations of crime scenes—plans, models and photographs—were expected only to be surrogates for the space, a scaled down imaginative aid in the courtroom.

As the trial progressed and 48 witnesses were called, those who referred to evidence or events in the bungalow repeatedly pointed to the model to reference locations, most in preference to the photographs and many in preference to the item itself. Use of the miniature is recorded in the transcript as, for example, 'Q The door here? (Indicating on the model) A. That is so.'[49] This was important even for rooms unfurnished on the model, to situate evidence and narrative in space. Expert witnesses, scientists John Webster and Bernard Spilsbury, referred to the model repeatedly in their testimony, unprompted, the latter regarding both what he had seen in the bungalow at first hand and what he had examined only at his laboratory.[50] When the defendant took the stand, he too offered to use the model, in one instance asking the prosecution

> ... [Mahon:] I cannot see the position. Could you do it with the model?
> [Henry Curtis Bennett:] Certainly. There is the fireplace, there is the armchair. You place the cauldron there?
> [Mahon:] Between the chair and the wall.
> [Bennett:] There?
> [Mahon:] Yes.[51]

Modern evidentiary standards would demand a time-stamped forensic photograph of the cauldron *in situ* before the crime scene was disturbed. In 1924, however, the model and photographs functioned instead to set the scene, to help the jury picture competing narratives about the location and significance of the cauldron and other items in the bungalow sitting-room. The miniature crime scene was prioritized over photographs and plans by every actor in court, representing a tiny stage set: *aide-mémoire* to witnesses and *aide à l'imagination* to the jury.

Direct comparison between the crime scene photographs and those of the model show that Shelah missed many opportunities to showcase his skills of miniaturization and tiny decorative effects, or more likely had yet to develop in some areas. The one photograph of the sitting-room interior (Fig. 3.3) shows that the chintz covers on the miniature armchairs and settee only approximated the real thing, the oversized florals pasted on with adhesive, unedged, rather than hemmed and sewn with minute stitches. Many lamps, ornaments and vases of dried flowers covered all available surfaces but were not copied on the model (Fig. 3.2), which

Fig. 3.3   Crime scene photograph 'No. 4: Interior of sittingroom' by Detective Inspector William McBride, Metropolitan Police, 3 May 1924. TNA: MEPO 3/1605: Metropolitan Police; Officer of the Commissioner: Correspondence and Papers: Murder of Emily Beilby Kaye by Patrick Herbert Mahon. Used with permission of the Metropolitan Police Service and the Mayor's Office for Policing and Crime

could be attributed to restrictions of scale, limits of the medium, or lack of necessity because these objects played no part in the narrative. On the other hand, neither did the pictures on the walls but these were faithfully captured, not simply drawn on, but standing out from the wall in tiny frames. The wallpaper also captured something of the original: hand-painted, featuring tiny potted trees, but not the bouquets between. It is likely that Shelah, when he made his measurements, made a sketch of the decorative features of the room and worked from this. He almost certainly did not work from the crime scene photograph. The exterior of the bungalow, however, had been photographed and printed on the front page of national newspapers (Fig. 3.4), providing an easy reference for Shelah making the model at home. Yet trellises of roses and ivy covered

Fig. 3.4   Crime scene photograph 'No. 1: The Officer's House, Langney Bungalows' by Detective Inspector William McBride, Metropolitan Police, 3 May 1924. TNA: MEPO 3/1605: Metropolitan Police; Officer of the Commissioner: Correspondence and Papers: Murder of Emily Beilby Kaye by Patrick Herbert Mahon. Used with permission of the Metropolitan Police Service and the Mayor's Office for Policing and Crime

the walls of the life-size bungalow but not the model, though it depicted exactly the right number of chimney pipes at the correct relative heights and even the same number of rows of roof tiles. Shelah's later work, for he made at least one more crime scene miniature, suggests he developed his skills and honed his craft considerably over the next few years. It is important to note, however, that these comparisons look for accuracy, facsimile, in a way the contemporary courtroom and application of the model did not.

The miniature interior decorations of the sitting-room were not required to be like-for-like facsimiles, but they did play a role in communicating subtle meanings about the space. The comfortable furnishings and plentiful decorations depicted in the miniature sitting-room and photographs helped to define this as a large, middle-class, seasonal second home. Mahon's regular family living arrangements were of no legal relevance to the murder case, but counsel questioned him about them anyway.[52] The implication here was that Mahon's faithful wife and daughter lived in just one room in a boarding house in London, while he rented a nine-roomed, fully furnished seaside cottage for his mistress. Thus, the bungalow represented part of the defendant's moral transgressions—a liar and adulterer pretending to belong to a social class he had no right to occupy, particularly because he had recently served time in prison for burglary and violence (also against a woman). But his previous convictions could not legally be revealed until the trial was over. As far as the jury was concerned, the more explicit question was: were the exhibits (including objects from the bungalow and depositions of witnesses) consistent with pre-planned murder as argued by the prosecution, or self-defence and accident as argued by the defence?[53] They answered this question with a verdict of guilty of murder and Patrick Mahon was hanged at Wandsworth Prison on 3 September 1924.

Conclusion: Reconstructing the Crime Scene in the Courtroom

In this chapter I have explored the previously neglected English crime scene miniature and shown how it was specifically fashioned for the courtroom; to spatialize evidence and narratives. Unlike more recent depictions of crime scenes in popular culture, early-twentieth-century English miniatures of murder did not claim to accurately depict clues at the crime scene. There were no miniscule bone fragments, doll-sized body-parts, tiny murder weapons or blood trails in Shelah's model of the Officer's House bungalow or the miniature of Carriage 269. Rather, these surrogate spaces helped jurors to situate and imagine the narratives of murder and investigation presented to them in court. English crime scene miniatures and transcripts that show them in use call on historians and criminologists to re-investigate the history of the crime scene as a conceptualized, bounded space, opening up the possibility that visual representations of crime scenes have a history separate from that of investigative techniques and photography for identification.

The significance of transcripts in interpreting visual representations of crime scenes can be widened to apply to other evidence. Each item in a long list of exhibits of various types was introduced, positioned in the narrative and the three-dimensional space represented by model, plan or photograph, and discussed, debated and weighed against other items. Such negotiations took place live, in the courtroom in front of the jury. In addition, visuals of crime scenes communicated more subtle implied meanings about class and respectability. This is important because many historians writing about crimes in the twentieth century have used depositions; dossiers of all paper evidence collected at the police or magistrates court before it was negotiated at trial. But it is only transcripts at the higher court that give context to utterances, meanings to objects and evidence is put in its proper place. Neglecting this vital context, the institutional stage for which each piece was made, can skew the value of evidence and the historical record of the crime. Trial transcripts, though imperfect, achieve a closer reconstruction of the place of the crime scene in the courtroom and highlight its central significance in proceedings. They allow us to view not only the limitations of forensic evidence in the past, and the 'CSI effect' more recent visuals of crime bring to bear, but also the limits and possibilities of contemporary understandings of evidence. As illustrated by miniatures of murder, it is possible to under or overstate meanings of exhibits compared to their application in the courtroom. Early twentieth-century crime scene miniatures were not intended to be read for 'clues' but to represent a space. This demonstrates the need for a thorough and fully realized historicization of crime sources, a framing that considers the bureaucratic and intellectual moment and the figurative and literal space in which a case was tried, a photograph taken, a murder made miniature.

Notes

1. *Daily Mirror*, 17 July 1924, p. 8.
2. Grateful thanks to Dr Katherine Watson for this observation.
3. For a summary of this literature and an excellent history of crime scene photography see A. Bell, 'Crime scene photography in England, 1895–1960', *Journal of British Studies*, 2018, 57: 53–78; also A. Neale, *Photographing Crime Scenes in Twentieth-Century London: Microhistories of Domestic Murder*, London: Bloomsbury, 2020.
4. East Sussex Record Office (ESRO): SPA 2/37: Sussex Police Authority: 'Papers for criminal conviction: R v Patrick Herbert Mahon', 1924; *Daily Mirror*.
5. *Historic England Archive*, BB012367&8: 'Lewes Crown Court Interior' by Sid Barker, 1988, https://archive.historicengland.org.uk/SingleResult/Print.aspx?id=3656443, 15 December 2018; ESRO: SPA 2/37/39-40: Press photographs of Mahon in the dock, 1924.
6. E. Wallace (ed.), *The Trial of Patrick Mahon* (Famous Trials Series), London: Geoffrey Bles, 1924, p. 27.
7. The National Archives (TNA): DPP 1/78: Director of Public Prosecutions Case Papers, MAHON, P.H., Murder, 1924, Index of Exhibits.
8. *Taunton Courier*, 23 July 1924, p. 1.
9. T. Hitchcock, R. Shoemaker, C. Emsley, S. Howard, J. McLaughlin, et al., *The Old Bailey Proceedings Online, 1674–1913*, www.oldbaileyonline.org, version 8.0, March 2018: Trial of Elizabeth Canning (t17540424-60), 1754, 30 October 2018.
10. Ibid., examples include Trials of William Williams (t18070408-90), 1807; Mary Harrison, (t18131027-27), 1813; James Haley (t18241202-1), 1824; Charles Thomas White (t18261026-54), 1826.
11. Ibid., Trials of Elizabeth Ross alias Cook and Edward Cook (t18320105-22), 1832; Benjamin Cole (t18510915-1818), 1851; William Palmer (t18560514-490), 1856; Sarah Jane Wiggins (t18591128-35a), 1859; John Wiggins (t18670923-884), 1867.

12. Ibid., Trial of Francois Courvoisier (t18400615-1629), 1840.
13. For examples trials of Patrick Mahon at Lewes, reported *Pall Mall Gazette*, 1 February 1901, p. 8; William Podmore, Southampton, *Daily Mail*, 3 March 1930, p. 10; Sidney Fox, Lewes, *Midland Daily Telegraph*, 17 March 1930, p. 1; John Loughnan, Manchester, *Northern Daily Mail*, 21 November 1933, p. 8; James Camb, Southampton, *Coventry Evening Telegraph*, 17 November 1947, p. 1.
14. *Old Bailey Online*, Trials of Elizabeth Gibbons (t18841215-126), 1884; Harry John Surtees (t18830730-737), 1883; Adelaide Bartlett and George Dyson (t18860405-466), 1886; Daniel Stewart Gorrie (t18900519-444), 1890; Patrick Duffy and Thomas Rushton (t18910406-355), 1891; Marie Herman (t18940528-509), 1894.
15. *The Police Journal*, 1928–2018, for examples A.J. Quirke, 'The evidence of the camera', 1933, 6: 72–83; W.J. Hutchinson, 'Plans and photographs', 1937, 10: 42–51; J. O'Brien, 'Simple photography for policemen', 1936, 9: 63–71, 173–182, 331–342, 468–472.
16. S. Stewart, *On Longing: Narratives of the Miniature, the Gigantic, the Souvenir, the Collection*, Durham: Duke University Press, 1993, pp. 54–65.
17. *Pall Mall Gazette*, 1 February 1901, p. 8.
18. Science Museum Group, 'Model railway carriage, 3rd class smoking compartment. Ref. 1999–7037', *Science Museum Group Collection Online*, https://collection.sciencemuseum.org.uk/objects/co489466, Accessed 15 December 2018; *City of London Police Museum Blog*, 'The Houndsditch Murders and the Siege of Sidney Street', https://cityoflondonpolicemuseum.wordpress.com/2018/06/11/the-houndsditch-murders-and-the-siege-of-sidney-street/, accessed 7 October 2019.
19. M. Byers and V.M. Johnson (eds.), *The CSI Effect: Television, Crime, and Governance*, Plymouth: Lexington, 2009.
20. J. Keily and J. Hoffbrand, *The Crime Museum Uncovered: Inside Scotland Yard's Special Collection*, I.B. Tauris and Museum of London, 2015, pp. 76–77.
21. TNA: ASSI 36/37/6: Assize Court Deposition Files, P Mahon, Murder, 1924: List of Exhibits; MEPO 3/1605: Metropolitan Police Papers and Correspondence, Murder of Emily Beilby Kaye, 1924: Report, Chief Inspector Percy Savage to Superintendent J.H. Ashley, 6 May and 13 June 1924. See also discussion of cauldron DPP 1/78: MAHON, 1924: Trial transcript [Savage cross-examined by Mr. Cassels for defence], pp. 19–20.

22. ESRO: SPA 2/37/2-41: Mahon, 1924—archived thanks to a Scotland Yard Detective's personal collecting and letters to his mum. See also A. Sutton-Vane, 'Murder cases, trunks and the entanglement of ethics: The preservation and display of crime scene material', in A. Adam (ed.), *Crime and the Construction of Forensic Objectivity from 1850*, Cham, Switzerland: Palgrave Macmillan, 2020, pp. 279–301.
23. I. Burney and N. Pemberton, *Murder and the Making of English CSI*, Baltimore: Johns Hopkins Press, 2016, p. 63.
24. K. Biber, *In Crime's Archive: The Cultural Afterlife of Evidence*, Abingdon: Routledge, 2018, pp. 39–61.
25. S. D'Cruze, '"The Damned Place was Haunted": The Gothic, middlebrow culture and inter-war 'Notable Trials', *Literature and History*, 2006, 15: 37–58.
26. Ibid., p. 39; C. Emsley, T. Hitchcock and R. Shoemaker, 'The value of the proceedings as a historical source', *Old Bailey Online*, https://www. oldbaileyonline.org/static/Value.jsp, Accessed 16 January 2019; K.D. Watson, 'Love, vengeance and vitriol: An Edwardian true crime drama', in A. Kilday and D. Nash (eds.), *Law, Crime and Deviance Since 1700: Micro-studies in the History of Crime*, London: Bloomsbury, 2017, pp. 107–123.
27. Watson, 'Love, vengeance and vitriol', pp. 114–118.
28. This is a criticism Biber has levelled at twenty-first-century legal treatment of photographs, see Biber, *In Crime's Archive*, pp. 13–38, esp. p. 15.
29. K. Fink (Dir.), *CSI: Crime Scene Investigation* (TV), Season 6, esp. *Built to Kill Parts 1 & 2*, 2006.
30. W.J. Turkel, 'The crime scene, the evidential fetish, and the usable past' in Byers and Johnson, *CSI Effect*, pp. 133–146.
31. S. Marks (Dir.), *Of Dolls and Murder* (documentary film), 2012.
32. Biber, *In Crime's Archive*, pp. 39–61; C.M. Botz, *The Nutshell Studies of Unexplained Death*, New York: Monacelli Press, 2004.
33. Byers and Johnson, *CSI Effect*.
34. P. Savage, *Savage of Scotland Yard: The Thrilling Autobiography of Ex-Superintendent of the C.I.D.*, London: Hutchinson & Co., 1934, pp. 165–186.
35. Ibid.
36. TNA: DPP 2/78: 'Director of Public Prosecutions Case Papers: MAHON, P', Exhibit 75: Statement of Mahon (2 May 1924), Exhibit 78: Further statement of Mahon (3 May 1924), Exhibit 79: Further

statement of Mahon (5 May 1924), Exhibit 80: Additions to Statement Exhibit 79 (5 May 1924).

37. Ibid.; Savage, *Savage of Scotland Yard*, 168; TNA: DPP 1/78: Trial transcript [Detective Sergeant Thomas Frew cross-examined by Cassels], p. 27. Comparing these documents shows something of how interviews were conducted and statements made, that police had different understanding of 'verbatim' than might be supposed, and that their own questions were not recorded.

38. DPP 1/78: Police report, Savage to Ashley, 6 May and 13 June 1924, p. 18.

39. Ibid.; Trial transcript [PC Shelah], pp. 3–4.

40. Ibid.; Memo to counsel 2 July 1924; Statement of PC Shelah, 30 June 1924.

41. L. Seal, *Capital Punishment in Twentieth-Century Britain: Audience, Justice, Memory*, London: Routledge, 2014, pp. 24–26.

42. DPP 1/78: Police report.

43. Ibid.; Trial transcript, [Mahon, examined and cross-examined], pp. 145–244; [Judge's summing up], pp. 248–272. Mahon claimed he bought the chef's knife to cut meat, unaware of a carving knife amongst the bungalow inventory when he rented it, he bought the meat saw to change a lock on a wooden door.

44. Ibid. Some exhibits were introduced to identify Kaye as the deceased, including her possessions, hotel registers and statements of staff who recognized her from photographs in life, statements by her sister and friends about her gentle personality and plans to marry, receipts and account statements showing purchase of foreign currency and withdrawal of promissory banknotes Mahon spent in false names.

45. DPP 1/78: Trial transcript [Shelah], pp. 3–6; *Trial of Patrick Mahon*, p. 34.

46. DPP 1/78: Transcript [Shelah], pp. 2–4. Note that this closed questioning and short answer is typical of police courts and trial courts. At the former, questions and answers were written into prose to form depositions which were then treated as verbatim at the latter, though they were not. Similarly, *Old Bailey Proceedings* and published Great and Famous Trials can be compared to transcripts to show that questions were largely edited out, forming inaccurate accounts of courtroom exchanges.

47. Ibid., p. 4.

48. Biber, *In Crime's Archive*, pp. 13–38, esp. 15.

49. DPP 1/78: Transcript [Savage], p. 122, emphasis and parentheses as original.
50. Ibid. [Webster], p. 111; [Spilsbury], p. 119.
51. Ibid. [Mahon], pp. 221–222.
52. Ibid., pp. 238–239.
53. DPP 1/78: Transcript [Judge's summing up], pp. 248–273.

Archives

East Sussex Record Office at the Keep, Falmer:

Findmypast and The British Library, *The British Newspaper Archive*, www.brit-ishnewspaperarchive.co.uk, 2018, Accessed 15 December 2018.
Historic England Archive, https://archive.historicengland.org.uk, 2018, Accessed 15 December 2018.
SPA: Sussex Police Authority Papers concerning Rex v Mahon

UK National Archives, Kew:

ASSI: Assize Court Deposition Files, CRIM: Central Criminal Court Deposition Files, DPP: Director of Public Prosecutions Case Papers, MEPO: Metropolitan Police Papers and Correspondence

Newspapers

Coventry Evening Telegraph
Daily Mail
Daily Mirror
Midland Daily Telegraph
Northern Daily Mail
Police Journal
Taunton Courier

Bibliography

Bell, A., 'Crime scene photography in England, 1895–1960', *Journal of British Studies*, 2018, 57: 53–78.

Biber, K., *In Crime's Archive: The Cultural Afterlife of Evidence*, Abingdon: Routledge, 2018.

Botz, C.M., *The Nutshell Studies of Unexplained Death*, New York: Monacelli Press, 2004.

Burney, I. and Pemberton, N., *Murder and the Making of English CSI*, Baltimore: Johns Hopkins Press, 2016.

Byers, Michele and Val Marie Johnson (eds.), *The CSI Effect: Television, Crime, and Governance*, Lexington: Plymouth, 2009.

D'Cruze, S., '"The Damned Place was Haunted": The Gothic, middlebrow culture and inter-war 'Notable Trials'', *Literature and History*, 2006, 15: 37–58.

Emsley, C., Hitchcock, T. and Shoemaker, R. 'The value of the proceedings as a historical source', *Old Bailey Online*, https://www.oldbaileyonline.org/static/Value.jsp, Accessed 16 January 2019.

Fink, K. (Dir.), *CSI: Crime Scene Investigation* (TV), 2006.

Hitchcock, T., Shoemaker, R., Emsley, C., Howard, S., McLaughlin, J. et al., *The Old Bailey Proceedings Online, 1674–1913*, www.oldbaileyonline.org, version 8.0, March 2018, Accessed 30 October 2018.

Hutchinson, W.J. 'Plans and photographs', *The Police Journal*, 1937, 10: 42–51.

Keily, J. and Hoffbrand, J. *The Crime Museum Uncovered: Inside Scotland Yard's Special Collection*, London: I.B. Tauris and Museum of London, 2015.

Kilday, A.-M. and Nash, D. (eds.), *Law, Crime and Deviance Since 1700: Microstudies in the History of Crime*, London: Bloomsbury, 2017.

Marks, S. (Dir.), *Of Dolls and Murder* (documentary film), 2012.

Neale, A., *Photographing Crime Scenes in Twentieth-Century London: Microhistories of Domestic Murder*, London: Bloomsbury, 2020.

O'Brien, J., 'Simple photography for policemen', *The Police Journal*, 1936, 9: 63–71, 173–182, 331–342, 468–472.

Quirke, A.J., 'The evidence of the camera', *The Police Journal*, 1933, 6: 72–83.

Savage, P., *Savage of Scotland Yard: The Thrilling Autobiography of Ex-Superintendent of the C.I.D.*, London: Hutchinson & Co., 1934.

Science Museum Group, *Science Museum*, https://www.sciencemuseum.org.uk/, Accessed 15 December 2018.

Seal, L., *Capital Punishment in Twentieth-Century Britain: Audience, Justice, Memory*, London: Routledge, 2014.

Stewart, S., *On Longing: Narratives of the Miniature, the Gigantic, the Souvenir, the Collection*, Durham: Duke University Press, 1993.

Sutton-Vane, A., 'Murder cases, trunks and the entanglement of ethics: The preservation and display of crime scene material', in A. Adam (ed.), *Crime and the Construction of Forensic Objectivity from 1850*, Cham, Switzerland: Palgrave Macmillan, 2020, 279–301.

Turkel, W.J., 'The crime scene, the evidential fetish, and the usable past', in M. Byers and V. M. Johnson (eds.), *The CSI Effect: Television, Crime, and Governance*, Lexington: Plymouth, 2009: 133–146.

Wallace, E. (ed.), *The Trial of Patrick Mahon* (Famous Trials Series) London: Geoffrey Bles, 1924.

Watson, K.D., 'Love, vengeance and vitriol: An Edwardian true crime drama', in A. Kilday and D. Nash (eds.), *Law, Crime and Deviance Since 1700: Microstudies in the History of Crime*, London: Bloomsbury, 2017: 107–123.

4

The Biggar Murder: 'A Triumph for Forensic Odontology'

Alison Adam

Introduction

Early in the morning of Monday, August 7, 1967, the body of fifteen-year-old, Linda Peacock was found in a cemetery in Biggar, a small town in the Scottish borders. She had been strangled with a ligature and hit on the head with a heavy object. She was partially clothed but had not been raped. A number of items found at the crime scene were to form circumstantial evidence and these, coupled with a mark on her body, understood to be a human bite-mark by the police and the medical expert witnesses and which was matched to an individual in the course of the investigation, formed the basis of important evidence in the case which led to an arrest and conviction. The mark was clear and distinctive and a number of photographs were taken. As the investigation proceeded, dental impressions were taken from staff and youths at Loaningdale, the nearby approved school (a residential institution for young offenders, supervised

A. Adam (✉)
Sheffield Hallam University, Sheffield, UK
e-mail: a.adam@shu.ac.uk

© The Author(s) 2020   **69**
A. Adam (ed.), *Crime and the Construction of Forensic Objectivity from 1850*, Palgrave
Histories of Policing, Punishment and Justice,
https://doi.org/10.1007/978-3-030-28837-2_4

but not secure, with thirty-five residents aged from fifteen to seventeen). Gordon Hay, a seventeen-year-old youth with unusual dental features, became the chief suspect when his dental impressions were matched to the bite-mark by dental experts. The dental evidence was combined with the other circumstantial evidence to build the case against Hay and he was subsequently charged with the murder and convicted in March 1968. The case was one of the earliest in the UK and the first in Scotland where results deriving from forensic odontology investigations formed the decisive evidence in the trial. At the time, the case was hailed as a triumph for forensic odontology, at least by police and criminal justice officials and in the press.[1] For some, the case was a sign that the Scottish legal system was finally taking heed of science, having apparently lagged behind the criminal justice system of England and Wales in terms of the acceptance of scientific evidence.[2]

My aim in this chapter is not to acclaim the Biggar case as a landmark in forensic scientific evidential techniques, indeed the history of forensic odontology has mirrored that of other forensic techniques which were initially held to offer a high degree of certainty, but have been significantly challenged in subsequent decades.[3] Forensic objectivity was framed through an assemblage of the procedures surrounding the crime scene and criminal enquiry, including the deployment of evidential and representational techniques and the use of expert witnesses alongside a complex institutional setting and political climate, against which objectivity was created and maintained. The story of the Biggar murder stretches from the opening of Loaningdale School and its effect on the Biggar community from 1963 through the murder, investigation and trial in 1967 and 1968 and beyond in later articles, books and media reports.[4] The criminal justice narrative centres on police, expert witnesses, the criminal investigation and trial in conjunction with the civil and political narrative which involved the people of Biggar, reflected in the Town Council's expressed concerns, and the reactions of the local MP, Scottish Office, Social Work Department and the Loaningdale School Management Board.[5] These concerns were reflected in media reports on the terrible events in Biggar perpetrated by a boy from Loaningdale, a school which was 'an absolute disaster from the word go.'[6]

Civil and Political Background

Space permits only the briefest discussion of the social and political back-cloth to the Biggar murder. Nevertheless, an understanding of the political climate of 1960s Scotland in relation to child welfare and justice helps to frame the overall setting for the crime and also goes some way to explain the reluctance of politicians to offer an inquiry, close the school or even admit that the murder demonstrated, in the most shocking way possible, that Loaningdale School as an approved school with a modern, therapeutic, participative regime, was a failure.[7]

Post-war Britain saw a widespread spirit of reform in social policy, especially with respect to children's and youth provision; 1960s Scotland was regarded as unusually progressive.[8] The catalyst for Scotland's forward-looking approach to children's welfare and 'juvenile delinquency' (now termed youth offending) was the Report of the Committee on Children and Young Persons, initiated by the Secretary of State for Scotland in 1961 and which reported to the UK Parliament in 1964.[9] The committee was chaired by the Scottish judge, Lord Kilbrandon and its report became known as the Kilbrandon Report.[10] The Kilbrandon Report was seen as significant and far-reaching in creating '…a radical flagship policy which reformers would subsequently rally around.'[11]

The Kilbrandon Report was informed by a Scandinavian view which emphasized child-centred welfare rather than punishment and by the new social sciences which were coming into vogue in a number of British universities, notably the London School of Economics.[12] According to Smith: 'The [Kilbrandon] report reflected a faith that the social sciences might offer a means through which to understand and intervene in the social world in a similar way that the natural sciences offered a window on the physical world…. The belief that we might eradicate or at least substantially reduce juvenile delinquency through his proposals for social education… reflecting a wider *zeitgeist* in Scottish society.'[13] The Scottish Office of this period encouraged innovation and it was within this climate that Loaningdale School was opened in 1963: 'the idea was to see if you could operate in a more open and participative way with selected young people.'[14]

Judith Hart was one of the Scottish Office ministers appointed by Harold Wilson's new Labour government in 1964. Although Hart spent less than two years at the Scottish Office, she was a graduate of the London School of Economics where she had imbibed the new social sciences, was a strong supporter of the sociological approach and was an active and involved advocate for the reform of social services in Scotland.[15] Her role as a Junior Minister in the Scottish Office was crucial. Brodie et al. describe her as 'particularly devoted to the social work cause' and with a 'belief that social work would play a pivotal role in a fifty-year struggle to overcome the problems of modern society.'[16] Loaningdale was in Judith Hart's parliamentary constituency, Lanark.

In the wake of the shocking murder, suspicion quickly fell on the boys at Loaningdale. Through the mouthpiece of the Biggar Town Council, speaking on behalf of the people of the town, there were calls for a public inquiry into the running of the school, a demand which was refused by Under Secretary of State for Scotland, Bruce Millan, who was the minister responsible for education in Scotland and who thought a public inquiry was unnecessary.[17] The Town Council also pressed for a significant tightening in the school's security and for the school to be shut down.[18] While the murder was being investigated, a number of meetings took place between Biggar Town Council and Judith Hart, and between the Town Council, Bruce Millan, the Social Work Services Group and the Board of Managers of Loaningdale School.[19] The Town Council was highly critical of the school and its criticisms were reiterated at meetings and in the local and national Scottish press. The substance of the Town Council's criticisms spread comprehensively across the whole ethos and operation of the school, centring on the selection of boys, their discipline and behaviour in the school, including alleged violence, behaviour while out in the town, security and the management and organization of the school.[20] The Town Council listed a catalogue of petty crimes and other incidents attributable to the boys at the school, a list which they claimed they could corroborate.[21] It was well known that girls from the town willingly and, quite often, met boys from the school. Before the terrible events of August 1967, the back door of the school was never locked and the windows were not secure. Although the headmaster claimed that abscondings were rare and the absence of a boy would be quickly noticed, stories abounded of unsupervised cinema visits, boys coming and going as they pleased, often being found in the town at 11 p.m.[22] As it transpired during the trial, on the night of the murder, Gordon Hay had had no difficulty in leaving Loaningdale for some half an hour or so from around 10 p.m., long enough to meet and murder Linda Peacock and return undetected.

The local MP and Secretary of State, as representatives of the state and members of the Town Council, as representatives of the local people, well aware of the unique and experimental nature of the school often referred to it as the Loaningdale 'experiment.'[23] In the Town Council's view, the experiment was clearly a failure. However, Hart and Millan were understandably reluctant to admit that the experiment had failed even when it was becoming clear that the chief suspect was a boy from Loaningdale School. Interestingly, given her belief in the positive power of the school's ethos, Judith Hart was able to separate the philosophy of the school from its implementation believing that the ideas represented by the former were not wrong even if there were questions about how the school impacted the community.

Anxious to point to statistics as a form of objective data to bolster her argument as to the perceived success of the Loaningdale 'experiment', Hart wrote to Millan on behalf of the Town Council to request data as to the success/failure rate of Loaningdale in terms of recidivism compared to other approved schools managed on more orthodox lines.[24] If a former pupil was not found guilty of an offence within three years of release his stay in an approved school was regarded as a success. On this measure, based on one year's data (and given that average detention time was significantly lower than usual in Loaningdale), Loaningdale's success rate was 47% against a national overall success rate of 40%.[25] However, this data was based on a very short timescale and was likely to have been derived from considerably fewer than fifty pupils hence can hardly be regarded as statistically significant.

Millan seemed reluctant to acknowledge the devastation that the murder had caused the townspeople as his argument against a public inquiry centred on the claim that it would have 'little positive value either in removing such grounds as there may be for the criticisms…' and he expressed the hope that changes in organization could take place 'without vitiating the important experiment which the school was undertaking.' Acknowledging the Town Council's criticisms: '... I would hope that the Town Council and the community generally could be led to a greater appreciation of what the school is trying to do and... be encouraged to a more tolerant and co-operative attitude.'[26] When these words were written it would be some months before Hay's trial and guilty verdict, nevertheless it is surprising that Millan retained such optimism as to the possibility of future town-school relations given the direction of the criminal enquiry.[27] Millan's and Hart's views appeared to demonstrate a desire to separate the theoretical foundation of an experimental, therapeutic school based on central tenets of the new social work approach which had been embraced in Scotland, from its implementation, to retain a belief in the former despite problems in the management of the school, problems which had apparently contributed to the opportunity for a boy from the school to murder a local girl. As the police enquiry proceeded and focus increasingly centred on Gordon Hay, it was in the establishment's interest that sufficient resource was concentrated on decisively securing his conviction, so that Loaningdale (and by implication its place in the community) could move on from this terrible murder. Thereby, the reputation of the therapeutic regime which Loaningdale represented, and which was central to the ethos of Scottish social services in the 1960s, could be restored.

Indeed there was a public outcry after Hay was found guilty on March 7, 1968, and a good deal of the blame, in the opinion of the Scottish press, centred on the running of the school and its lack of security with headlines immediately after the trial such as: 'Close School Demand at Biggar: Experiment "a disaster"' and 'Rid us of killer's school says Linda town.'[28] These headlines made Bruce Millan's and the Loaningdale Management Board's hopes that eventually the town would come to accept the school seem impossibly naïve. Nevertheless, Loaningdale School continued to operate and must have been a cloud hanging over Biggar for years to come. Ironically, a study in the early 1970s showed that Loaningdale's reoffending rates were no different from other approved schools (by then known as 'List D' schools), probably because of patchy after-care and a return to inadequate family relationships rather than the school's regime itself and it was this and financial concerns which would eventually signal the school's closure rather than the shocking murder and the people of Biggar's demands.[29]

The Criminal Justice Narrative

The criminal justice narrative surrounding the Biggar case can be understood in terms of a combination of legal, policing and scientific arguments made in the course of the investigation and trial which is largely the 'official' story to be found in accounts of the trial and in a lengthy technical paper in the *Journal of the Forensic Science Society*.[30] The latter outlines aspects of the criminal enquiry, including sections of the trial transcript and the dental evidence. A number of other articles were written by the chief actors in the case.[31] As the trial transcript is not available, for the most part it is the readily available *Journal of the Forensic Science Society* paper, coupled with the memoirs of the officer in charge of the case, Detective Chief Superintendent (DCS) Muncie, from Lanarkshire Police, a well-known figure in Scottish policing who was to achieve somewhat legendary status by the end of his career for his ability to secure convictions,[32] which have filtered into later accounts including magazine and newspaper articles, 'true crime' books and even student presentations.[33]

It would be tempting to regard the *Journal of the Forensic Science Society* paper as the canonical view of the case because of its apparent comprehensiveness and its description of material not currently available elsewhere (such as the trial transcript). Nevertheless, this article is, at least to some extent, a history told by the victors and a range of other sources provides a form of triangulation This is especially important given that some details of procedure in the criminal enquiry are skated over or not described at all either in scientific journal papers or memoirs—such details emerge elsewhere. To some extent, this is the typical story of representation in an academic, scientific or technical paper without all the tacit knowledge that goes into making a skilled technical and scientific analysis where the procedural aspects, the nuts and bolts, packaging, soldering, wiring and so on, or in this case the skilled work involved in taking dental impressions and making appropriate models, are not usually regarded as part of the 'science'.[34] There are hints of this in the *Journal of the Forensic*

Science Society paper. For instance, the original dental models obviously had to be handled a great deal, a problem for plaster models which were easily damaged, so the second set was made from acrylic resin. The need for further, confirmatory details prompted making a third set of impressions from the chief suspect. Harvey, the chief prosecution dental witness, described examining the models produced by the defence 'in appalling circumstances of light and haste.'[35] However, if such forensic evidence is to be admissible in court and is to stand up to the scrutiny of cross-examination, the method of obtaining and constructing it has to be accepted scientifically by the court and the chain of custody of an item of evidence must be explicit and subject to agreed protocols.[36] Hence, procedures which do not have to be explicit in other kinds of academic or official texts may well need to be made explicit in a criminal case. This is part of what Lynch has characterized as 'administrative objectivity' in the context of scientific evidence in a legal setting.[37] The agreed administration of physical evidence, especially the way it is transformed, represented and displayed to the court, is as much a part of what counts as objectivity as the scientific analysis itself. At the end of the *Journal of the Forensic Science Society* paper, the authors somewhat cryptically point out that, after the trial, they had reflected upon the ideal procedure in a bite-mark case and offered an eleven-point suggested protocol for future cases.[38] There was no admission that their own procedures had been wrong (to make this explicit could have undermined the prosecution case), nevertheless it is notable that the proposed procedures are quite different from the sequence of events which unfolded in the Biggar case, notably in respect of requirements for a forensic dentist to see the bite-mark *before* a body is moved, for photographs to be taken of the marks alongside a metric scale, for swabs to be taken of dried saliva found around the bite-mark for blood-grouping of the assailant and for impressions of the area of the body containing the bite-mark to be taken in an alginate or rubber material.[39] Indeed, the Biggar murder sparked the development of protocols in Scotland to deal with bite-marks over the next few years, where procedures were initiated to link twenty-five dentists with the police in the main Scottish cities so that victims would be seen at the first available opportunity by a dentist, police photographer and pathologist.[40]

Physical Evidence and the Problem of Identification of Suspects

The Biggar murder presented immediate problems for the identification of suspects. There were no eyewitnesses to the murder although Linda had been seen about the town earlier in the evening. A witness had seen a male and female at the cemetery gate at around the appropriate time but thought that they must be a 'courting couple' and did not get a clear view; screams had also been heard.[41]

The cause of death was strangulation; there had been ligatures round her neck and wrist where there was also a burn mark caused by a petrol cigarette lighter. There had been two blows to the head with a heavy, blunt instrument. These, along with the marks on the breast formed the main injuries to the body. There was blood at the scene from the wounds to Linda's head. There was a fibre of sisal string under one of her fingernails and a piece of sisal string, knotted at each end and with a slip knot was hanging from a nearby tree.[42] It quickly became clear that there was little by way of physical evidence that might link a perpetrator definitively to the crime.[43]

In the early days of the investigation, with no eyewitnesses, no clear trace evidence to link the crime definitively to its perpetrator and no direct leads, the net was cast very wide. Linda Peacock was murdered on the night before the Scottish August bank holiday and schools were still on their summer break. It was still light in the evening, it would have been twilight at the time of the murder, and many people were enjoying the holiday weekend and the attractions of a travelling funfair which was in town. All these people had to be traced, including the staff from the funfair which had already packed up and left. Almost all those who were interviewed 'went through the sieve' as DCS Muncie put it.[44] As potential subjects were quickly eliminated, suspicion centred on the teenage boys from the local approved school, Loaningdale which was a very short walk or run, from the crime scene.[45]

The main non-dental evidence which was presented at the trial included the string found at the crime scene; Gordon Hay had shown a considerable amount of interest in a kind of 'cat's cradle' string trick that weekend in Loaningdale School and had put some sisal string in his pocket. He also had a petrol cigarette lighter which a housemother had let him keep. A heavy metal boat-hook which had been found on a camping trip by one of the boys from the school, and which Hay had admired, had mysteriously disappeared from a wardrobe and then was returned after the time of the murder.[46] On the evening of Saturday, August 5, Hay had spoken briefly to Linda Peacock at the funfair and later made a lewd comment to his friend indicating he wanted to have sexual intercourse with her.[47] Hay's defence of alibi, he claimed he was in the school at the time of the murder, eventually collapsed at the trial when other boys admitted he had been missing from the school at the crucial time on Sunday, August 6.[48] He had returned with muddy jeans, sweating and with his hair blown about as if he had been gardening, in time to get into bed for lights out so the housemaster did not notice his absence. Hay's jeans, which may have held vital clues were routinely washed the next day, hence potential evidence was lost.[49]

Dental Evidence: The Bite-Mark

There was some initial hesitation in acknowledging the potential significance of the alleged bite-mark, demonstrating that the path from the crime to 'a triumph for forensic odontology' (the title of Muncie's article) was far from linear. DCS Muncie's recounting of the sequence of events merely mention that 'assistance was sought regarding the bite mark' while other enquiries were ongoing.[50] Two police surgeons first examined the body, undertook the post-mortem and produced a joint report: Dr James Imrie, Lecturer in Forensic Medicine at the University of Glasgow saw the body in the cemetery on the day of its discovery and arranged for it to be moved to the City Mortuary in Glasgow where he undertook the post-mortem the same day with Dr Walter Weir, Consultant Pathologist at the Royal Alexandra Hospital, Paisley.[51] Both were experienced police surgeons; in particular, Imrie had very lengthy experience of police work having been appointed in 1936 as physician to the Glasgow Police.[52]

Although a number of photographs had been taken of the bite-mark, given that the two medical men did not explicitly think about linking it to the identification of the perpetrator at that stage, a dental expert was not immediately contacted.[53] Muncie's writing gives no clue as to the steps involved in deciding to call in a dental expert but the *Journal of the Forensic Science Society* paper suggests that it was Detective Inspector (DI) Osborne Butler from Glasgow Police's Identification Bureau who pressed this line of enquiry.[54] Butler had over fifteen years' experience of traumatic injuries left on bodies by tools or weapons and had seen several bite-marks in his career.[55]

Muncie paid tribute to the painstaking photography of police photographer, Detective Sergeant (DS) Jack Paton.[56] However, DS Paton had done more than merely record the bite-mark photographically. Towards the end of the *Journal of the Forensic Science Society* article, the authors note that DS Paton considered the marks on the body to be a bite-mark and, hence, took several photos.[57] Professor Keith Simpson recounts in his biography that although the police surgeon and pathologist thought that the mark on the breast was a bite-mark, '…it was Sergeant Paton alone who grasped its possible importance.'[58] Paton took fifteen photographs of the mark in the churchyard and later in the mortuary. He sent an urgent message to DI Butler at Glasgow Police headquarters, who received the message about the bite-mark as he was about to have morning coffee. His cup was left untouched as he hurried to the mortuary to see the marks himself and to arrange for more photographs to be taken.[59] He was lucky to arrive before the post-mortem began. Although he 'knew nothing about teeth and teeth marks'[60] he immediately suggested that dental help should be sought and this was agreed. Butler tried to contact Dr Warren Harvey who was attached to Glasgow Dental Hospital and was Lecturer in Forensic Dentistry to the Scottish Police. Butler was on a motor caravan holiday in Northern Ireland and could not immediately be contacted but he made contact with Glasgow Police on Thursday, August 10, offering to return immediately; this was not deemed necessary as Linda's funeral had taken place that morning.[61] This, of course, meant that Harvey, the chief dental witness, never saw the actual bite-mark on the body; indeed no dentist saw the bite-mark in the flesh.[62]

As, by now, suspicion was centring on the boys of Loaningdale School, permission was granted by the school and by the staff and boys themselves, individually, for Glasgow Dental Hospital staff to take sets of dental impressions and make plaster casts of their teeth.[63] Each cast was known only by a number, so dental staff examining the casts did not know the names of those from whom the casts were made. Ronald Laird, also from Glasgow Dental Hospital was part of the Crown dental team and John Furness, Home Office Lecturer in Forensic Dentistry from Liverpool was also called in.[64] Starting on August 22 comparisons of the dental casts were made with a transparency of the marks on the breast. Matches were rejected when models showed teeth were too regular or where there were dentures (teeth also too regular) and hence a 'sieving' process produced a short-list of five pairs of dental models of which no. 14 seemed to be the most likely fit at that stage.[65] As there were basically three distinctive marks within the overall bite-mark it began to look as if it might be difficult to convince a jury of a match and hence Keith Simpson, Professor of Forensic Medicine at Guy's Hospital, was contacted for help. Simpson was one of the foremost forensic pathologists in the UK and had more experience of dealing with bite-marks than any other British forensic expert.[66] His word carried considerable weight. Indeed, the first UK case where a murderer was identified by their teeth marks was made by Simpson in 1948 when he matched Robert Gorringe's teeth to a mark on the breast of his wife, Phyllis Gorringe.[67] Although Simpson was undoubtedly an expert forensic pathologist with considerable experience of bite-marks and identification of human remains by dental means, it is notable that his two most significant earlier bite-mark cases, the Heath and Gorringe cases involved clear chief suspects, a lover and husband, respectively,[68] and in both cases there was other evidence to support conviction. A 1956 bite-mark murder case where Simpson was involved and where there was no clear suspect, hence an open population of suspects, never produced a conviction.[69] Harvey and Butler carried their twenty-nine plaster models, photographs and models on a train to London to show them to Simpson.[70] He agreed with them that model no. 14 seemed the most likely fit where the largest mark on the overall bite-mark could have been formed by more than one tooth.

A second set of dental impressions was made from a short-list of five possible matches. These models were made of acrylic resin and were set up on articulators or hinges. Particular attention was given to how the upper and lower teeth bit together, and also the direction from which the bite-mark was made on Linda Peacock's body was considered further. A test of trial bites was made with the models on a suitable female body in the mortuary.[71] It then became clear that model no. 14 could not have made the bite-mark.[72] Only at this stage, quite far on in the timescale of the investigation, were two small ring marks which were part of the overall bite-mark, regarded as significant. The dental team agreed that the orientation of the bite was from behind, over the girl's shoulder. The upper and lower right canines of model no. 11 had pits in their tips and if that model were pressed into a nail bed, circular marks, similar to those on the actual bite-mark could be seen. The other twenty-eight original dental models were examined but only no. 11 had pits in the tops of the upper right and lower right canines. Although there were other distinctive dental features indicated by the bite-mark (broken incisor and filling partially missing causing a larger mark than the two ring marks), the police were warned of the numerical scarcity of points on which the identification was being made.[73] There was a clear intention to make an analogy with fingerprinting where, in many jurisdictions, there had to be a minimum number of matching points to consider that a fingerprint constituted a match with an individual. In Scotland, at this time, the requirement for fingerprints was sixteen matching points.[74]

Only at this stage was the dental team informed that model no. 11 was that of Gordon Hay, an individual of considerable interest to the police.[75] The ring marks were so unusual in normal light that Simpson was contacted again, and he suggested preparing scaled 'overlay transparencies.'[76] Steps were taken to take a third confirmatory cast of Hay's teeth and an application was made for a sheriff's warrant to authorize this.[77] A third impression of Hay's teeth was made on September 27 and his teeth were examined in considerable detail. It was noted that the right canines were not able to come into contact with each other so wear could not have caused the pits. The pits were not caused by dental decay but were probably caused by an illness in early childhood while the teeth were forming—Hay had had measles and mumps at the age of three.[78] By this stage the dental team believed that the ring marks on the breast had been caused by the upper and lower right canines of Hay's teeth biting against the tissue.[79] Although Harvey and the dental team believed that the pitting in the canines was unusual, a jury would need to be convinced. With no information from the literature or from colleagues on such pitting in canines Harvey undertook an extensive research project to examine the teeth of boys of a similar age to Hay. Harvey studied 1000 canines in almost 350 boys aged sixteen to seventeen.[80] He found only two teeth with pits similar to those of Hay and none in opposing canines in the same mouth.[81] Harvey was unable to find any other sets of teeth which could have produced the marks on the girl's breast.[82] John Furness, a further dental witness for the Crown examined 90 boys between sixteen and eighteen to test the rarity of pits such as those in Hay's right canines and found only one with a pit in the lower left canine.[83] Although Harvey and Furness undertook extensive research to demonstrate the rarity of canine pits, they did not attempt to express their results statistically in terms of the probability of an individual male of that age having this particular dental feature.[84] Similarly, their research did not prove that individual dentitions are unique and even if they are unique this does not mean that individuals will produce forensically distinguishable bite-marks. Nevertheless, it seems reasonable to accept that that their research lent considerable weight to the belief that pits of this sort in opposing canines were rare.

Meanwhile, Professor Keith Simpson was consulted once again as Harvey brought his latest set of dental exhibits to London. Simpson told him that had never seen such clear bite-mark photography. *'A jury should have no difficulty in understanding this evidence, and appreciating its simple strength. It is akin to tool-marking evidence or fingerprints.'*[85] He emphasized the importance of the standard, documented procedures in taking impressions and making casts and declared that no. 11 was *'an exact "fit"'* … *'…this bite-mark is such a striking detailed reproduction of the "bite" of No. 11 that no doubt could exist as to who bit the girl's breast. It happened "close to the time of her death".'*[86] Gordon Hay was arrested on November 24, 1967, whereupon he lodged a special defence of alibi, claiming he was in Loaningdale School at the time of the murder.[87]

There were different ways in which the match between dental model and bite-mark could be demonstrated and the Crown team decided to present dental evidence of potential matches between dental models and the bite-mark in court by superimposing transparencies of the dental impressions onto photographs of the bite-mark, a method that had been used in court before, including by Professor Simpson.[88] The fact that such methods had been used before, and by such an eminent expert witness as

Professor Keith Simpson, was important as the more the analysis and presentation of scientific evidence was seen to be following standard, tried and accepted procedures the more likely it was to be accepted in court—once again, part of the story of 'administrative objectivity'.[89]

The Crown (prosecution) team prepared extensively for the trial by preparing books of superimpositions of transparencies of the models from the third set of the teeth onto photographs of the breast with the bite-mark.[90] By that stage, and with the more detailed third dental cast, they were able to demonstrate sixteen points of comparison. They also produced comparisons with the second set of casts, although these casts were not as detailed as the final set, as they had been alerted to the possibility of the defence team challenging the manner in which the final set of impressions was obtained.

At the trial, a challenge was indeed made, by the defence, to the way that the third set of dental impressions was acquired on the basis that the dental evidence had been obtained, by means of a warrant, before charges were brought.[91] This was not a challenge to the admissibility of the dental evidence and the science involved as such, rather it was a question of admissible *procedure* in the Scottish criminal justice system. After consideration by a bench of three judges, in the middle of the trial and without the jury present, in itself a highly unusual procedure mid-trial, the objection was dismissed and the trial proceeded with the evidence from the third set of casts deemed admissible.[92] Two months after the trial a formal appeal was lodged by the defence on the basis of the admissibility of this evidence, once again, but the appeal was also dismissed.[93] Such was the significance of this ruling that it is cited in relation to the law of evidence of Scotland where, in taking evidence from the person of an individual who is not yet in custody, a warrant may be granted to take evidence from the person in circumstances where public interest is balanced against the interest of the individual.[94]

At the trial, DI Butler stated that although he had fifteen years' experience of examining marks made by tools, weapons and firearms this was the first time he had examined tooth marks in detail. As an experienced photographer, he had prepared the books of photographs to demonstrate the comparison between Hay's teeth and the bite-mark and to show where the pits in Hay's teeth could have caused the curious ring marks.[95] He was, of course, one of the relatively few people, to have seen the bite-mark on the body. It is notable that DI Butler's evidence as to the match between dental impressions and bite-mark was not reported in the *Journal of the Forensic Science Society* paper, however, George Saunders, the chief law correspondent to *The Scotsman* at the time, whose book on cases he had covered in his long career contained a chapter on the Biggar murder, outlined Butler's responses which were surprisingly definite given his lack of dental qualifications.[96]

The two dental expert witnesses for the defence were George Beagrie, Professor of Restorative Dentistry at the University of Edinburgh, and Torquil McPhee,[97] Head of the Department of Periodontology, also at Edinburgh. Beagrie stated that he could not believe that pits such as those found in Hay's teeth were rare as he had found twenty defects in the canines of ten of the prosecution models. Both defence witnesses thought that the bite-mark was ill-defined and that although Hay's teeth could have made the bite-mark there could have been others in Great Britain who had made the mark, hence the match of the mark to Hay's teeth was not proved beyond reasonable doubt. The two defence witnesses had spent four and four and a half hours respectively on the case and this coupled with the fact that they did not agree over whether cast no. 14 could be eliminated must have significantly weakened the defence case.

Simpson was an extremely important expert witness for the Crown. In thirty years' practice Simpson stated he had seen many bite-marks, both in his own and others' cases. 'I would say that in more than 30 years practice… that I have not seen a bite-mark with better defined details than this.' He claimed never to have seen rings in a bite-mark like those in this case so they could not be common.[98] Unsurprisingly, Simpson was asked whether it would have been an advantage if the dental experts could have seen the body. 'I am not quite sure about this. I have seen in many cases both the body and photographs, and I have seen photographs which more clearly displayed the marks on the skin than the body; this is a little difficult to understand but the shadows that lie in the skin are sometimes more clearly seen in the photographs in black and white, than they are in pink and rose colour in the skin.' Simpson also stated that if the bruising is fresh then colour photographs do not help at all.[99]

He did not think that there should be a fixed number of points of comparison between dental model and bite-mark 'but the more points of comparison that can be pointed to the more certain the truth, and the fewer the less certain.'[100] Bite-mark identification was quite different to fingerprints. It was not difficult to get sixteen to eighteen points of comparison with fingerprints whereas in dental markings 'one is lucky if one has half a dozen points of comparison.'[101] There are different types of comparisons to be made between patterns so when you do get a number of points of comparison on a dental mark it is of much greater value—as it was in this case—and it depends on how distinct and how unusual the marks are. The peculiarity of a particular point 'would be of the greatest possible significance.'[102] He said that if an explanation were forthcoming for the ring marks (which, of course, he had not seen before) 'I would regard it as quite remarkable evidence, positive evidence… I did see them, they are undoubtedly there.'[103]

As Mnookin argues, judges often have to decide whether an appropriate analogy can be made between a new technology which is brought before the courtroom and an existing technology and if so which is the appropriate technology for the analogy.[104] This can permit a new technology to be assimilated but it does not necessarily mean that the understanding of the new technique will be made purely in terms of the analogy with the older accepted, evidentiary technique. Here, Simpson made the analogy between bite-mark analysis and fingerprint analysis, in terms of number of points of comparison, but at the same time emphasizing that inevitably there were fewer points available in dental marks hence *each point was much more significant.* He was therefore able to use the analogy, or rather the lack of analogy between the two techniques, to his advantage.

As the headline expert witness, there were a number of aspects of Simpson's evidence which were very significant. The fact that the scientific analysis pre-trial and demonstration of evidence at the trial were made by means of photographs and transparencies, where a transparency of a photograph of the dental model was superimposed on a photograph of the bite-mark, is an illustration of just how well-accepted crime scene photography was in relation to producing an objective record of what exists, in the criminal justice system by then, even to the extent that Simpson was able to claim, without challenge, that colour photography would not have been helpful.[105] As Bell notes, crime scene photography had been used by the police since the middle of the nineteenth century and was an accepted documentary form where black and white photographs were seen as 'the definitive format for conveying the truth to the viewer.'[106] Black and white photographs were regarded as more objective than colour prints, and were still used in the 1960s in the UK, so in arguing that colour photography would not have been useful, Simpson was conforming to contemporary norms of forensic photography.[107]

The validity of each of the representational steps involved in accepting photographic evidence which was at some remove from the actual thing itself (photograph of bite-mark, teeth, model of teeth, photographic transparency of model of teeth) had to be accepted in its own right. The idea that a photograph could 'bring out' certain features not seen in real life makes a photograph appear more objective than the thing it represents. This is demonstrated by Simpson's claim that a photograph could bring out something not visible on the body and in Imrie's answers under cross-examination where on the one hand he stated that the photograph of the bite-mark was as he saw it in real life but shortly after said that the photograph brought out certain features which he had not seen at the time.[108] The models of suspects' teeth and the material in which they were modelled, plaster of Paris, acrylic resin and even copper also show a need for a considerable level of representational acceptance given that different substances show different things—harder substances such as acrylic resin and copper are less subject to wear. Considerable work in terms of representational acceptance was involved. This accords with Mnookin's description of the 'culture of construction' which developed from the middle of the nineteenth century in courtrooms in relation to the use of photographic evidence[109] which changed the ways that evidence was assembled.[110] Models could be made and photographs taken especially for the trial itself so evidence could be actively constructed and representations created. '…[P]resenting a case entailed not only telling a story, but depicting it visually, whether through photographs, diagrams, or models, in order to bring matters directly to the senses of the jury… These forms of visual evidence were often especially persuasive, for they let jurors see for themselves, rather than hearing secondhand the reports of percipient witnesses'[111] and this 'evidence turned jurors themselves into virtual witnesses.'[112] Undoubtedly, in this trial, in relation to the matching of a transparency of the dental model to a photograph of the bite-mark, the jurors were invited to see and understand the evidence, or at least accepted representations of the evidence, for themselves.

At the trial, Dr Imrie was cross-examined as to the significance of the bite-mark.[113] Imrie and Weir were the only medical specialists to have seen the body and the other expert witnesses had worked solely from photographs of the marks. Imrie stated that did not have it in mind that an identification could be made from the bite-mark, when he first saw it on Linda's body, even though he was asked this several times and in different ways.[114] Although not explicitly stated, the implication must be that he did not think, at the time, that an identification of assailant from the bite-mark was possible.[115] This view was confirmed by Dr Weir, under cross-examination.[116]

During the trial Imrie stated that what he saw on the photograph handed to him was the same as he saw on the body.[117] He was asked about tooth marks with white centres (ring marks). 'Looking at the photograph now I do see that there is a peculiarity in the sense there is a ring, a central clear area. Q.—What form of tooth would make that sort of mark? A.—A tooth with a hollow in its cutting edge.'[118] Hence Imrie was being invited to say that he saw something in the photograph that he had not seen on the body thus confirming, as Simpson had done, the ability of the photograph not just to reflect forensic reality—he had said under cross-examination that the photograph was as he saw the mark in the flesh—but to somehow amplify reality. This was confirmed when he was asked to consider the white lines across the bruising visible on the photo (probably tags of skin tissue). 'At the moment I don't recollect having noticed that at the time but it would be there because we photographed it. You did not particularly notice it?—The camera has picked it up.'[119]

Conclusion

There is no doubt that the Biggar murder was an important case. Lord Grant, the judge presiding over the trial, described it thus: 'It has been a grave, serious, and in some ways a unique case, difficult and puzzling.

… a classic example of circumstantial evidence, not enough to prove the suspect guilty; for this reason the dental and pathological evidence is of paramount importance.'[120] It was remarkable on a number of levels, not least because, the Scottish court accepted the dental evidence and the techniques and procedures and all the links in the evidential chain, whereby it was obtained, analysed and presented, with remarkable ease. This required accepting a representational chain from the mark on the body to the teeth of the accused which involved several steps including black and white photographs, dental impressions, dental models in different materials and transparencies of photographs of dental models fitted over a photograph of the mark. Each of these steps required acceptance that the representational artefact which was produced, photographic or otherwise, was an objective representation of what was really there. The act of appointing dental expert witnesses was very nearly an afterthought given that the police medical officers examining the body *in situ* and performing the post-mortem did not call in a dental expert at that stage. It was left to the quick thinking of DS Paton, the police photographer to contact his colleague, DI Butler at the Glasgow Police Identification Bureau to set in train the dental investigation. If Paton had not contacted DI Butler and if Butler had not arrived at the mortuary before the post-mortem, it is possible that vital evidence would have been lost making it far more difficult for the dental evidence to be convincing. The weak procedural aspects of the initial handling of the dental evidence were underscored by the later set up of considerably strengthened procedures to deal with bite-mark evidence in Scotland.[121] In addition to taking dental impressions, making dental models and matching transparencies of models against photos of the bite-mark, the hours spent by the Crown dental team in what was effectively a large dental research project to show that pitting in canines was very rare, coupled with the assuredness of the star expert witness, Keith Simpson, stood in contrast to the relative weakness of the defence. And as I have argued above, at least some of the reason for the Crown to have put such a level of resource into the prosecution's case lay with the significance of the Loaningdale 'experiment' and the need to secure a decisive conviction which would then permit a line to be drawn between the actual murderer and the reputation of the therapeutic regime represented by Loaningdale.

By contrast, the time spent on the case by defence expert witnesses was surprisingly minimal; the defence may not have had sufficient resource to mount a more lengthy expert witness examination of evidence. The defence concentrated on challenging the way in which the third set of dental impressions was obtained; if the objection had been upheld by the court, that evidence would have been disallowed and this might have weakened the prosecution case. The defence team spent little more than a day's effort in examining the dental evidence, did not challenge the procedural aspects of the way in which the defence team obtained the dental evidence and also seemed unable to take advantage of the views of a visiting Danish dental expert who had seen the Crown evidence and was sceptical that the mark on the girl's body was a bite-mark.[122] A number of sources cite the Biggar murder as the first case where dental evidence was used to convict in a murder case in the UK, which clearly underscores its perceived significance. This is not quite correct; it was the first such case in Scotland,[123] and it was the first case in the UK where a conviction was secured on only three main, although highly unusual, marks forming part of a bite-mark on a breast.[124]

But this is all the more significant, given that the therapeutic social science culture under which Loaningdale was instituted and managed was especially strong in Scotland, given that Scottish courts were believed to be more reluctant to accept scientific evidence than English courts at that time and had accepted a fairly new scientific technique without protest and given that the important third set of dental impressions could have been rendered inadmissible in court as Scots law is somewhat different to English law in relation to taking evidence from the person before arrest.[125] The Biggar case may have been a 'triumph for forensic odontology' but only because a number of links in the evidential chain (some of which were quite fragile) and its presentation in court held together without breaking.

Notes

1. W. Muncie, 'The murder of Linda Peacock: A triumph for forensic odontology', *Police Journal*, 1968, 41: 319–340.

2. W. Harvey, O. Butler, J. Furness, and R. Laird, 'The Biggar murder. Dental, medical, police and legal aspects of a case "in some ways unique, difficult and puzzling"', *Journal of the Forensic Science Society*, 1968, 8(4): 157–219.
3. M.J. Saks et al., 'Forensic bitemark identification: Weak foundations, exaggerated claims', *Journal of Law and the Biosciences*, 2016, 3(3): 538–575.
4. For example, see R. McKay, 'The Tell-Tale Toothmark', *Daily Record*, 19 October 2007; A. Gaw, 'The Biggar murder & Warren Harvey', *Forensic Dentistry Online*, 2015; G. Saunders, *Casebook of the Bizarre: A Review of Famous Scottish Trials*, Edinburgh: John Donald, 1991, pp. 17–39.
5. See NRS ED15/347/1 Loaningdale School, Biggar.
6. For other newspaper reports example see *The Scotsman*, 8 March 1968, 'Close School' demand at Biggar. Experiment 'a disaster' quoted words from Mr. James Stephen, a local garage proprietor and Honorary Treasurer of the burgh who once employed Hay for a week before dismissing him. Also see *Scottish Daily Express*, Friday 8 March 1968, 'The boy who killed Linda Peacock', complied by David Scott.
7. See P. McMichael, 'After-care, family relationships and reconviction in a Scottish approved school', *British Journal of Criminology*, 1974, 14(3): 236–247. The article makes no mention of the Biggar murder.
8. J. Murphy and G. McMillan, *British Social Services: The Scottish Dimension*, Edinburgh: Scottish Academic Press, 1992.
9. Ibid., p. 118.
10. *Children and Young Persons, Scotland, 1964* Cmnd. 2306. Also see S. Asquith (ed.), *The Kilbrandon Report. Children and Young Persons in Scotland*, Edinburgh: HMSO, 1995.
11. I. Brodie, C. Nottingham and S. Plunkett, 'A tale of two reports: Social work in Scotland from 'Social Work and the Community' (1966) to 'Changing Lives' (2006)', *British Journal of Social Work*, 2008, 38(4): 697–715, p. 699.
12. Murphy and McMillan, *British Social Services*, p. 129.
13. M. Smith, 'Something lost along the way: Changing patterns of leadership in Scottish residential schools', *Scottish Journal of Residential Child Care*, 2015, 14(2): 1–16, p. 2.
14. Ibid., p. 7.
15. Murphy and McMillan, *British Social Services*, p. 135.
16. Brodie, Nottingham and Plunkett, 'A tale of two reports', p. 700.

17. '...my own view that an inquiry would be of little positive value.' NRS ED15/347/1 Letter from Bruce Millan to Judith Hart, 17 November 1967. Also See William Harrold, 'Millan 'No' to School Probe' by William Harrold, *Scottish Sunday Express*, 19 November 1967.

18. NRS ED15/347/1 The Loaningdale School Company. Note of Meeting with Representatives of the Scottish Education Department, held at 41 Mansionhouse Road, Edinburgh, held on Saturday 25 November 1967.

19. While the murder was being investigated, a number of meetings took place between Biggar Town Council and Judith Hart, the local MP, between the Town Council, Bruce Millan of the Scottish Office, the Social Work Services Group and the Board of Managers of Loaningdale School. See file for NRS ED15/347/1. These items are not separately catalogued.

20. NRS ED15/347/1 347/10 Notes of Meeting with Biggar Town Council, Friday 27 October 1967.

21. The Town Council listed a catalogue of petty crimes and other incidents attributable to the boys at the school, a list which they claimed they could corroborate. NRS ED15/347/1 Loaningdale School: Notes of a meeting of Judith Hart and with Biggar Town Council, Friday 25 October 1967, p. 3.

22. For example, see NRS ED15/347/1 Loaningdale School: Notes of a meeting of Judith Hart and with Biggar Town Council, Friday 25 October 1967, p. 2.

23. See McMichael, 'After-care' on the social milieu therapy regime.

24. NRS ED15/347/1 Draft letter for Bruce Millan to send to Judith Hart (presumably drafted by R.D.M. Bell of the Scottish Education Department) n.d.

25. NRS ED15/347/1 Loaningdale's success rate was 47% set against a national overall success rate of 40%. NRS ED15/347/1 Draft letter from Bruce Millan to Judith Hart, n.d., 'an ex-pupil is regarded as successful if he is not found guilty of an offence in the three years following release. Even this arbitrary and unreliable yardstick can be applied as yet to only a very small number of boys in view of its short life; for boys released in the year to 31st March 1964 the Loaningdale success rate is 47 per cent as against an overall rate of 40 per cent.'

26. NRS ED15/347/1 Letter Bruce Millan to Lord Birsay (Chair of Loaningdale Management Board), 17 November 1967.

27. NRS ED15/347/1 Letter to Mr Millan, cc Solicitor General, p. 1. From R.D.M. Bell (Scottish Education Department) 5 February 1968.
28. *The Scotsman*, 8 March 1968 'Close School' Demand at Biggar: Experiment "a disaster"; *Scottish Daily Mail*, Friday 8 March. 'Rid us of killer's school says Linda town' by Ian Ramsay and Ron Flockhart.
29. Bloor et al. in M. Bloor, N. McKeganey and D. Fonkert, D., *One Foot in Eden: A Sociological Study of the Range of Therapeutic Community Practice*, London and New York: Routledge, 1988 state that after McMichael's study showing that Loaningdale's reconviction rates were no lower than other approved schools 'Loaningdale was subsequently closed', p. 22 but they do not give a date for the school's closure.
30. Harvey et al., 'The Biggar murder'.
31. For example, see R. Laird, 'The Biggar murder—Some personal recollections', *Dental History Magazine*, 2010, 4(1): 8–14. Muncie, 'The murder of Linda Peacock'; W. Muncie, *The Crime Pond. Memoirs of William Muncie*, Edinburgh: Chambers, 1979, chapter 10, pp. 137–165; K. Simpson, *Forty Years of Murder. An Autobiography*, London: Harrap, 1978, chapter 25, pp. 270–278.
32. Muncie, *The Crime Pond*. See chapter 6 for details of the Manuel murders.
33. Records of Scottish criminal trials in the High Court of Justiciary are closed to the public for 100 years. See https://www.nrscotland.gov.uk/research/guides/crime-and-criminals.
34. H. Collins, *Tacit and Explicit Knowledge*, Chicago and London: University of Chicago Press, 2010.
35. Harvey et al., 'The Biggar murder', p. 194.
36. Ibid., p. 192. There are hints of this when Simpson said dental impressions were obtained by accepted methods. 'Q. "Thus far, are you as a pathologist satisfied that the methods and techniques carried out have been recognised and correct ones?" A. "I have seen nothing unorthodox or unusual about them; they follow the usual pattern."'
37. M. Lynch, 'Science, truth and forensic cultures: The exceptional legal status of DNA evidence', *Studies in History and Philosophy of Science Part C*, 2013, 44(1): 60–70.
38. Harvey et al., 'The Biggar murder', p. 211.
39. Ibid., p. 213.

40. Saunders, *Casebook of the Bizarre*, p. 37.
41. Muncie, *The Crime Pond*, pp. 140, 142.
42. Muncie, 'The murder of Linda Peacock', pp. 319–320.
43. Ibid., pp. 322–323.
44. Ibid., p. 322.
45. Ibid., p. 323.
46. Ibid., p. 324.
47. Harvey et al., 'The Biggar murder', p. 159.
48. Ibid., p. 190.
49. Ibid., p. 160.
50. Muncie, 'The murder of Linda Peacock', p. 324.
51. NRS AD99/7/5 Extracts from trial of Gordon Hay, Volume II, p. 275.
52. M.A. Crowther and B. White, *On Soul and Conscience. The Medical Expert and Crime. 150 Years of Forensic Medicine in Glasgow*, Aberdeen: Aberdeen University Press, 1988, p. 84.
53. NRS AD99/7/5, pp. 291–292.
54. Harvey et al., 'The Biggar murder', p. 161. The Identity Bureau was the section of the Glasgow Police which handled scenes of crimes, fingerprints, tool-marks and other marks relating to crimes.
55. Laird, 'The Biggar murder', p. 9.
56. Muncie, 'The murder of Linda Peacock', p. 340.
57. Harvey et al., 'The Biggar murder, p. 214.
58. Simpson, *Forty Years of Murder*, p. 272.
59. Ibid., p. 272; Laird, 'The Biggar murder' p. 9.
60. Simpson, *Forty Years of Murder*, p. 272.
61. Harvey et al., 'The Biggar murder', p. 161.
62. Ibid., p. 214.
63. Ibid., p. 164.
64. Ibid.
65. Ibid., p. 167.
66. Ibid., p. 164.
67. R.M. Bruce-Chwatt, 'A brief history of forensic odontology since 1775', *Journal of Forensic and Legal Medicine*, 2010, 17(3): 127–130, p. 129; Simpson, *Forty Years of Murder*, pp. 270–271.
68. K. Simpson, 'Dental evidence in the reconstruction of crime', *British Dental Journal*, 1951, 91(9): 229–237.
69. Simpson, *Forty Years of Murder*, p. 172.

70. Ibid., p. 273.

71. Ibid.

72. Harvey et al., 'The Biggar murder', p. 167.

73. Ibid., p. 197.

74. A requirement for sixteen points matching for fingerprints was still in operation in Scotland, England and Wales at this time. By the 1980s the sixteen-point standard was coming under criticism in the UK for being neither statistically nor scientifically valid and was abandoned in England and Wales in 2001 See I.W. Evett and R.L. Williams, 'Review of the sixteen points fingerprint standard in England and Wales', *Journal of Forensic Identification*, 1996, 46(1): 49–73. In Scotland, the sixteen-point standard was abandoned after the controversy surrounding the Shirley McKie case—see https://archive.parliament.scot/business/committees/justice1/reports-07/j1r07-03-vol1-01.htm.

75. Harvey et al., 'The Biggar murder', p. 170.

76. Simpson, *Forty Years of Murder*, p. 275.

77. Harvey et al., 'The Biggar murder', pp. 170, 172.

78. Ibid., p. 172.

79. Ibid., p. 177 and Gaw, 'The Biggar murder.'

80. Harvey et al., 'The Biggar murder', p. 177.

81. Harvey et al., 'The Biggar murder', p. 177.

82. Ibid., pp. 194–195.

83. Ibid.

84. See C.G.G. Aitken and F. Taroni, *Statistics and the Evaluation of Evidence for Forensic Scientists*, 2nd ed., Chichester: Wiley, 2004, pp. 101–102.

85. Harvey et al., 'The Biggar murder', p. 180. Italics in original.

86. Ibid. Italics in original. If Linda had lived for much longer bruising would have spread causing the bruising and the bite-mark would have lost definition.

87. Ibid., p. 183.

88. Ibid.

89. For example, see Lynch, 'Science, truth and forensic cultures.'

90. Harvey et al., 'The Biggar murder', pp. 184–185.

91. Harvey et al., 'The Biggar murder', p. 206; NRS AD99/7/5 Extracts from trial of Gordon Hay, Volume II, pp. 307–344.

92. Harvey et al., 'The Biggar murder', p. 206; NRS AD99/7/5 Extracts from trial of Gordon Hay, Volume II, pp. 346–434.

93. Harvey et al., 'The Biggar murder', pp. 206–207.
94. M. Ross and J. Chalmers, *Walker and Walker. The Law of Evidence in Scotland*, 3rd ed., Haywards Heath and Sussex: Tottel, 2009, p. 330, 18.2.3.
95. Harvey et al., 'The Biggar murder', p. 191. Preparing books of photographs was standard evidentiary procedure. See A.H. Bell, 'Bodies in the bed: English crime scene photographs as documentary images', in A. Adam (ed.), *Crime and the Construction of Forensic Objectivity from 1850*, Cham, Switzerland: Palgrave Macmillan, 2020, 17–41.
96. Saunders, *Casebook of the Bizarre*, chapter 2, 'The Biter bit', pp. 17–39.
97. Harvey et al., 'The Biggar murder', pp. 195–196.
98. Ibid., pp. 191–192.
99. Ibid., p. 192.
100. Ibid., p. 194.
101. Ibid.
102. Ibid.
103. Ibid.
104. J.L. Mnookin, 'The image of truth: Photographic evidence and the power of analogy', *Yale Journal of Law & the Humanities*, 1998, 10(1), Article 1: 1–74, p. 6.
105. Ibid.; Bell, 'Bodies in the bed.'
106. Bell, 'Bodies in the bed', p. 31.
107. Ibid.
108. NRS AD/99/7/5, p. 293; Harvey et al., 'The Biggar murder', p. 192.
109. Mnookin, 'The image of truth', p. 5.
110. Ibid., p. 65.
111. Ibid.
112. Ibid., p. 66
113. NRS AD99/7/5, p. 289.
114. Ibid., p. 292.
115. Ibid., p. 294.
116. Ibid., p. 303.
117. Ibid., p. 287.
118. Ibid.
119. Ibid., p. 293.
120. Harvey et al., 'The Biggar murder', p. 158.
121. Saunders, *Casebook of the Bizarre*, p. 37.

122. S. Keiser-Nielsen, 'The Biggar murder', (Letters to the Editor), *Journal of the Forensic Science Society*, 1969, 9(3-4): 222–223.
123. For example, J. Hinchcliffe 'Forensic odontology, part 4. Human bite marks', *British Dental Journal*, 2011, 210(8): 363–338 states that Hay was the first person to be convicted by forensic dentistry in the UK.
124. Harvey et al., 'The Biggar murder', p. 215.
125. Ibid., pp. 206–207.

Archives

National Records of Scotland, NRS AD99/7/5 Extracts from trial of Gordon Hay, Volume II
National Records of Scotland, NRS ED15/347/1 Loaningdale School, Biggar

Newspapers

The Daily Record
The Scotsman
Scottish Daily Express
Scottish Daily Mail
Scottish Sunday Express

Bibliography

Aitken, C.G.G. and Taroni, F., *Statistics and the Evaluation of Evidence for Forensic Scientists*, 2nd ed., Chichester: Wiley, 2004, 101–102.
Asquith, S. (ed.), *The Kilbrandon Report. Children and Young Persons in Scotland*, Edinburgh: HMSO, 1995.
Bell, A.H., 'Bodies in the bed: English crime scene photographs as documentary images', in A. Adam (ed.), *Crime and the Construction of Forensic Objectivity from 1850*, Cham, Switzerland: Palgrave Macmillan, 2020, 17–41.
Bloor, M., McKeganey, N. and Fonkert, D., *One Foot in Eden: A Sociological Study of the Range of Therapeutic Community Practice*, London and New York: Routledge, 1988.

Brodie, I., Nottingham, C. and Plunkett, S., 'A tale of two reports: Social work in Scotland from 'Social Work and the Community' (1966) to 'Changing Lives' (2006)', *British Journal of Social Work*, 2008, 38(4): 697–715.

Brownlie, A.R. '12(2) 1972: There is a time to speak', in N. Nic Daéid (ed.), *Fifty Years of Forensic Science: A Commentary*, Chichester: Wiley, 2010, 204–207.

Bruce-Chwatt, R.M., 'A brief history of forensic odontology since 1775', *Journal of Forensic and Legal Medicine*, 2010, 17(3): 127–130.

Collins, H., *Tacit and Explicit Knowledge*, Chicago and London: University of Chicago Press, 2010.

Crowther, M.A. and White, B., *On Soul and Conscience. The Medical Expert and Crime. 150 Years of Forensic Medicine in Glasgow*, Aberdeen: Aberdeen University Press, 1988.

Evett, I.W. and Williams, R.L., 'Review of the sixteen points fingerprint standard in England and Wales', *Journal of Forensic Identification*, 1996, 46(1): 49–73.

Gaw, A., 'The Biggar murder & Warren Harvey', *Forensic Dentistry Online*, 2015, http://www.forensicdentistryonline.org/the-biggar-murder-warren-harvey/, Accessed 7 May 2019.

Harvey, W., Butler, O., Furness, J. and Laird, R., 'The Biggar murder. Dental, medical, police and legal aspects of a case "in some ways unique, difficult and puzzling"', (with a note on the law by A.R. Brownlie and a foreword by K. Simpson, *Journal of the Forensic Science Society*, 1968, 8(4): 157–219.

Hinchliffe, J., 'Forensic odontology, part 4. Human bite marks', *British Dental Journal*, 2011, 210(8): 363–338.

Keiser-Nielsen, S., 'The Biggar murder', (Letters to the Editor), *Journal of the Forensic Science Society*, 1969, 9(3-4): 222–223.

Laird, R. 'The Biggar murder—Some personal recollections', *Dental History Magazine*, 2010, 4(1): 8–14.

Lynch, M., 'Science, truth and forensic cultures: The exceptional legal status of DNA evidence', *Studies in History and Philosophy of Science Part C*, 2013, 44(1): 60–70.

McMichael, P., 'After-care, family relationships and reconviction in a Scottish approved school', *British Journal of Criminology*, 1974, 14(3): 236–247.

Mnookin, J.L., 'The image of truth: Photographic evidence and the power of analogy', *Yale Journal of Law & the Humanities*, 1998, 10(1), Article 1: 1–74, https://digitalcommons.law.yale.edu/yjlh/vol10/iss1/1, Accessed 8 May 2019.

Muncie, W., 'The Murder of Linda Peacock: A triumph for forensic odontology', *Police Journal*, 1968, 41: 319–340.

Muncie, W., *The Crime Pond. Memoirs of William Muncie*, Edinburgh: Chambers, 1979.

Murphy, J. and McMillan, G., *British Social Services: The Scottish Dimension*, Edinburgh: Scottish Academic Press, 1992.

Ross, M. and Chalmers, J., *Walker and Walker. The Law of Evidence in Scotland*, 3rd ed., Haywards Heath and Sussex: Tottel, 2009.

Saks, M.J., et al., 'Forensic bitemark identification: Weak foundations, exaggerated claims', *Journal of Law and the Biosciences*, 2016, 3(3): 538–575.

Saunders, G., *Casebook of the Bizarre: A Review of Famous Scottish Trials*, Edinburgh: John Donald, 1991.

Simpson, K., 'Dental evidence in the reconstruction of crime', *British Dental Journal*, 1951, 91(9): 229–237.

Simpson, K., *Forty Years of Murder. An Autobiography*, London: Harrap, 1978.

Smith, M., 'Something lost along the way: Changing patterns of leadership in Scottish residential schools', *Scottish Journal of Residential Child Care*, 2015, 14(2): 1–16.

5

Making Forensic Evaluations: Forensic Objectivity in the Swedish Criminal Justice System

Corinna Kruse

Forensic objectivity is an issue that is very much alive in forensic practice today. The underlying difficulty is the same as it was in the past: practitioners must deliver legally secure and useful results despite dealing with inescapable uncertainty. How this legal security, usefulness, and uncertainty are understood changes between contexts and with time, but forensic practitioners are always expected to give a professional opinion on matters about which their knowledge is inevitably limited. In the laboratory, forensic scientists cannot know with absolute certainty whether the match they have established between a trace from the crime scene and a comparison sample is due to connection or coincidence. At the crime scene, crime scene technicians cannot know with absolute certainty how

I am deeply grateful to my interlocutors for opening their world and generously giving of their limited time to me, to the Swedish Research Council and the Swedish Foundation for Humanities and Social Sciences for funding this research, and to my *Body, Knowledge, Subjectivity* colleagues for their invaluable comments.

C. Kruse (✉)
Department of Thematic Studies - Technology and Social Change,
Linköping University, Linköping, Sweden
e-mail: Corinna.Kruse@liu.se

© The Author(s) 2020   **99**
A. Adam (ed.), *Crime and the Construction of Forensic Objectivity from 1850*, Palgrave Histories of Policing, Punishment and Justice,
https://doi.org/10.1007/978-3-030-28837-2_5

the traces they find have come into being. However, both the match in the laboratory and the technicians' observations at the crime scene are valuable information for the investigation—if the uncertainty is made manageable.

It is this uncertainty that makes forensic objectivity necessary. As it is impossible to achieve absolute certainty, there is no way of knowing or measuring how accurate a piece of forensic evidence is; thus, validity cannot be achieved through absolute accuracy. Instead, validity is a matter of producing evidence in a way that is accepted as reliable and legally secure. In the contemporary Swedish context—as in many others—a crucial part of this acceptable way is 'objectivity;' a notion shared across the criminal justice system's different professions, but sometimes understood in different ways.

I will discuss contemporary Swedish forensic objectivity at two different and separate sites with their separate and different professions: the forensic scientists in the laboratory—the National Forensic Centre (NFC)—and the crime scene technicians at the crime scene. Both sites' evaluation practices rely, albeit in different ways, on Bayesian reasoning, a mathematical-statistical concept used for assessing probabilities. The NFC's forensic scientists have used Bayesian reasoning since 2008; it has been introduced more recently to the crime scene technicians' work.

My empirical basis is ethnographic fieldwork, mainly interviews with staff at the NFC as well as with crime scene technicians (some of them former crime scene technicians). I set this material against the background of earlier ethnographic work in the Swedish criminal justice system, where I have studied forensic evidence since 2008, first its production,[1] then how the criminal justice system organizes for interprofessional cooperation through crime scene technician training, and recently the movement of knowledge objects such as expert statements and crime scene reports.

My theoretical point of departure is Lorraine Daston and Peter Galison's tracing of objectivity through the history of science[2] and of 'how and why objectivity emerged as a new way of studying nature, and of being a scientist'.[3] They write,

The history of the various forms of objectivity might be told as how, why, and when various forms of subjectivity came to be seen as *dangerously subjective*.[4]

Their point is that objectivity is neither a given nor a constant. Instead, scientific objectivity has taken different shapes as scientists have seen different dangers to the validity of their work. However, instead of treating forensic objectivity as yet another example of a particular form of objectivity constituting the answer to a particular danger, I will argue that *forensic objectivity*, a notion that is rooted in the criminal justice system as a whole and shared across professions, is filled with (sometimes differing) meaning in different sites and contexts. I will first discuss forensic objectivity in the laboratory—whose evaluation practices are the template for those at the crime scene—before moving to the crime scene with its sometimes different meanings and ways of striving for the 'same' forensic objectivity.

Evaluation in the Laboratory

The NFC is Sweden's main forensic science laboratory, with a central laboratory in Linköping and smaller regional laboratories in Stockholm, Gothenburg, and Malmö.[5] It is part of the police and therefore run by the state, but although its forensic scientists are employed by the police, most of them do not have police training and experience; instead they typically have science backgrounds combined with in-house training in one (or a few) forensic specializations. Their work takes place predominantly in the laboratory; only in exceptional cases do they accompany crime scene technicians to crime scenes. Forensic scientists analyse the traces recovered by the crime scene technicians, producing written expert statements that state their findings and the result of their evaluation of these findings—an evaluation made with a Bayesian approach.

Using a Bayesian approach in the forensic science laboratory is not exclusive to Sweden. Similar approaches are used to varying extents in forensic science laboratories in, for example, England, Ireland, the Netherlands, Belgium, Spain, Poland, and New Zealand. This use is not entirely undisputed, however; there are lively discussions on whether and how Bayesian reasoning should be used, for example recently in the journal *Science & Justice*.[6]

In practice, the NFC's Bayesian approach means that the forensic scientists, after having obtained a match—between, say, a shoe mark recovered from a crime scene and a shoe seized from a suspect—evaluate how strong conclusions can be drawn from the match. This is necessary because a match far from equals identity. The shoe matches the mark, but so might quite a number of other shoes with the same sole pattern. Wear and damage decrease the likelihood of these other matches, but, as the forensic scientists cannot possibly exclude all other shoes (or even know how many pairs of shoes with this particular pattern exist), analysis can never completely remove all doubt that the trace and the comparison sample bear a relation to each other. 'We weren't there when it happened', forensic scientists say, 'so we can't know for certain'.

Hence, the evaluation produces a probabilistic result.[7] The forensic scientist compares the probability of obtaining a match given that the mark was made by the suspect's shoe with the probability of obtaining a match given that the mark was made by another shoe. That is, she or he evaluates two propositions—the so-called main proposition that the mark was made by the shoe in question as opposed to the so-called alternative proposition that the mark was made by a different shoe—against each other in the light of the match between the shoe and the trace, arriving at a likelihood ratio (or an interval of likelihood ratios).[8] In analytic terms, the evaluation makes inescapable uncertainty manageable—quantified uncertainty is still not certainty, but it has been turned into a known quantity.

For DNA evidence, the likelihood ratio can be calculated based on a reference database. For other types of evidence, such precision is unattainable; in such cases the forensic scientist estimates an order of magnitude for the likelihood ratio and chooses the corresponding interval from a predefined scale. A number of factors affect the result of that estimation. For evaluating a shoe mark, important factors are how many details beyond the pattern itself the forensic scientists have been able to find; how clear and complete the crime scene mark is; how soon after the suspected crime the shoe has been seized (as a shoe's sole changes with wear);

how common this specific kind of sole is (as shoes typically are mass produced, there may be quite a number of them in circulation); and whether all kinds of shoe are used as a reference population or only those of the same make.

These factors are not determinate. The details found depend on the forensic scientist's analysis and skill (and the time they can spend on the case); the quality of crime scene marks varies; the exact number of shoes with a specific sole pattern in circulation is (in the majority of cases) impossible to know; there is no given reference population but one must be chosen.[9] In other words, even though the Bayesian approach provides a framework and rules for evaluating laboratory results, this evaluation also depends on personal (and therefore to some extent inevitably subjective) judgment and decisions.

Accordingly, experience is regarded as valuable to the laboratory and as a crucial part of producing solid forensic evidence. But despite of this valued experience's inevitably personal nature, forensic scientists want to avoid arbitrary or biased decisions, seeing a danger of over- or underrating matches, of unwitting partiality, and of idiosyncrasies affecting the result. As a counterweight, the NFC aims to standardize forensic practice across specializations and to thus make the expert statements commensurable. Of course, the different forensic specializations perform different analyses and base their evaluation on different criteria, but apart from fingerprint analysis they all produce probabilistic evidence and report their results on the same scale.[10]

Balancing Judgment

Through the lens of Daston and Galison's work, what constitutes dangerous subjectivity in the forensic laboratory appears to be primarily the forensic scientist's individual idiosyncrasies as well as her, potentially biased or even partial, choices and judgments.[11] Forensic objectivity seems to be a matter of restraining such subjectivity through the institution of rules.

Using a Bayesian approach for these rules is by no means unique; statistical-mathematical methods of calculating in particular probabilities have historically been developed and regarded as a way of being rational about risk.[12] Quantification and statistics engender trust in, or rather through, numbers.[13] This trust could be seen as a version of mechanical objectivity,

> the form of objectivity that strives to eliminate all forms of human inter-
> vention in the observation of nature, either by using machines … or by
> mechanizing scientific procedures, as in deploying statistical techniques to
> choose the best of a set of observations.[14]

In other words, mechanical objectivity combats subjective judgment and decisions by standardizing the scientific gaze through encasing it in mechanical devices or through implementing explicit rules or statistical procedures. Formal rules and statistical methods—like the Bayesian approach in the forensic science laboratory—invoke impartiality by replacing a potentially subjective, and thus potentially partial, decision:

> A decision made by the numbers (or by explicit rules of some other sort)
> has at least the appearance of being fair and impersonal. Scientific objectiv-
> ity thus provides an answer to a moral demand for impartiality and fair-
> ness. Quantification is a way of making decisions without seeming
> to decide.[15]

Personal judgment, potentially biased and flawed, is replaced with the impersonal result of calculating. Porter draws parallels to making judgment in court, emphasizing an association with morality:

> In most contexts, objectivity means fairness and impartiality. Someone
> who "isn't objective" has allowed prejudice or self-interest to distort a judg-
> ment. The credibility of courts depends on an ability to elude such charges.
> … Both these senses of objectivity imply that rules should rule, that profes-
> sional as well as personal judgment should be held in check.[16]

In other words, (impersonal) quantification that follows rules, for example how to arrive at a likelihood ratio interval, is perceived as objective in the sense of being fair and impartial. Thus, the adoption of the Bayesian approach suggests that personal decisions and interventions are a concern for forensic scientists—this is further underlined by forensic scientists' stressing their obligation to be impartial.

This does not mean to say that their output is necessarily correct in an absolute sense. The forensic scientists themselves point out that arriving at the same numbers 'does not mean that they are correct'—such certainty is unattainable. This caveat resonates with Daston and Galison's assertion that mechanical objectivity does not equal accuracy; as they put it, '[n]onintervention, not verisimilitude, lay at the heart of mechanical objectivity'.[17] In other words, where forensic objectivity counteracts personal idiosyncrasies and biases, there might still be mistakes or systematic bias.

The numbers generated by the Bayesian approach may of course still suggest accuracy; Lynch et al., for example, note that 'the apparently precise measures of uncertainty provided by probability figures [for DNA evidence] became a source of credibility'.[18] That is, the seeming precision of a number—especially if it comes with the authority of (mechanically) objective calculation—further contributes to the perceived reliability of forensic evidence.

Thus, forensic objectivity in the laboratory could be understood as striving for mechanical objectivity in an enterprise that depends on personal judgment and skill and that thus cannot delegate important parts of the work to machines. Subjectivity in the form of personal judgment is balanced by striving towards uniformity and standardization without eliminating personal experience and skill. This standardization also makes practitioners exchangeable and minimizes personal intervention; to put it another way, it distances the individual that is the source of subjectivity from the evaluation. In addition, counteracting subjectivity is, through its roots in statistical methods, intertwined with associating the evaluations with science and thus the reliability and trustworthiness attributed to science.

The Bayesian approach that this forensic objectivity is based on is also the foundation for forensic objectivity at the crime scene. However, by analogy with Bruno Latour's distinction between 'science in the making' and 'ready made science', one could say that forensic objectivity in the laboratory has already been turned into ready-made forensic objectivity whose '[u]ncertainty, people at work, decisions, competition, controversies'[19] have been resolved or hidden away as evaluation practices have been established, disseminated, and made routine in the laboratory. Forensic objectivity at the crime scene, on the other hand, is presently in many ways forensic objectivity in the making—forensic objectivity that is still being worked out and negotiated.

Extending Probabilistic Reasoning to the Crime Scene

In Sweden, crime scenes are examined by crime scene technicians (*kriminaltekniker*), police officers with policing experience and subsequent specialist training, both by a kind of 'apprenticeship' with senior colleagues and, subsequently, formally from the NFC.[20] Crime scene technicians are often dispatched to a crime scene by themselves; they document the site, search for and recover traces that can give clues to what happened at the site (and become evidence later in the process), give the investigation leader advice on which traces to send to the NFC, and write crime scene reports that make their examination and conclusions—the latter in the form of a so-called 'concluding judgment'—accessible to the investigation.[21]

Unlike in forensic laboratory contexts, where Bayesian approaches are quite widespread, using a Bayesian approach for crime scene analysis appears to be unique to Sweden. The NFC, who has been involved in crime scene technicians' work through organizing and carrying out their training since 1998 and with overall responsibility for their crime scene work since 2015,[22] saw a need to harmonize crime scene reports and make them, in their words, 'scientifically sustainable.' In the past, each crime scene technician wrote reports in their own way, which meant that the same expression could have quite different meanings and could create uncertainty for the recipients. To remedy this, the NFC developed a model for analysing crime scenes and writing crime scene reports, developed from the laboratory's own evaluation practices. The model, whose development involved crime scene technicians, is still in the process of being disseminated[23] and adjusted; in the NFC's words, it is a 'work in progress'.

Like the evaluation in the laboratory, the crime scene model uses propositions that are evaluated against each other. In practice, that means that crime scene technicians are taught to ask themselves 'a lot of questions' about what can have happened at the crime scene and, as one of the developers of the model explained,

> make a list of all the answers whatsoever that you can come up with to those questions. Some of them are far-fetched, some are highly natural. And one answer is definitely the one you believe in the most, because that one was your first impulse, … something like this ought to have happened here.

This 'first impulse' can be, for example, that a fight has recently taken place in a disarranged corner of a room, that a window has been prised open in the course of a break-in, or that someone has touched a bloody hand to a wall. There are other possibilities, of course. The room might always look like that, the window might have been damaged independently from the break-in, and the blood might have been transferred to the wall by another object.

To evaluate, the technicians are to turn these possibilities into propositions: a fight has taken place, the room is always in disorder, the window has been prised open in the break-in, the damage to the window is old, a bloody hand has touched the wall, some object has transferred blood to the wall. Starting with the proposition based on their 'first impulse', the technician then looks more closely at the crime scene—and only the crime scene, using 'outside' information is not allowed—looking for what the model calls 'detailed traces' that can reject or confirm the proposition. For example, fresh scuff marks in the dust on the floor of the disarranged corner of the room would strengthen the proposition that a fight has taken place, and so would dust under the furniture in disarray but not on the presumably newly horizontal surfaces. Conversely, an even film of dust on all horizontal surfaces suggests that the room has been in disarray for a while; such findings contradict the fight proposition, as the model developer explains:

> If you don't find any contradictory traces, then you have confirmed the main proposition. If you find contradicting traces, you have to think about replacing the main proposition, and if you can't really, it almost doesn't matter which you choose as your main proposition, there are always

contradicting traces, you just have to leave it. Then you can't say anything about this.

At the end of this process, ideally the crime scene technician is left with one main proposition for every aspect of the crime scene and one alternative proposition composed of all the alternative propositions pertaining to that aspect. These can be, for example, that the room was disarranged in the course of a fight versus that the room was disarranged unrelatedly to the presumed crime. What remains to be done is to assess these propositions' probabilities. By now, the main propositions are more probable—and often also more specific—than their alternatives, otherwise they would not be main propositions, but that in itself does not say very much. So, the next step is to go through the detailed finds again and weigh them against the alternative proposition in what the model calls 'endpoint anchoring'. The technician is to ask her—or himself, 'would I be able to get those traces—would I be able to make this observation if the alternative proposition were true?' They choose their answer out of four possible prefabricated answers: *Yes, it's fully possible; It's not expected, but it could be like this; It's exceedingly odd, but not impossible;* and *No, it's impossible.* The process starts with the endpoints—hence the name 'endpoint anchoring'—of the scale:

> If my first impulse is no, I start, a little daringly, *No, it's impossible.* But then I ask, is it impossible? If it isn't, I go to *It's exceedingly odd but not impossible* and stay there.

In the same manner, if the technician's first impulse is yes, they are to start with *Yes, it's fully possible* and then to consider whether *It's not expected, but it could be like this* is a better-fitting answer. Again, they are to stop there:

> [E]xactly that stop, that's important to remember. It's there that you listen to your first impulse but you challenge it. … You can't just take it straight off, you have to challenge it. But … if my first impulse is yes, you can't lower that to that it's exceedingly odd but not impossible. … Something's not holding together if you have to go that far.

In numbers, the one extreme—*Yes, it's fully possible*—is attached to a likelihood of at least 50% that the alternative proposition is true, whereas the other extreme—*No, it's impossible*—is attached to a likelihood of 0%. The intermediary answers are attached to likelihoods of less than 50% (*It's not expected, but it could be like this*) and 1% (*It's exceedingly odd, but not impossible*). It is important to note that this endpoint anchoring refers to the alternative proposition—thus, what is deemed *impossible* or *fully possible* in the light of the detailed observations is that the alternative proposition is true, not the main proposition. Thus, the answer that gives most certainty is *No, it's impossible*, as it in effect rules out everything but the main proposition, while the other extreme contains most uncertainty. This is tied to standardized expressions that the crime scene technicians are expected to use in their crime scene reports. When it is deemed impossible that the alternative proposition can be true, the technicians are taught to report this as the results of the crime scene examination 'showing' that the event specified in their main proposition happened. For example, if the detailed observations the crime scene technician makes in the disarranged corner of the room—perhaps scuff marks in the dust on the floor and drops of blood—have convinced them that every other explanation than a fight is impossible, they will write that their examination shows that a fight has taken place there. If they arrive at the conclusion that *It's exceedingly odd, but not impossible* that the alternative proposition is true, they are to write that their examination gives 'strong support' to a fight having taken place. The expressions that match *It's not expected, but it could be like this* and *Yes, it's fully possible* are that the crime scene examination gives 'support' to and that it speaks 'neither for nor against' the main proposition.

In a similar way to the Bayesian approach in the laboratory, the crime scene model thus incorporates personal skill and experience into mathematical-statistical thinking (although the model is packaged in a way so as to not require its users to handle numbers or theories), balancing the need for personal judgment against the dangers of intervention. Like its 'sibling' in the laboratory, the crime scene model evokes the rationality and mechanical objectivity associated with probabilities and statistics. However, a closer look at how different practitioners discuss the model reveals quite different understandings of what forensic objectivity at the crime scene means and how it should be performed.

Biases and Impulses

Just as in the laboratory, subjectivity is seen as dangerous at the crime scene. However, where personal interventions and decisions carry the danger of subjectivity in the form of arbitrariness in the laboratory, subjectivity at the crime scene is less clear-cut. By law, a crime scene examination must be impartial in the sense of equally seeking to incriminate and to exonerate, but different practitioners describe the dangers to this forensic objectivity differently. The type of subjectivity the crime scene model explicitly is meant to counteract is overconfidence in first impulses or the 'gut feeling' based on personal experience. In this, experience seems to be regarded rater ambivalently: In giving first impulses the prominent place as point of departure, the model acknowledges the importance of experience. Yet, experience is also perceived as prone to bias, for example in the shape of prejudice, incompleteness, or getting too invested in a first impression; thus it is held in check by formalized questions and rules.

Another danger to forensic objectivity that the model highlights is the danger of letting one's crime scene assessment be influenced—in other words, biased—by the rest of the investigation that proceeds simultaneously. Avoiding this danger is tightly interwoven with the report (at least in expectation) withstanding the test of time. In the words of the model developer:

> [T]here shouldn't be elements in that concluding judgment that can change when new facts appear. That's the most important thing. Because then, the concluding judgment contains things that are more speculative, I think, and … there can absolutely not be something like that. … [W]hat you say here needs to still hold in two months. You have to be as convinced that it is like this in two years [as you are when writing].

That is, if crime scene technicians follow the model and its ban on bringing 'outside' information (i.e. information not only outside of the crime scene but, therefore, also outside of the technicians' immediate control) into their analysis, they will produce unbiased—and unshak-able—reports. Conversely, building one's analysis on outside information is akin to speculating; and information from the investigation poses the risk of being influenced by the investigation leader's perception of the case. Even though also investigation leaders must be impartial, the crime scene technicians cannot delegate their own impartiality to them. In addition, the crime scene technicians can and should only take responsi-bility for their own work, not that of others.

In other words, by advancing a forensic objectivity that emphasizes standardized practices as a counterweight to the bias seen as inherent in individual skill and experience, the technician as an individual loses importance. The model could thus also be understood as a part of profes-sionalizing crime scene technicians through standardizing and de-personalizing their work.

Frictions and Complexity

The crime scene technicians I have interviewed about the model—by no means a representative sample—talked about forensic objectivity (although they did not use the term) at the crime scene in a different way. Some of them had been loosely involved in the model, some had recently moved on from the crime scene division, none of them were novices. All of them emphasized that the crime scene model was a 'useful' way of thinking about both specific cases and their work in general. In addition, it gave them not only legitimacy but also an external aid to lean on. As one crime scene technician put it,

> I think it's good that you at least can say when you're standing in court that we've followed a model that's being taught … You don't just want your own concoction…

Even though this statement may sound like the model serves primarily as a 'fig leaf', the opposite is the case: the technician can say they followed a model because they did. The individual technician may still make mis-takes, but they can lean on a shared model and no longer are left to their own devices for crime scene analysis. However, the crime scene technicians also criticized aspects of the model. This could, of course, be seen as discontent with professionalization from the outside,[24] but it also illuminates how differently crime scene technicians and the model's developers conceive of the dangers to and, consequently, the accomplishment of forensic objectivity. In other words, these differences open a window to forensic objectivity in the making;[25] forensic objectivity in the process of being negotiated.

One concern was that the crime scene model introduces instead of counteracts bias; the particular danger the crime scene technicians saw was confirmation bias. By focusing on generating propositions early on, a technician explains,

> you run the risk, I think, of narrowing yourself down in a way that you can't take yourself out of. And it's here that I see an enormous risk … that you can get stuck in a way of thinking that you can't get out of. Because you're being steered to try to restrict yourself [to specific propositions] at an early stage.

That is, he felt the model might limit one's ability to see the crime scene without committing to an interpretation. Instead,

> what I would like, that's that … you only take in the facts, that's how I work. When I go into a crime scene, … no matter whether it's a break-in into a house or a murder or a rape or whatever, I first want to take in the facts. I note what it looks like, I note how things lie. And refrain from trying to speculate, trying to connect a cause to that it looks like it does, I want to take in everything first. Then I can start trying to sort things out. Because then, I have it in here [points to his temples] when I start sorting.

When crime scene technicians speak about 'facts', they refer to things that can be observed at the crime scene. For example, a door standing open when they arrive is such a fact; why, when, and by whom it was opened is a completely different question and not part of the fact. This definition of 'fact', specific to crime scene technicians as a profession, reflects technicians' concern to keep apart (unchangeable) facts and their (changeable) explanations.

The careful and constant separation of fact and explanation is the technicians' way of counteracting bias in the shape of rushing to conclusions and subsequently succumbing to confirmation bias and seeing the crime scene in the light of the rushed conclusion. By 'taking in' the crime scene as a whole while refraining from conclusions—in the words of one of the technician's colleagues, early conclusions are 'deadly dangerous'—the technician counterbalances bias with restraint. This restraint serves a similar purpose to the model's endpoint anchoring; both prevent the technician's rushing to conclusions. And indeed, another crime scene technician stressed this as a strong point of the model: as it forced one to question one's perception, it counteracted committing oneself too early.

An additional worry for some crime scene technicians was the potential for partiality in the alternative propositions:

> I don't see any problem in setting up a main proposition. I see the problem in setting up a working alternative proposition. *That's* where you've got the problem. If you are to choose an alternative proposition, how is that supposed to be formulated to kind of, have similar value, because we are supposed to be impartial.

He is concerned with how the choice of alternative proposition affects the outcome of the crime scene analysis: choosing an alternative proposition that is easily dismissed favours the main proposition.

In addition, some technicians stressed that, in a perfectly impartial world, these alternative propositions should be supplied by the defence, both because the original Bayesian approach speaks about the prosecutor's proposition being assessed against the defence's proposition[26] rather than, as in their Swedish translation, the main against the alternative proposition, and because impartiality, in their opinion, includes taking the defence's version into account. Not doing so may constitute a further danger to impartiality. It also means that the crime scene assessment may become obsolete if (or when) the defence supplies their own version of events. In consequence, their previous work might be all for nothing; also, the crime scene report does not remain stable over time (a concern that echoes the developers' aiming for lasting reports).

What they would prefer, in order to combat biases and to produce lasting reports, would be for forensic evaluations to keep to the source level, that is, to only give an opinion on whether a trace and a suspected source can have belonged together, not on which activities may have caused the trace to come into being. The latter is called the activity level; ideally, the technicians' concluding judgment is expected to reach up to that level. As one of the technicians explains, her preferred solution would be

> when you do these evaluations, you always deliver an opinion on the source level. … On request, then—I can understand that it's sometimes important—you can also deliver [an opinion] on the activity level. … But that it's two different requests, that—the source level is always there, that is all done, because then, if [new information makes the assessment on the activity level obsolete], at least that is left.

In other words, she does not resist or reject forensic evaluations or a Bayesian approach *per se*,[27] but she wishes for a different implementation, one that fits her concerns about forensic objectivity better.

All crime scene technicians with whom I talked about the crime scene model voiced doubts that the 'lab thinking' they saw in the model could always be smoothly transferred to the crime scene. Their doubts can be summed up in terms of the complexity of the crime scene as opposed to the laboratory's focus on single traces as well as the laboratory's controlled environment that lends itself much more easily to standardization than the greatly varying crime scenes. 'The problem', one of them said,

> comes with complexity. A crime scene contains such a tremendous lot of information, and it's *there* that I think it's difficult to apply this [model] well.

That is, he did not think that the crime scene model could do justice to the complexity of crime scenes—laboratories are heavily controlled and standardized environments, whereas crime scenes are messy. This concern was shared, in almost identical wording, by another technician, who underlined that this complexity meant that, unlike a forensic scientist, a crime scene technician must be able to sift the relevant from the irrelevant (e.g. traces of everyday life from those related to the crime).

A further issue with extending the laboratory's forensic objectivity to the crime scene that the technicians pointed out was that it was not always possible not to use information from the investigation and still work usefully and efficiently. While it was possible, one of them explained, to examine a fingerprint in the laboratory with a completely open mind, a crime scene posed different challenges. Witness and other information—which is not part of the crime scene model in its strict sense—could, for example, be crucial for narrowing down a crime scene to a feasible size. A completely open-minded examination would take a both impractically and unjustifiably long time and perhaps still not turn up anything useful—usefulness always has to do with the larger investigation and the questions it turns up. This is one reason why crime scene technicians typically are in dialogue with the investigation leader and information and questions travel back and forth. The other reason is that crucial information about the 'facts' at the crime scene sometimes has to come from the outside: as one technician explained, he might, for example, find damage to a living room wall; the crime scene examination itself may not be able to determine whether the damage has any connection to the presumed crime. Witness statements—produced by the police investigators' interrogations—on the other hand, may, for example when a janitor or visitor has seen the damage prior to the crime. (Of course, he immediately added, witnesses varied in reliability and trustworthiness, so using witness information required a critical mindset.) Thus, an important aspect of forensic objectivity at the crime scene is the necessity of balancing the need for contact with the 'outside' against the danger of being influenced—a necessity that places high demands on the crime scene technician.

As an additional factor to the complexity, the same technician highlighted that crime scene analysis is performed 'in the head' and is thus both invisible and difficult to document. In contrast, laboratory work can rely on technology and machines, making at least part of it external and thus more tangible and less personal. The crime scene model, he explained, partly remedies that—writing down possible propositions and their assessment could, for example, document and make visible some of the 'internal' work, thus also making it less solitary. (This ties, of course, into the de-personalization of forensic work.)

Again, none of these objections is necessarily representative or widespread; talking to other crime scene technicians might have generated a different response. However, what still makes these crime scene technicians' criticisms pertinent to thinking about forensic objectivity is that they illustrate that forensic objectivity does not necessarily travel easily. Even though practitioners in the laboratory and at the crime scene strive for objectivity of a similar shape—avoiding partiality and biases—perspectives differ on what threatens that forensic objectivity and how to respond to these threats. In other words, there is friction on *how* to do forensic objectivity. The NFC emphasizes a standardized model for evaluating and assessing, striving for forensic objectivity through standardizing and de-personalizing forensic practice. The crime scene technicians, on the other hand, tend to underline continuous personal restraint and the importance of delaying assessment until after all the 'facts' are in.

Conclusion: Performing Forensic Objectivities

The discussions around the crime scene model illustrate that forensic objectivity is by no means an unambiguous concept but one that requires negotiation, particularly since the implementation of the model is still ongoing. In the criminal justice system, the differences must be, and, according to the NFC, are, worked at; one example is that the model is being adjusted to accommodate taking in (and documenting) outside information when absolutely necessary.

Analytically—unlike the scientific objectivity traced by Daston and Galison[28]—forensic objectivity does not seem to be the answer to a distinct threat but rather the point of departure that is set in opposition to different dangers and thus filled with different meanings and performed differently in different forensic sites and by different forensic professions. In the laboratory (and the crime scene model based on laboratory evaluation practices), forensic objectivity is a matter of de-personalizing forensic practices. For crime scene technicians, forensic objectivity seems to be not only a matter of following rules but also, and importantly, a matter of personal restraint and ethics: They emphasize consciously observing the obligation to be impartial and investigate 'both sides' without rushing to conclusions or becoming influenced by necessary contact with the investigation. They seem to understand forensic objectivity as not rooted (only) in a model but as of necessity anchored in and continuously upheld by the individual crime scene technician.

Placing emphasis on the person of the crime scene technician also resonates with others' focus on their personal qualities. For example, Kelty et al. describe the key attributes of Australian 'top crime scene examiners' as 'knowledge, life experience, professionalism, approach to life, communication, cognitive abilities, and stress management'[29] and from a historical perspective, Burney and Pemberton[30] enumerate physical attributes as well as intellectual capabilities as crucial for crime scene work. In earlier fieldwork, I have noted that developing and displaying certain personal qualities is an important part in crime scene technician training.

The difference in where forensic objectivity is placed—in internal qualities or in rules and standards outside of the practitioner—may not only have to do with different self-understandings. Establishing and maintaining shared standards is easier in the laboratory, when working within easy reach of each other: a forensic scientist can always ask colleagues for advice (and will always have her or his work scrutinized by at least one colleague), whereas crime scene technicians typically work alone or in pairs. Another reason for the difference may be the laboratory's focus on single traces where the crime scene examination takes in the site as a whole. Bias in its different forms is a concern in both, but 'investigating both sides', that is, looking for contradiction as well as for confirmation, may be more easily formalized in rules when it comes to clearly demarcated traces than it is for crime scenes, both because they contain much more than one trace and because they hold much more variation. That is, these differences in understanding forensic objectivity may also have to do with differing work practices and conditions.

To put it differently, instead of opposing a distinct form of subjectivity,[31] forensic objectivity opposes a variety of different subjectivities: arbitrariness, confirmation and other biases, partiality, preconceptions, hastiness. This variety—intertwined with the different work practices and conditions—makes it difficult for forensic objectivity to travel smoothly from the laboratory to the crime scene. This does not mean that either laboratory or crime scene practices are invalid; instead the friction reveals the work required to establish a shared forensic objectivity. In addition, practices like the emphasis placed on personal restraint illustrate how forensic objectivity must be actively and continuously maintained. That is, even after shared forensic objectivity has been established and negotiated and practitioners have reached (transient) agreement on how to understand and perform it, forensic objectivity still requires continuous work. It is never a closed chapter.

Notes

1. C. Kruse, *The Social Life of Forensic Evidence*, Oakland: University of California Press, 2016.
2. L. Daston, 'The moral economy of science', *Osiris*, 1995, 10: 2–24; L. Daston and P. Galison, *Objectivity*, New York: Zone Books, 2007.
3. Daston and Galison, *Objectivity*, p. 17.
4. L. Daston and P. Galison, 'The image of objectivity', *Representations*, 1992, 40: 81–128; italics in original.
5. The NFC describes its responsibilities as forensic science outside of the human body; forensic medicine is performed by The National Board of Forensic Medicine.
6. See *Science & Justice*, 2017, 57(6).
7. See A. Nordgaard, R. Ansell, W. Drotz and L. Jaeger, 'Scale of conclusions for the value of evidence', *Law, Probability and Risk*, 2012, 11(1): 1–24; C. Kruse, 'The Bayesian approach to forensic evidence: Evaluating, communicating, and distributing responsibility', *Social Studies of Science*, 2013, 43(5): 657–680.
8. The choice of alternative proposition—wide or specific—affects, of course, the likelihood ratio and can be quite controversial.
9. For practices of population, see A. M'charek, 'Technologies of population: Forensic DNA testing practices and the making of differences and similarities', *Configurations*, 2000, 8: 121–158.
10. For more about these evaluations, see Kruse, 'Bayesian approach'; Kruse *Social Life*, chapter 4; Nordgaard et al., 'Scale'.
11. Cf., Daston and Galison, 'Image', p. 82ff.

12. L. Daston, *Classical Probability in the Enlightenment*, Princeton: Princeton University Press, 1988.
13. Cf., T.M. Porter, *Trust in Numbers—The Pursuit of Objectivity in Science and Public Life*, Princeton: Princeton University Press, 1995; Daston, 'Moral economy'; Daston and Galison, *Objectivity*.
14. Daston, 'Moral economy', p. 19.
15. Porter, *Trust*, p. 9.
16. Ibid., pp. 4–5.
17. Daston and Galison, 'Image', p. 120.
18. M. Lynch, S.A. Cole, R. McNally and K. Jordan, *Truth Machine—The Contentious History of DNA Fingerprinting*, Chicago: The University of Chicago Press, 2008, p. 345.
19. B. Latour, *Science in Action—How to Follow Scientists and Engineers through Society*, Cambridge, MA: Harvard University Press, 1987, p. 4.
20. See also C. Kruse 'Being a crime scene technician in Sweden', in I. Gershon (ed.), *A World of Work—Imagined Manuals for Real Jobs*, Ithaca: Cornell University Press, 2015.
21. See Kruse, *Social Life*, chapter 5.
22. The point with this close link between laboratory and crime scene, as stressed by the NFC, is to ensure the best forensic evidence and thus the greatest legal security possible. Putting the NFC in charge of crime scene work makes it possible to develop and establish standards for the recovery and transport of traces that enable and support subsequent analysis.
23. The model was introduced at the crime scene technicians' annual national conference in 2013 and into their basic training in 2015; familiarity with the model may still vary.
24. For the implications of such a professionalization on crime scene technicians' professional identity as well as their work, see D. Wilson-Kovacs, '"Backroom boys": Occupational dynamics in crime scene examination', *Sociology*, 2014, 48(4): 763–779 or C. Kruse 'Swedish crime scene technicians: Facilitations, epistemic frictions and professionalization from the outside', *Nordic Journal of Criminology* 2019, https://Doi.org/10.1080/2578983X.2019.1627808.
25. Cf Latour, *Science*.
26. For example, N. Fenton, 'Assessing evidence and testing appropriate hypotheses', *Science and Justice*, 2014, 54: 502–504.
27. When crime scene technicians are critical of the Bayesian approach itself (as used in the laboratory), they name the lack of databases on which to

base the assessment of probabilities and how the evaluation is not transparent to defence attorneys and courts who, consequently, may not understand forensic evidence correctly.

28. Daston and Galison, *Objectivity*.
29. S.F. Kelty, R. Julian and J. Robertson, 'Professionalism in crime scene examination: The seven key attributes of top crime scene examiners', *Forensic Science Policy & Management*, 2011, 2: 175–186, p. 175.
30. I. Burney and N. Pemberton, *Murder and the Making of English CSI*, Baltimore: Johns Hopkins University Press, 2016, p. 11ff.
31. Cf., Daston and Galison, 'Image'.

Bibliography

Burney, I. and Pemberton, N., *Murder and the Making of English CSI*, Baltimore: Johns Hopkins University Press, 2016.

Daston, L., *Classical Probability in the Enlightenment*, Princeton: Princeton University Press, 1988.

Daston, L., 'The moral economy of science', *Osiris*, 1995, 10: 2–24.

Daston, L. and Galison, P., 'The image of objectivity', *Representations*, 1992, 40: 81–128.

Daston, L. and Galison, P., *Objectivity*, New York: Zone Books, 2007.

Fenton, N., 'Assessing evidence and testing appropriate hypotheses', *Science and Justice*, 2014, 54: 502–504.

Kelty, S.F., Julian, R. and Robertson, J., 'Professionalism in crime scene examination: The seven key attributes of top crime scene examiners', *Forensic Science Policy & Management*, 2011, 2: 175–186.

Kruse, C., 'The Bayesian approach to forensic evidence: Evaluating, communicating, and distributing responsibility', *Social Studies of Science*, 2013, 43(5): 657–680.

Kruse, C., 'Being a crime scene technician in Sweden', in I. Gershon (ed.), *A World of Work—Imagined Manuals for Real Jobs*, Ithaca: Cornell University Press, 2015.

Kruse, C., *The Social Life of Forensic Evidence*, Oakland, University of California Press, 2016.

Kruse, C., 'Swedish Crime Scene Technicians: Facilitations, Epistemic Frictions and Professionalization from the Outside', *Nordic Journal of Criminology*, 2019, DOI: 10.1080/2578983X.2019.1627808.

Latour, B., *Science in Action—How to Follow Scientists and Engineers through Society*, Cambridge, MA: Harvard University Press, 1987.

Lynch, M., Cole, S.A., McNally, R. and Jordan, K., *Truth Machine—The Contentious History of DNA Fingerprinting*, Chicago: The University of Chicago Press, 2008.

M'charek, A., 'Technologies of population: Forensic DNA testing practices and the making of differences and similarities', *Configurations*, 2000, 8: 121–158.

Nordgaard, A., Ansell, R., Drotz, W. and Jaeger, L., 'Scale of conclusions for the value of evidence', *Law, Probability and Risk*, 2012, 11(1): 1–24.

Porter, T.M., *Trust in Numbers—The Pursuit of Objectivity in Science and Public Life*, Princeton: Princeton University Press, 1995.

Wilson-Kovacs, D., '"Backroom boys": Occupational dynamics in crime scene examination', *Sociology*, 2014, 48(4): 763–779.

Part II

The Professional Development of Forensic Investigation

6

The Police Surgeon, Medico-Legal Networks and Criminal Investigation in Victorian Scotland

Kelly-Ann Couzens

At 8 p.m. on Wednesday 23 November 1859, Edinburgh city police surgeon Henry Duncan Littlejohn, was about to retire to his home in York Place when an urgent message arrived.[1] Local police required his immediate attendance at the scene of an attempted child murder in the city's New Town.[2] Littlejohn's journey to the suspected crime scene was unusually short on this occasion, for the injured infant was discovered only a few hundred metres away from the surgeon's own home, in a house on the junction between York Place and Elder Street.[3] On arrival, Littlejohn was led to the downstairs rooms of the property to find the landlady Mrs Watts and her tenant George Gibson, attempting to nurse a mortally injured male newborn by the fire.[4] The child had been found by Watts on the sill outside Gibson's window, where it had broken the glass pane after its fatal descent from the adjacent rooms above.[5] Suffering from a broken arm, lacerations and a severely fractured skull, the child survived for only twenty minutes after Littlejohn's arrival.[6] Police were keen to identify the

K.-A. Couzens (✉)
University of Western Australia, Perth, WA, Australia

© The Author(s) 2020
A. Adam (ed.), *Crime and the Construction of Forensic Objectivity from 1850*, Palgrave
Histories of Policing, Punishment and Justice,
https://doi.org/10.1007/978-3-030-28837-2_6

whereabouts of the mother of the dead infant, and to determine the circumstances that led to the child's brutal death. However, with the mother nowhere to be found and investigations still ongoing, Littlejohn directed the child's body be removed to the dead house of the city Police Office and made his way back home as the clock passed nine.[7]

In the hours to follow, police made inquiries within the surrounding neighbourhood to ascertain the whereabouts of the child's recently delivered mother. Criminal officer John Youdall had managed to track the suspected woman, Ann McQue, to the premises of her mistress, in nearby rooms.[8] When inside, Youdall saw marks of blood in both the water closet and attic in which McQue slept and made haste to call Littlejohn back to the scene. It had now passed 11 p.m. and accompanied by Youdall, Littlejohn examined the bloody traces on the attic windowsill and surrounds before turning his attention to McQue.[9] Lying in disordered sheets, surrounded by bloody traces on the floor and bed, it was evident to Littlejohn that McQue had recently delivered and destroyed her child immediately after its birth by throwing the infant from her attic window.[10] When confronted by the doctor's suspicions of her state, McQue initially denied she had been delivered of a child and vehemently claimed, 'This is a respectable house, there's nothing of that sort'.[11] Concerned over the potential instability of McQue's mental state following the birth of her child and that 'any undue excitement…might have been attended with serious consequences', Littlejohn refrained from directly questioning her further about the events of that night.[12]

Over the following five days, Littlejohn continued to visit McQue at her room in York Place until her physical health had returned and her mental stability was assured.[13] Although concerned that McQue recover physically as soon as possible, Littlejohn also had a duty to the state as police surgeon to investigate and testify in criminal matters. Thus, his daily visits to McQue also aided him in forming an expert forensic opinion of his patient's mental state at the time of the killing.[14] In his precognition (pre-trial) interview with Scottish prosecutors on 29 November 1859, he noted that 'I have seen no symptom of aberration of her mind from the very first. She was perfectly collected when I first saw her and has continued so and in a few days I have no doubt she will be quite well'.[15] Given the weight of physical, expert and circumstantial evidence against McQue, the initial stages of investigation were brought to a close when prosecutors charged the nineteen-year-old domestic servant with the crime of child murder.[16]

As the McQue case demonstrates, the core forensic duties of the police surgeon were demanding and varied. As a medical practitioner affiliated to the city police and responsive to the demands of legal officials, the police surgeon worked daily at the intersection between differing professional collectives and communities. Conducting physical examinations of assaulted parties, undertaking post-mortem dissections in cases of suspicious or sudden death and certifying cases of mental insanity formed the cornerstone of the police surgeon's daily diet of forensic work in Victorian Edinburgh. Thus, this forensic doctor occupied an instrumental role in the production and evolution of forensic knowledge and practice within the landscape of British criminal justice. In addition, the police surgeon was frequently on call day or night (and in any weather) to the local force. Accordingly, this practitioner often became the vital first point of medical contact with victims (and suspects) in cases of homicide or assault in the nineteenth century. Yet, despite the pivotal role this practitioner occupied as a forensic expert in the Victorian city, relatively little scholarship has been dedicated to analysing the contribution and nature of the police surgeon's medico-legal work.[17] However, analysis of the career and life of one Scottish police surgeon indicates that the experience gained from the regular practice of medical jurisprudence was vital in developing and maintaining an authoritative medico-legal presence both within and outside the courtroom.

The investigation of violent crime in Scotland generally followed an established pattern of procedure that remained distinct from that of her neighbour south of the border. Unlike the English system of criminal procedure—marked out by the jurisdiction of the coroner and the public inquest—suspicious death in Scotland was investigated in private by legal officials and police on behalf of the state.[18] The procurator-fiscal played a key role in this process. This lawyer was responsible for liaising between police, the sheriff and other legal officials in suspected criminal enquiries and for collecting and transmitting witness precognitions (pre-trial interviews) in all cases that would likely warrant further legal proceedings.[19] Furthermore, the fiscal was also chiefly responsible for ordering post-mortems in cases of suspected foul play.[20] In instances of serious crime—such as suspected murder or sexual assault—the written interviews and reports collected by legal officials were the major basis by which a group of state advocates, known as Crown Counsel, would determine whether to prosecute, drop or remit a criminal case.[21] In consequence, the records detailing the steps taken from reporting to trying major crimes are particularly rich within the Scottish context.[22]

In particular, records suggest that the surgeon of police collaborated with constables, detectives and prosecutors to facilitate the investigation and prosecution of violent crime. Sometimes this collaboration would be procedural and routine, such as directing officers to remove bodies to the mortuary of the police chambers. At other times, these practitioners worked closely with the local force and legal officials in more complex and influential ways that blurred the professional and practical boundaries between medicine, policing and criminal investigation. In addition, the nature of Scottish procedure in suspicious deaths also forced the police surgeon to co-operate with a diverse range of medical practitioners in the examination and certification of death, injury and lunacy in the Scottish city. Sometimes, resolving inconsistencies in medical evidence could be a core part of the police surgeon's role when consulted by the Crown. On other occasions, working in partnership with other doctors to establish an informed, robust and objective medical opinion of a case was vital to the consolidation of the police surgeon's medico-legal authority.

This chapter analyses the contribution of one such Victorian police surgeon—Sir Henry Duncan Littlejohn—to the practice of forensic medicine in nineteenth-century Scotland. Littlejohn was an influential figure within the fields of public health and forensic medicine in Edinburgh, holding the dual posts of medical officer of health and police surgeon to the city from 1862 to 1908. Although scholars such as Brenda White, Ian Levitt, Paul Laxton and Richard Rodger have emphasized Littlejohn's contribution to the practice of state medicine in the decades after mid-century in Britain, these writers have focused predominantly on his significance as an advocate of sanitary reform, rather than as a forensic practitioner and expert witness.[23] The lack of extensive research into Littlejohn's career as a medico-legal investigator is all the more surprising given his routine appearances as an expert witness before the Scottish High Court of Justiciary during this period.[24] Nevertheless, his influential role as a medico-legal investigator and expert consultant can patently be evidenced by turning to the surviving criminal and press records that narrate the process of criminal investigation in nineteenth-century Scotland. While this study does not claim to provide an exhaustive account of either Littlejohn's career as a forensic examiner—or that of the British police surgeon in general—it does seek to sketch the integral role this medical man played within medico-legal networks in the Scottish city by focusing on revealing criminal cases and core personal interactions that occurred during his extensive professional career.

Henry Duncan Littlejohn: 'The Best Man for the Office'

Henry Duncan Littlejohn was born in Scotland in 1828, the son of a successful rusk and biscuit maker who resided at 33 Leith Street, Edinburgh.[25] Evidently a talented student, Littlejohn graduated from the University of Edinburgh with distinction and followed his Scottish medical education by studying for a time at France's prestigious Sorbonne.[26] While preparing for the MD in Edinburgh, Littlejohn was taught by some of the leading forensic practitioners in the country, such as Thomas Stewart Traill (Regius Professor of Medical Jurisprudence and Medical Police) and the famous toxicologist, Sir Robert Christison.[27] Following the conclusion of his medical education, the young practitioner briefly established himself in private practice in the border town of Selkirk.[28] However, by the early 1850s, Littlejohn decided to pursue a public career through the holding of key official medical offices in the Scottish capital.[29] The first official post Littlejohn pursued was that of surgeon of police to the city of Edinburgh, in August 1854.

Election to the position of city police surgeon during the first half of the nineteenth century was made by canvassing the city's Police Commissioners. The Police Commission was a civic body that existed in tandem to Edinburgh's other major municipal authority, the Town

Council.[30] Between 1805 and 1856 the elected members of the
Commission responded to propertied householder's concerns not only
over matters pertaining to crime but also to matters of civic order, cleanliness and health within the Scottish city.[31] The power of the Commission
extended to appointing the role of city police surgeon. Following a long
running conflict between the city's former surgeon of police—Dr George
Glover—the Police Commission and the Edinburgh press, the position
of police surgeon was made newly vacant in July 1854.[32] The requirements of applicants to be between twenty-five and forty-five years of age
and the small salary of £155 per annum[33] had been critiqued in the published July correspondence of *The Scotsman*, as restricting too severely the
pool of potential candidates.[34] In addition, post-mortem examinations—
the likes of which attended the daily work of a police surgeon—were
challenging and menial work, that was considered unlikely to attract a
high-quality applicant. As Jane Robins has observed within the context of
twentieth-century England, post-mortem examinations were 'physically
demanding, low status and unpleasant. Knives, saws, chisels and mallets
were the rougher tools of the trade, used to cut through bone and open
up difficult areas such as the skull. And the equipment for putting the
body back together at the end of an autopsy was similarly prosaic, nee-
dles, twine, sponges and sawdust'.[35]

Notwithstanding the limited pay and poor status of the work,
Littlejohn was in a favourable position for nomination to the office of
city police surgeon. At only twenty-eight years of age and residing in the
New Town, only a short-distance from police chambers, Littlejohn met
the age and residency requirements prescribed by the Commission for the
position. In addition, Littlejohn had received strong recommendations
for the post from respected members of the medical profession, garnering
a reference from the future Edinburgh University Chair of Medical
Jurisprudence, Sir Andrew Douglas Maclagan.[36] Indeed, the city's major
newspaper—*The Scotsman* would report to its largely professional middle-
and-upper-class readership,[37] that Littlejohn's:

> testimonials were of the highest order, better, indeed than could have been
> expected considering the lowness of the salary and the nature of the duties.
> These testimonials were from gentleman of the highest professional stand-

ing in the city—men whose opinions were entitled to the greatest possible consideration, and they all spoke of Dr Littlejohn's attainments in the most flattering manner.[38]

In spite of the often unpleasant nature of the work and the apparent merits of Littlejohn's youth and qualifications, his appointment to the position of surgeon of police was tainted by claims that nepotism and 'jobbing' were instrumental in his election (Fig. 6.1). *The Scotsman* remarked on this point that:

> The Lord Provost, before the vote was taken, alluded to an article which appeared in the *Evening Post* of Saturday, charging his Lordship with perpetrating a job in the election of a Police Surgeon, by having been instrumental in creating a vacancy for the purpose of getting a relation of his own

Fig 6.1 Photograph of Sir Henry Duncan Littlejohn (Credit: Wellcome Collection)

appointed....Dr Littlejohn was certainly a relative of his so far as that he was a cousin of his late wife's; but he was yet to learn that such a relationship was yet to deter him from giving him his vote should he prove to be the best man for the office. He (the Lord Provost) had carefully read over the testimonials of both candidates...Dr Littlejohn'[s] were immeasurably beyond those of the other candidates. This was the impression made on his mind from reading them, and such being his impression, he would vote on it.[39]

Despite the toxic atmosphere surrounding Littlejohn's canvass for the position, the Commission voted for his successful election to the role by seventeen votes to nine.[40] He would remain in the position of city police surgeon for the following five decades, until his retirement in March 1908.[41]

In the years to follow, Littlejohn would be an active force in the advancement of both forensic medicine and public health causes within nineteenth-century Britain. One year after his appointment to city police surgeon, Littlejohn became a lecturer at the Royal College of Surgeons, teaching the subject of medical jurisprudence at the Edinburgh Medical School until 1896.[42] In 1862, he was appointed Medical Officer of Health for Edinburgh and three years later would produce an extensive and innovative report into the public health of the city. The report received wide public acclaim and produced changes in the administration and legislation of sanitary concerns in Scotland.[43] Littlejohn's ongoing work as police surgeon brought him into regular contact with state prosecutors and the Scottish judiciary. On his resignation of public office in 1906, *The Scotsman* noted: 'for many years there was no great criminal trial in the High Court in which he did not figure as a Crown witness. In that capacity, his experience, his nimble mind and his ready wit put him on a perfect equality in fencing with the cleverest cross-examining advocates'.[44] In consequence of his adept skill as a medical witness and forensic examiner, he was also employed as medical adviser to the Crown in criminal cases.[45] While in 1895, Littlejohn's exemplary career and contribution to the state was officially recognized through a knighthood by Queen Victoria.[46]

The year 1897 saw Littlejohn appointed by the Crown to the Regius Chair of Forensic Medicine at the University of Edinburgh, following a tide of public support for his canvass.[47] In Edinburgh alone, 3200 signatures were garnered from the medical and legal profession in support of his appointment.[48] Littlejohn's was noted to be a popular teacher whose distinctive sense of humour and practically focused pedagogical approach left a strong impression on his students. Famous writer, physician and anti-eugenicist Dr Halliday Sutherland, was a student in Littlejohn's lectures on forensic medicine during his term as Regius Professor at the University of Edinburgh.[49] In his 1934 memoir *A Time to Keep*, Sutherland recalled that:

> Sir Henry was a dapper little man, with white hair, sharp features, and expressive hands. Sir Henry's class at 9 a.m. was always crowded, and he told of us of the murder trials of the last century in which he had played his part. It was Lord Young who said, "There are four kinds of witnesses—liars, damned liars, expert witnesses, and Sir Henry Littlejohn." Sir Henry's wit was Rabelaisian, and he was brightly cynical.[50]

Littlejohn had long argued that his position as police surgeon and forensic witness complemented his teaching as lecturer on medical jurisprudence. In his opening address as Professor of Forensic Medicine at the Edinburgh University on 4 May 1897, Littlejohn was reported by *The Scotsman* to have observed, that:

> He had...found in practice that the investigation of a criminal case in a practical manner lent an interest to the subject matter of his lectures which enabled the student to enter with zest into fuller discussions, and to render him a more satisfactory witness when called upon to give evidence in a Court of Law...Daily engaged as he was in the investigation of cases of sudden death and in the detection of crime, it would be his duty to take them into his confidence (applause)—and to discuss each case in such a manner as to justify the option he had been led from experience to adopt.[51]

Despite a controversial beginning to his forensic career, Littlejohn's dedication, ability, extensive practice and public reputation elevated him to a position of established authority within the Scottish medico-legal community by the close of the nineteenth century. Ever keen to advocate on behalf of his fellow police surgeons, Littlejohn served as President (and later Vice-President) to the United Kingdom of Police Surgeons' Association in the late 1890s.[52] Only in 1908, at the age of eighty, would Littlejohn finally resign his public office as police surgeon for Edinburgh.[53]

The Police Surgeon and Criminal Investigation in Edinburgh

In instances of suspicious death, the initial path taken to reporting the crime to officials depended largely upon the circumstances of the victim's passing. In instances where bodies were discovered outside of a home or dwelling—in the street, or in public spaces like parks or bodies of water—passers-by and neighbours were instrumental in the reporting of the case to local police. We see this particularly clearly in both the McQue case, which opened this study and in the violent death of Louisa Purdie in March 1872. Purdie's body was first discovered by James Stables, a boot-closer residing in North St James Street, Edinburgh.[54] Stables' attention was attracted to the scene by the presence of dog that was '"sporting" about' twenty yards from Arthurs Street.[55] On walking over to see what was attracting the dog's interest, Stables came across the semi-naked and exposed body of Purdie in Queen's Park. His next actions were to report the discovery to the police.[56] In this case, Stables told local constable William Reid—who was just coming off-duty—of the finding of the body nearby.[57] Reid conducted some initial observations of the scene, spreading Purdie's discarded petticoat over her exposed corpse before seeking further assistance from other officers.[58] By approximately 10.40 a.m., a little over an hour since police had first been alerted of Purdie's death, Littlejohn arrived on scene to conduct a provisional exam-ination of the state of the body *in situ*.[59] The corpse was removed to the police chambers, where the following day Littlejohn and Dr David Wilson made a post-mortem examination of Purdie.[60]

    In cases of suspicious death, the precognition records and certified medical reports reveal that bodies were most often removed from the crime scene to the mortuary or dead house located in the police chambers on High Street.[61] Removing bodies to this site was likely done for two central reasons. Firstly, the police chambers were located in the centre of Edinburgh city, on the main thoroughfare connecting the Canongate and Old Town Districts with the civic heart of the capital. As Dominique Kalifa, Andrew Brown-May and Simon Cooke have noted within the settings of nineteenth-century Paris and Melbourne respectively, mortuary location was often centralized within nineteenth-century cities in order to ensure the easy traffic of witnesses to identify a corpse.[62] Yet locating the dead house at the heart of city also served a second functional purpose. As city police surgeon, Littlejohn was based in the police chambers, alongside local officers and criminal detectives.[63] In consequence, conducting forensic and post-mortem examinations, receiving information from the public and directing enquiries from a centralized location, facilitated the smooth running of criminal investigations in an era in which the detection of crime was becoming increasingly professionalized and publicly scrutinized within Britain.[64]

In other instances, in which the site of the post-mortem is listed, medical institutions held a key role. This can be seen in the enquiries into the death of Elizabeth Chantrelle, whose body was examined in Edinburgh's Royal Infirmary.[65] In this case, Littlejohn was called in to see the dying Mrs Chantrelle in early January 1878 by fellow doctor, James Carmichael.[66] At the time, Chantrelle's husband Eugene had suggested to doctors that his wife's worsening condition and comatose state, was a result of accidental coal gas poisoning.[67] After briefly examining the half-dead Elizabeth, Littlejohn advised that she be sent directly to the Royal Infirmary[68] which had a dedicated ward for cases of poisoning.[69] By early afternoon of the same day, then Chair of Medical Jurisprudence and lecturer on Clinical Medicine, Douglas Maclagan, was walking the wards of the Infirmary when he observed his assistants attempting to resuscitate the unconscious Mrs Chantrelle.[70] On observing the condition of her body, Maclagan provisionally concluded that opium poisoning, not gas, had occasioned her illness and death.[71] The following day, a post-mortem would be conducted on the body of Elizabeth Chantrelle by both Littlejohn and Maclagan at the infirmary that would challenge Eugene's assertions that carbon monoxide poisoning had been the cause of his wife's death.[72] Outside the city, settings for conducting post-mortems varied depending on the facilities available to the forensic practitioner. Littlejohn and his fellow medical examiners were expected to adapt to these conditions and deliver results accordingly. For example, in the investigations into the case of the Kirriemuir poisoning in 1893, Littlejohn travelled to Dundee in order to conduct a post-mortem on the exhumed body of Mary Anne Webster.[73] The medical report in the case lists the place of the forensic examination as being 'in the mortuary of the Constitution Church Yard, Dundee'.[74]

Conducting a post-mortem examination could often be an unpleasant experience. Such examinations were seen to be physically demanding, low status and messy work, that brought the practitioner into direct physical contact with the putrefying matter of the body.[75] However, for police surgeons like Littlejohn, post-mortem examinations were a regular part of the professional remit of this forensic practitioner. Contact with the corpse was made chiefly through touch. This could be made directly—chiefly in the form of the examiner's hand, touching, exposing and holding physical remains—or indirectly through the use of medical instruments, such as saws, scalpels, forceps and chisels, that could probe, dissect and lay bare the inner workings of the body.[76] Importantly, interaction with the body was made without the use of barrier protection such as gloves, gowns or scrubs, meaning that the medical examiner made direct physical contact with the corpse both internally and externally throughout a post-mortem examination. Such contact could risk injury to police surgeon themselves. Indeed, Littlejohn reminded readers of the *Edinburgh Medical Journal* in 1876, that care needed to be taken in the conduct of post-mortem examinations, especially:

As the majority of cases of sudden or suspicious deaths investigated in large towns are of persons who have been addicted to the immoderate use of spirits, strong adhesions exist between the cranium and the membranes, it is no easy matter to separate them without injuring the fingers. It is well known that there is no more fruitful source of whitlow and blood poisoning than such wounds, which, in the hurry of a dissection, are apt to be occasionally overlooked.[77]

Given the acknowledged physical demands, graphic nature and potential danger associated with conducting post-mortem examinations, it is unsurprising that forensic pathology exemplified more calculated butchery than scientific art in the Victorian period.

The duties of daily forensic work required the city police surgeon to attend all manner of violent physical and sexual injury authorized by local officials too. Sometimes, examinations would be conducted in the centralized city police chambers, but in other cases, Littlejohn attended victims in their homes or in situ at the suspected crime scene. This occurred most often when injuries left victims immobile or close to death. In July 1902, for example, Littlejohn was called out by police at midnight to attend to Mary Hastie, who was lying in bed, dying, following a severe beating by her neighbour, John Adamson.[78] The scene confronting Littlejohn was graphic:

> I found the deceased lying in bed in the house in question. Her face was much bruised and swollen…She had evidently lost a good deal of blood as evinced by extensive blood staining of the pillows on which she was lying and bed clothing adjoining as also her own clothing.…I saw that her injuries were fatal and that medical assistance was of no avail, but she survived for three hours after.[79]

Littlejohn was not the first medical practitioner on the scene; instead local police had called for a Dr Linton to attend.[80] Linton stayed with Hastie for thirty minutes before returning home.[81] By contrast, Littlejohn, then approaching his mid-seventies, stayed with her for three hours until her death.[82]

As has been observed within the English context by Victoria Bates, Ivan Crozier, Gethin Rees and Louise Jackson, the police surgeon was one of the most commonly called medical attendants in instances of suspected rape.[83] Doctoral research conducted by the author within the context of nineteenth-century Edinburgh, confirms these findings within the Scottish context too.[84] Physical examinations conducted by the police surgeon upon rape victims and suspected rapists was necessarily intimate, often involving the repeated exposure, examination and probing of private parts. This is demonstrated clearly in the 1874 case of Elizabeth

Henrietta Aitken.[85] Aitken was a fifteen-year-old domestic servant who, in late July 1874, was subjected to an opportunistic attack by John Walker, a twenty-one-year-old journeyman baker, while on an errand for her employer in the parish of Torphichen. Aitken had been bruised and violated by the attack and had also lost a tooth in the right side of her mouth, following a blow sustained from Walker.[86] Three separate rape examinations by attending doctors occurred over the period of a month following her reporting of the attack to authorities. In the third examination dated 31 August 1874, Littlejohn travelled to Linlithgow, to examine Aitken in the local Courthouse buildings.[87] He reported in his medical examination that 'Her private parts were unusually well developed. Menstruation was going on, and the parts in question were moistened with a bloody discharge. The vagina admitted the forefinger with ease, and no obstruction was felt in its passage'.[88]

For the survivors of sexual assault, sensitivity to pain—whether it be as a result of the assault itself or attendant on the physical examination conducted on the complainant's body by doctors—was subject to the observations and documentation of the police surgeon. When Margaret Ross was examined by Littlejohn in the city police chambers in October 1876 after being attacked by William King on the street that same night, it was detailed in the medical report that:

> She was much agitated and complained of pain in the neck, throat and also in the private parts. The front of the neck was swollen and disfigured by numerous scratches and abrasions of the skin—all of which were moist and therefore quite recent. The act of swallowing was accompanied with pain....Internally, the entrance to the vagina was very red and was very painful to the touch....The injuries to the neck were such as I am familiar with in cases of garrotting.[89]

Thomas Lacqueur has suggested that autopsies and medical case histories formed part of a cluster of 'humanitarian narratives' that 'bridged the gulf between facts, compassion and action' as they emerged during the eighteenth and nineteenth centuries in the West.[90] The focus upon 'pain, suffering or death' in such narrative mediums, inspired a path to 'ameliorative action' to avoid and redress such suffering.[91] Thus, the sensitivities to the victim's response to pain in the Ross case, worked both as important evidentiary proof that sexual connection had been effected violently and forcibly, while also grounding the attack by King in terms of pain and trauma that inspired sympathy and connection to the rape victim's plight. Given that medical reports formed an important source in the Crown's precognition material and were read before the court at trial, Littlejohn's narrative of the violation on Ross can be argued as working to inspire a path to ameliorative action through the criminal justice system. King subsequently pleaded guilty to the assault at trial in December 1876 and was sentenced to eighteen months hard labour by the presiding judge, Lord Young.[92]

Working with Police

Aside from being necessarily responsive to a victim and suspected accused's physical and mental state, Littlejohn's forensic career points to a strong collaboration with the city's local police force. This is perhaps of little surprise given that the duty of a police surgeon extended not only to investigating criminal cases of murder, assault or insanity but also to attending to (and monitoring) the health of the force itself.[93] Such directions were encapsulated in the small pamphlet entitled, *The Duties and Emoluments of the Police Surgeon*—a document given to Littlejohn by the Police Commission on his appointment to the role of surgeon of police in 1854.[94] The police surgeon's role in maintaining the health of the city constabulary extended to testing the medical fitness of new recruits as well. Directive fourteen required the police surgeon to '…examine all persons who are candidates for employment in the Watching Department, as to their health and bodily strength and report to the superintendent as to their fitness for the Police Service'.[95]

   While Haia Shpayer-Makov has emphasized the parallels between journalists and police detectives in Victorian England, similarly detailed research that analyses the relationship between police and police surgeons has yet to be completed from a Scottish perspective.[96] Nevertheless, provisional research within the Scottish context indicates many similarities between the two occupations. Police work and forensic practice required commitment to the job at all hours, with both professions needing to be available at any time day or night to respond to potential complaints or inquiries. Precognition records attest to surgeons like Littlejohn being called out at dawn, at midnight and every hour in between often accompanied by constables and detectives. Sometimes, call outs could occur multiple times in the same night, as was demonstrated in the case of Ann McQue that began this chapter.

Police surgeons especially, worked closely with detectives and police officers, conducting and directing searches for evidence and examining suspected crime scenes. We see an example of such a case when Littlejohn was called to the Edinburgh police office to examine the dismembered remains of a thigh and leg from a newborn child in June 1882. The partial remains had been discovered after searching a drain in Blacket Place, near Holyrood Park.[97] In his precognition, Littlejohn remarked upon the success of his industry and co-operation with police and local civic authorities in the search for the remaining body parts, for:

> I at once got the assistant burgh engineer to accompany the police…to have the drain opened and examined. On the evening of the same day, I was shown…eleven fragments of a newborn child apparently in the same condition of the other two before mentioned.[98]

The accused Jessie Peattie was subsequently sentenced to two years' imprisonment, having pleaded guilty to the lesser charge of concealment of pregnancy at trial.[99]

A further fruitful example of collaboration between Littlejohn and Edinburgh police is revealed in the investigations into the poisoning of the infant William Walker in March 1860.[100] On a Friday evening in mid-March 1860, Elizabeth Smith Walker—a domestic servant and child's nurse—called on Littlejohn at his home to request the formal registration of the death of her son William.[101] Given the sudden nature of the child's death, Littlejohn agreed to register the child's death only after completing a post-mortem examination of the body. However, 'This the mother refused to allow, and her manner was so peremptory and peculiar that I determined to mention the case to the acting lieutenant of police that evening, and request him, on behalf of the authorities to make some inquiry into the circumstances of the case'.[102] While reporting the case to the lieutenant, two women from Walker's neighbourhood approached the police and city surgeon, detailing their suspicions that the child had died under suspicious circumstances.[103] On hearing this news, Littlejohn notes that he was asked by the lieutenant as to what the best course of action should be.[104] From Littlejohn's account of the case given in an article published in the *Transaction of the Medico-Chirurgical Society* in 1885, together he and the officer determined to instruct a plain-clothes detective to watch Walker's house, monitoring her conduct and ensuring that she did not destroy any evidence that could be instructive in establishing the means of the child's death.[105] Following the joint forensic examination of the body by Littlejohn and Dr Cowan (whom had also been unsuccessfully asked by Walker to certify the child's death), it was evident that William Walker had been poisoned by 'some irritant substance'.[106] On these findings, Littlejohn observed that he 'felt justified in instructing the officers to take the mother into custody'.[107]

Determining the exact cause of the child's death presented a challenge for investigators given that the police search of Walker's house revealed that the floor was scrubbed clean, with no traces of vomit surviving from the scene to chemically test.[108] In addition, the clothing worn by the toddler on the day of its death was soaking in a tub of water in the house, making analysis for traces of poison on the garments impossible. Initially, Littlejohn and toxicologist Andrew Maclagan were stumped as to the type of substance that had killed the child, for 'neither arsenic, mercury, antimony, lead, zinc, nor oxalic acid were present'.[109] However, the discovery of the child's booties by criminal officer William Angus in the recesses of a cupboard in Walker's lodgings changed the game.[110] For on returning to his home following the first day of unsuccessful test for the offending poison, Littlejohn was met by detective Angus. The officer pointed out his discovery of the child's boots and the trace of a crystallized substance around the toe of the shoes. Littlejohn recalled: 'The boots were produced from under his coat, and by means of the rather uncertain light from a street lamp I made out, but with difficulty, indications of a scanty crystalline deposit…with a lens the crystals were determined to be prismatic and fluted'.[111] Following consultation and tests with Maclagan the next morning, both doctors were able to confirm that the poison was nitrate of potash.[112] In consequence, Walker was officially brought before the sheriff and charged with the murder of her son.[113]

Advising Prosecutors, Policing Medical Practice

Perhaps one of the most interesting, though most concealed roles a forensic practitioner could occupy was as an expert consultant to Crown Council in criminal cases. In these instances, medical practitioners of professional esteem who had developed a strong and reliable working relationship with the Crown would be called upon to aid authorities in understanding or resolving tensions in medical evidence or in lending their support to the validity of arguments made by medical witnesses. Sometimes these unofficial reports would include anatomical sketches with which to visually aid the questions needed to be asked of medical practitioners, or as responses to the inquiries made by these consulting experts. Unsurprisingly perhaps, Littlejohn's extensive forensic practice as both police surgeon and lecturer on medical jurisprudence led to his appointment as adviser to the Crown in criminal cases.

We see the process of expert consultation particularly clearly in the case against Dr Edward Pratt Evatt for rape. Evatt was a surgeon-physician practising in the Scottish border town of Galashiels in the spring of 1882, when prosecutors alleged that he raped Eliza Blair—an eighteen-year-old millworker—while under the guise of performing a surgical operation on her to cut her hymen.[114] Littlejohn was consulted by Crown Counsel to review the medical reports and precognitions provided by the attending local doctors who examined Blair following her accusation of rape. Littlejohn wrote a memo in response to this official request, which responded to two core issues. The first was whether the operation performed upon Blair by Dr Evatt was classed as a legitimate treatment for excessive vaginal discharge. The second was whether Blair's body and behaviour was consistent with existing medical understandings about how the female body should look post-violation. The document included both written questions and responses, as well as sketched and labelled diagrams depicting different representations of hymen rupture within a female virgin.[115] So useful was Littlejohn's response that, Crown Counsel noted:

I think we might with advantage give the P[rocurator] F[iscal] copy of Dr Littlejohn's report & call his attention generally to the information described there and in particular to the description of the hymen its mode of rupture or division and the appearance of semen on the person of the girl…[116]

Thus, Littlejohn's report was used as a means by which the procurator-fiscal and his subordinates might 'ask better questions' of the examining medical men so that the true nature of the alleged offence could be elucidated. The results of this approach were reflected in the responses given by Dr William Henry Murray to the authorities. Murray had attended Blair and issued a medical certificate as to the physical appearance of her body on 20 April 1882—eight days after the alleged assault.[117] In Murray's response to the fiscal, he directly engages with Littlejohn's memorandum in his responses. This can be seen by comparing passages within the writings produced by Littlejohn and Murray for the case.

In his 'Answers to Crown Inquiries' dated 10 May 1882, Littlejohn wrote the following to prosecutors:

3. *Query No. 3*
The appearances described by the 2 doctors are those ordinarily met with after connection with an adult male. It will be observed that the doctors are not precise in their description of the hymen. Dr Murray says "the hymen was divided". Dr Somerville "the hymen was ruptured". These gentlemen will have been asked either to amend their reports or to have described in their precognitions (two in number!!) the exact appearance of the hymen. The usual appearance of the hymen is as A; and after connection as of B. if the hymen presented the abnormal appearances as depicted on page no. 1 then the result of recent connection would be very peculiar and may be thus delineated C and D. From the reticence of the medical men, I think it is highly probable that the torn hymen presented no unusual appearances. As to cutting. This must only have been partial & if followed…by an act of connection—it is impossible to detect it or to distinguish it from the tearing from the forcible introduction of the male organ.[118]

Dr Murray responds in his third precognition on 13 May 1882, as follows:

> the appearance presented by the hymen of the girl Blair on the morning of the 13th was such as is depicted by Dr Littlejohn in his report marked 'B'. Namely a normal semilunar hymen that had been ruptured, presenting the ragged edges seen in the drawing in his report marked 'B'.[119]

The process of consultation between medical experts and legal practitioners was vital in determining whether a case was strong enough to proceed to trial. If a prosecution case was constructed soundly—with compelling evidence elicited through pre-trial investigation and weaknesses in the case remedied early through clarification and expert consultation—the Crown would increase the chance of a successful prosecution in the High Court. That medical men like Littlejohn would want to be involved in this process too, is hardly surprising. As Anne Digby has noted, involvement in public office helped medical practitioners become known within local communities and compete for the share of an already competitive medical market.[120] In addition building relationships with the legal profession, in turn, galvanized the claims of forensic practitioners to their own elite status both within and outside the courtroom. Given how often courtroom trials were regarded as sources of embarrassment for the ill-experienced or complacent medical practitioner brought down to earth by the hostile exchanges of cross-examination, such pre-trial consultancy primed the medical witness and prosecutors in the specifics of forensic evidence in preparation for the arena of the criminal trial. Furthermore, the role Littlejohn occupied as a consultant expert for the Crown, demonstrates how valuable the forensic knowledge and practice acquired by a skilled police surgeon could be in helping to prosecute serious crime to the highest level.

The Wider Medical Profession

In March 1878, Dr Charles Kinane, an ex-student of Littlejohn's and police surgeon in Perth, wrote a short letter to his former lecturer asking for advice. A case of incest committed between an elder brother upon his seven-year-old sister had come before the doctor in his private capacity as a local practitioner. The nature of the offence was exacerbated by communication of gonorrhoea to the young girl from the rape effected by her eighteen-year-old brother.[121] The writer asked Littlejohn: 'What is my duty, if any, in a public capacity?'[122] This letter, along with a handful of others, was scrapbooked by Littlejohn in the private notebooks he kept during the latter decades of his professional practice, chronicling contemporary issues and debates in forensic medicine through newspaper and medical reports, legislative changes and received mail.[123]

Although we have no record as to whether Littlejohn responded to this or other enquiries, Kinane's attempt at correspondence with a fellow police surgeon and member of the Scottish forensic elite is revealing. On one hand, it highlights the imperfect nature of medical knowledge, even amongst qualified practitioners serving in authoritative roles within local communities. As Anne Crowther has argued, instruction in medical jurisprudence was vital in helping to educate the wider profession on its ethical duties and responsibilities towards patients, other doctors and the state throughout the nineteenth century.[124] In addition, letters of this kind demonstrate that trusted advice on medical matters was often derived from other practitioners who would turn to their own professional networks in order to resolve gaps in their understanding of medico-legal matters. That Kinane chose to correspond with Littlejohn specifically—years after receiving his medical qualifications and instruction—attests to the enduring strength and value placed upon able forensic teaching from within the profession. Further documentary evidence suggests that the lessons learnt within the classroom could have a powerful half-life within a medical practitioner's career. In describing the journey to his first medico-legal case in 1909, Halliday Sutherland recalled that:

> During the drive I tried to remember all the things I should observe. If this was to be the prelude to a criminal trial, what questions would be put to me. I remembered Sir Henry Littlejohn. A body washed up by the tide has not of necessity been drowned. A person may faint, fall into the sea, and die of shock...[125]

Thus, such evidence collectively helps demonstrate that the medical profession often made up for any deficits in education on medical jurisprudence, by the strength of the professional community it engendered and long-lasting impact the forensic elite exercised from their student's earliest university days. That Littlejohn kept such correspondence amongst his medico-legal scrapbooks is also suggestive. It is highly likely that enquiries of this kind helped indirectly shape Littlejohn's own teaching as a lecturer on medical jurisprudence. After all, the keeping of these letters suggests that they were valued by Littlejohn. Although speculative, it is probable that such correspondence provided a means by which the experienced police surgeon and lecturer could keep in touch with current issues that affected practitioners from across the country and so ensure his ongoing teaching and practice remained relevant and comprehensive too.

Conclusion

Throughout the second half of the nineteenth century, police surgeon Henry Duncan Littlejohn held an instrumental role in the teaching and practice of forensic medicine within Edinburgh. His influential legacy as a teacher and medico-legal expert was largely made possible by his sustained employment as the Scottish capital's premier police surgeon. Although detailed research that explores the history of the police in Britain during the nineteenth century remains to be conducted, the tentative findings in this chapter emphasize the central role this class of practitioner occupied within the medical, legal and wider social world of Victorian Scotland. Littlejohn's career as police surgeon instilled within him an enduring appreciation of the practical experience and knowledge acquired through direct encounter with the victims, suspects and investigators of major crime. The case histories and writings produced by Littlejohn as police surgeon particularly often cast the human body—disordered, wounded, bloodied and exposed—as a vulnerable, confronting and empathic symbol of the impact of violent crime. At times, the technical and dispassionate accounts of the findings of forensic examinations, especially in rape cases, casts the victim as little more than an object, scrutinized repeatedly at the hands of the police surgeon and other medical men in the name of 'justice'. Yet in other instances, the detail revealed within medical reports, trial testimony and precognition accounts, emphasized the suffering of the victim and the demanding medico-legal practice expected of the police surgeon in this period. The rich archival and press materials associated with the life and times of Littlejohn, emphasize the tangible challenges associated with investigating crime. The work of the surgeon of police was physically demanding, bloody, relentless and confronting. But it was also predicated upon collaboration, teamwork and trust between the various participants involved in criminal enquiries. In consequence, Littlejohn's professional success was founded not just on his distinct abilities as a forensic expert, but also on the strength of the collaborations and networks he established within the medical and legal communities of nineteenth-century Edinburgh.

Notes

1. 'Precognition of Dr Henry Duncan Littlejohn', 29 November 1859 in *Precognition Against Ann McQue for the Crime of Child Murder at York Place, Edinburgh*, Edinburgh: National Records of Scotland, 1860, GB234/AD14/60/260, p. 31.
2. Ibid.
3. At this time, Littlejohn lived at 67 York Place in the city's New Town.
4. See the witness statements made by George Gibson and Mrs Watts, as reported in: 'High Court of Justiciary: The York place child-murder', *The Scotsman*, Edinburgh, 13 March 1860, p. 4
5. Ibid., p. 4.
6. Henry Duncan Littlejohn's witness testimony as reported in ibid.
7. 'Precognition of Dr Henry Duncan Littlejohn', 29 November 1859 in *Precognition Against Ann McQue for the Crime of Child Murder*, p. 32.
8. 'High Court of justiciary: The York place child-murder', *The Scotsman*, p. 4.
9. 'Precognition of Dr Henry Duncan Littlejohn', 29 November 1859 in *Precognition Against Ann McQue for the Crime of Child Murder*, pp. 32–33.
10. It was also suggested in the indictment that the child may have received pre-mortem injuries to its body by being beaten by McQue prior to her disposal of the child from the attic window. However, isolating the

exact cause of such injuries was impossible in the case. See: Ibid., pp. 33–34.

11. 'High Court of Justiciary: The York place child-murder', *The Scotsman*, p. 4.

12. Precognition of Dr Henry Duncan Littlejohn', 29 November 1859 in *Precognition Against Ann McQue for the Crime of Child Murder*, pp. 33–34.

13. Ibid., p. 34.

14. Ibid.

15. Ibid.

16. 'Indictment' in *Precognition Against Ann McQue for the Crime of Child Murder*.

17. There remains only a very limited scholarship on the history and analysis of the police surgeon in Britain. This stands in relative contrast to the more extensive research conducted upon prison surgeons and other institutional doctors. Core studies to date that have explored the general history and work of the police surgeon, include: J. Bourke, 'Police surgeons and sexual violence: A history', *The Lancet*, 2017, 390(10094): 548–549; J. Bourke, 'Police surgeons and victims of rape: Cultures of harm and care', *Social History of Medicine*, 2018, 31(4): 711–731; Y. Bradshaw et al., 'A different sort of doctor: The police surgeon in England and Wales', *Social Policy & Administration*, 1995, 29(2): 122–134; S.P. Savage et al., 'Divided loyalties? The police surgeon and criminal justice', *Policing and Society*, 1997, 7(2): 79–98; R.D. Summers, *History of the Police Surgeon*, London: Association of Police Surgeons of Great Britain, 1988.

18. A particularly useful comparison between the English and Scottish system of prosecution is offered in M.A. Crowther, 'Crime, prosecution and mercy: English influence and Scottish practice in the early nineteenth century', in S.J. Connolly (ed.), *Kingdoms United? Great Britain and Ireland Since 1500: Integration and Diversity*, Dublin and Portland: Four Courts Press, 1999, pp. 225–238.

19. Ibid., pp. 225–226.

20. This point was observed in student notes taken during lectures on forensic medicine by Littlejohn; see 'Lecture X', 20 May 1906 in *Forensic Medicine: Volume of Notes on Forensic Medicine from Lectures Delivered, c. 1906 by Sir Henry Duncan Littlejohn, Physician, while Professor of Forensic Medicine at Edinburgh University, 1897–1906,*

National Library of Scotland, Edinburgh, 1906, GB 233/MS.19321, pp. 30 and 33 particularly.

21. M.A. Crowther, 'Criminal precognitions and their value for historians', *Scottish Archives*, 1995, 1: 76; P.T. Riggs, 'Prosecutors, juries, judges and punishment in early nineteenth-century Scotland', *Journal of Scottish Historical Studies*, 2012, 32(2): 168–172.
22. This was first observed by Anne Crowther in the above piece, published in *Scottish Archives* almost twenty-five years ago. Despite this, scholars have still yet to fully utilize the value of precognition records in the study of Scottish crime.
23. B.M. White, 'The police surgeon as Medical Officer of Health in Scotland 1862–1897', *The Police Surgeon*, 1989, 35: 29–37; I. Levitt, 'Henry Littlejohn and Scottish Health Policy, 1859–1908', *Scottish Archives*, 1996, 2: 63–77; P. Laxton and R. Rodger, *Insanitary City: Henry Littlejohn and the Condition of Edinburgh*, Lancaster: Carnegie Publishing Limited, 2013.
24. For a discussion of Littlejohn's performance as a medico-legal witness within the Scottish courtroom, see K.A. Couzens, 'Upon my word, I do not see the use of medical evidence here': Persuasion, Authority and Medical Expertise in the Edinburgh High Court of Justiciary', *History*, 2019, 104(359): 42–62.
25. 'The Late Sir Henry D. Littlejohn, M.D.: A Distinguished Public Official and Medical Jurist', *The Scotsman*, Edinburgh, 2 October 1914, p. 5; 'Littlejohn, Thomas', *Post Office Annual Directory*, Edinburgh, Postmaster General, 1828–1829, p. 103.
26. 'The Late Sir Henry D. Littlejohn, MD', *The Scotsman*, p. 5.
27. Laxton and Rodger, *Insanitary City*, p. 7.
28. Ibid., p. 8.
29. 'The Late Sir Henry D. Littlejohn, MD', *The Scotsman*, p. 5.
30. Laxton and Rodger, *Insanitary City*, p. 45.
31. Ibid., pp. 45–47.
32. Ibid., p. 72.
33. 'Surgeon Wanted for the Edinburgh Police Establishment', 2 August 1854, *The Scotsman*, Edinburgh, p. 1.
34. See Medicus, 'The Police Surgeon', *The Scotsman*, Edinburgh, 12 July 1854, p. 3; Medicus, 'The Police Surgeon', *The Scotsman*, Edinburgh, 15 July 1854, p. 3.
35. J. Robins, *The Magnificent Spilsbury and the Case of the Brides in the Bath*, London: John Murray, 2010, pp. 29–30.

36. Laxton and Rodger, *Insanitary City*, p. 75.
37. On the readership of the Scotsman, see: *The Scotsman, 1817–1955: Scotland's National Newspaper*, Edinburgh: The Scotsman Publications Limited, 1955, pp. 1–2.
38. 'Police Commission', *The Scotsman*, Edinburgh, 16 August 1854, p. 3
39. Ibid.
40. Ibid.
41. 'Resignation of Sir Henry D Littlejohn', *The Scotsman*, Edinburgh, 16 March 1908, p. 7.
42. Ibid.
43. 'The Late Sir Henry D. Littlejohn, MD', *The Scotsman*, p. 5. For an excellent recent contextual survey of Littlejohn's *Report* that also includes a reproduction of the original text, see: Laxton and Rodger, *Insanitary City*.
44. 'Resignation of Sir Henry D Littlejohn', *The Scotsman*, p. 7.
45. 'The Late Sir Henry D. Littlejohn, MD', *The Scotsman*, p. 5.
46. Ibid.
47. H.P. Tait, 'Sir Henry Duncan Littlejohn: Great Scottish Sanitarian and Medical Jurist', *The Medical Officer*, 21st September 1962, 108: 186.
48. Ibid.
49. H. Sutherland, *A Time to Keep*, London: Geoffrey Bles, 1934, p. 71.
50. Ibid.
51. 'Professor Sir Henry Littlejohn's Opening Lecture', *The Scotsman*, Edinburgh, 5 May 1897, p. 12
52. 'United Kingdom Police Surgeons' Association', *British Medical Journal*, London, 20 August 1897, pp. 492–493.
53. 'Resignation of Sir Henry D Littlejohn', *The Scotsman*, p. 7.
54. 'High Court of Justiciary—The Queen's Park Murder Case', *The Scotsman*, Edinburgh, 3 June 1872, pp. 6–7.
55. Ibid.
56. Ibid.
57. Ibid.
58. Ibid.
59. Ibid.
60. 'The Suspected Murder in the Queen's Park', *The Scotsman*, Edinburgh, 26 March 1872, p. 3.
61. On this point, see, for example, 'High Court of Justiciary—The Queen's Park Murder Case', *The Scotsman*, p. 7.

62. D. Kalifa, 'Crime scenes: Criminal topography and social imaginary in nineteenth-century Paris', *French Historical Studies*, 2004, 27(1): 177–178; A. Brown-May and S. Cooke, 'Death, decency and the dead-house: The city morgue in colonial Melbourne', *Provenance: The Journal of Public Record Office Victoria*, 2004, (3): 2 of 20 pages.

63. See, for example, Sutherland, *A Time to Keep*, pp. 70–71.

64. Although a study of the police detective in Scotland remains to be conducted, an excellent general discussion of the social and cultural history of the police detective within England can be found in H. Shpayer-Makov, *The Ascent of the Detective: Police Sleuths in Victorian and Edwardian England*, Oxford and New York: Oxford University Press, 2011.

65. See 'Report of the Post-Mortem Examination by Drs Maclagan and Littlejohn of body of Madame Chantrelle', 3 January 1878 in *Print of Declarations and Reports of Experts in the Trial of Eugene Marie Chantrelle for Murder* in *Trial Papers Relating to Eugene Marie Chantrelle for the Crime of Murder at 81a George Street, Edinburgh. Tried at High Court, Edinburgh*, Edinburgh: National Records of Scotland, 1878, GB234/JC26/1878/296/15, p. 20; 'Appendix IV. Report of Post-Mortem Examination by Drs. Maclagan and Littlejohn of Body of Madame Chantrelle', in A.D. Smith (ed.), *Trial of Eugene Marie Chantrelle*, Glasgow and Edinburgh: William Hodge & Company, 1906.

66. Testimony of Henry Littlejohn, as reported in Smith (ed.), *Trial of Eugene Marie Chantrelle*, pp. 82–83.

67. Ibid., pp. 83 and 95.

68. Testimony of Littlejohn, as reported in ibid., p. 84.

69. Ibid., p. 76.

70. Testimony of Douglas Maclagan, as reported in ibid., p. 94.

71. Testimony of Douglas Maclagan, as reported in ibid., p. 95.

72. See, for example, Testimony of Douglas Maclagan, as reported in ibid., p. 96.

73. Henry Duncan Littlejohn and George Clark, 'Medical report of the post-mortem of Mary Ann Webster', 27 November 1890 in *Precognition Against John Webster, John Webster for the Crime of Murder at Newtown Hotel, Southmuir of Kirriemuir, Forfarshire*, Edinburgh: National Records of Scotland, 1891, GB234/AD14/91/154, p. 399.

74. Ibid.

75. For a particularly pertinent discussion of 'disgust' and its relationship to the human body and physical waste, see W.I. Miller, *The Anatomy of Disgust*, Cambridge, MA and London, Harvard University Press, 1997.

76. For an excellent technical and diagrammatic account of how to conduct a post-mortem, see H.D. Littlejohn, 'On the practice of medical jurisprudence: No IV post-mortem examination. B. Internal examination', *Edinburgh Medical Journal*, 1876, XXI(VIII): 1112–1124.

77. Ibid., p. 1116.

78. 'High Court of Justiciary: The Potterow Case', *The Scotsman*, Edinburgh, 20 September 1902.

79. 'Precognition of Sir Henry Duncan Littlejohn, MD, Edinburgh', 2 August 1902 in *Precognition Against John Adamson for the Crime of Murder at 39 Potterrow, Edinburgh*, Edinburgh: National Records of Scotland, 1902, GB234/AD15/02/22, pp. 67–68.

80. 'Precognition of John Linton, MD', 4 August 1902 in *Precognition Against John Adamson for the Crime of Murder at 39 Potterrow, Edinburgh*, Edinburgh: National Records of Scotland, 1902, GB234/AD15/02/22, p. 83.

81. Ibid., p. 84.

82. 'Precognition of Sir Henry Duncan Littlejohn, MD, Edinburgh', 2 August 1902 in *Precognition Against John Adamson for the Crime of Murder at 39 Potterrow, Edinburgh*, Edinburgh: National Records of Scotland, 1902, GB234/AD15/02/22, p. 68.

83. V. Bates, '"So far as I can define without a microscopical examination": Venereal disease diagnosis in English courts, 1850–1914', *Social History of Medicine*, 2012, 26(1): 38–55, p. 42 particularly; I. Crozier and G. Rees, 'Making a space for medical expertise: Medical knowledge of sexual assault and the construction of boundaries between forensic medicine and the law in late nineteenth-century England', *Law, Culture and the Humanities*, 2012, 8(2): 285–304; L. A. Jackson, *Child Sexual Abuse in Victorian England*, London and New York: Routledge, 2000, pp. 71–89 especially.

84. Between the 1820s and 1900s, Edinburgh police surgeons such as Drs Tait, Black, Glover, Henry Littlejohn and Harvey Littlejohn, were routinely called as expert witnesses in rape trials at the High Court of Justiciary. See particularly, *Chapter 4: Rape* in the forthcoming: K.A. Couzens, *Medicine on Trial: Medical Testimony & Forensic Expertise in the Scottish High Court of Justiciary, c. 1822–1906*, Unpublished Doctoral dissertation, University of Western Australia, Perth, 2019.

85. 'Indictment' in *Trial Papers Relating to John Walker for the Crime of Rape and Assault with Intent to Ravish at Torphichen Village, Linlithgow. Tried at High Court, Edinburgh*, Edinburgh: National Records of Scotland, 1874, GB234/JC26/1874/400.

86. NOTE: No page numbers available for this source. 'Precognition of Elizabeth Henrietta Aitken', 3 August 1874 in *Precognition Against John Walker for the Crime of Rape and Assault with Intent to Ravish at Torphichen Village, Linlithgow*, Edinburgh: National Records of Scotland, 1874, GB234/AD14/74/307.

87. Linlithgow is approximately 30 kilometres from Edinburgh.

88. NOTE: No page numbers recorded in this source. 'Medical Report by Henry D. Littlejohn', 31 August 1874 in *Precognition Against John Walker for the Crime of Rape*.

89. NOTE: No page numbers recorded in this source. 'Report by Dr Littlejohn in Case of Wm King', 12 October 1876 in *Trial Papers Relating to William King for the Crime of Rape and Assault with Intent to Ravish. Tried at High Court, Edinburgh*, Edinburgh: National Records of Scotland, 1876, GB234/JC26/1876/313.

90. T.W. Lacqueur, 'Bodies, details, and the humanitarian narrative', in L. Hunt (ed.), *The New Cultural History*, Berkeley: University of California Press, 1989, p. 179.

91. Ibid., p. 178.

92. 'High Court of Justiciary', *The Scotsman*, Edinburgh, 5 December 1876, p. 3.

93. Anon., *Duties and Emoluments of Police Surgeon*, Edinburgh: Pamphlet Collection of the Royal College of Physicians, c. 1847, p. 2.

94. Ibid.

95. Ibid., p. 3.

96. H. Shpayer-Makov, 'Journalists and police detectives in Victorian and Edwardian England: An uneasy reciprocal relationship', *Journal of Social History*, 2009, 42(4): 963–987.

97. 'Precognition of John Bell, Constable of the Edinburgh City Police', 24 June 1882 in *Precognition Against Jessie Peattie for the Crime of Child Murder*, Edinburgh: National Records of Scotland, 1882, GB234/AD14/82/47, p. 19.

98. 'Precognition of Henry Duncan Littlejohn, MD', 26 June 1882 in ibid., pp. 43–44.

99. 'High Court of Justiciary: Concealment of Pregnancy', *The Scotsman*, Edinburgh, 25 July 1882, p. 3.

100. 'High Court of Justiciary: Charge of Child Murder', *The Scotsman*, Edinburgh, 11 May 1860, p. 4.

101. H.D. Littlejohn, 'A case of poisoning with nitrate of potash, with hints as to the conduct of medical practitioners in cases of suspected poisoning', *Transaction of the Medico-Chirurgical Society of Edinburgh*, 1885, 4: 25.

102. Ibid., p. 26.

103. Ibid.

104. Ibid.

105. Ibid.

106. See 'Report of the post-mortem examination of the body of William Walker' in H.D. Littlejohn, 'A case of poisoning with nitrate of potash', p. 27.

107. Ibid., p. 28.

108. Ibid.

109. Ibid., p. 29.

110. Ibid., p. 29. See also Testimony of William Angus, as reported in 'High Court of Justiciary: Charge of Child Murder', *The Scotsman*, p. 4.

111. Ibid., p. 29.

112. Ibid., p. 29. Nitre was typically used in this period for curing meats or in the production of match-paper. It was cheap and easily available.

113. Ibid., pp. 28–29.

114. 'Indictment' in *Trial Papers Relating to Edward Pratt Evatt for the Crime of Rape and Assault with Intent to Ravish. Tried at High Court, Edinburgh*, Edinburgh: National Records of Scotland, 1882, GB234/ JC26/1882/316.

115. Henry Duncan Littlejohn, 'Case of Edward Pratt Evatt: Answer to Queries of Crown Counsel', 10 May 1882 in *Precognition Against Edward Pratt Evatt for the Crime of Rape and Assault with Intent to Ravish*, Edinburgh: National Records of Scotland, 1882, GB234/ AD14/82/41, pp. 1–4.

116. 'Note by Crown Counsel', 13 May 1882 in ibid.

117. NOTE: No page numbers given in this source. 'Medical Certificate by Wm.Hy. Murray', 20 April 1882 in *Trial Papers Relating to Edward Pratt Evatt for the Crime of Rape*.

118. Note: Emphasis belong to the original text. See Littlejohn, 'Case of Edward Pratt Evatt: Answer to Queries of Crown Counsel' in *Precognition Against Edward Pratt Evatt for the Crime of Rape*, pp. 2–3.

119. 'Precognition of William Henry Murray', 13 May 1882 in ibid., p. 35.
120. A. Digby, *Making a Medical Living: Doctors and Patients in the English Market for Medicine, 1720–1911*, Cambridge and New York: Cambridge University Press, 1994, p. 50.
121. Note: No page numbers recorded in this source. Letter from Charles Kinane to Henry Littlejohn', 16 March 1878 in 'Infanticide Vol. I.' in *Notebooks of Sir Henry Duncan Littlejohn*, Edinburgh: Edinburgh University Library Special Collections, c.1880, 5 volumes, GB 237/ EUA IN1/ACU/F1/1.
122. Ibid.
123. Approximately five scrapbooks survive within the Edinburgh University Library Special Collections (EULSC) archive, with the two scrapbooks on 'Infanticide' the most fruitful for correspondence and material on medical jurisprudence. Despite their labelling, the content does not always correspond to the title of each book, and only three of the five notebooks include retained correspondence. See *Notebooks of Sir Henry Duncan Littlejohn*.
124. M.A. Crowther, 'Forensic medicine and medical ethics in nineteenth-century Britain', in R. Baker (ed.), *The Codification of Medical Morality*, Dordrecht, Boston and London: Kluwer Academic Publishers, 1995, pp. 173–190.
125. Sutherland, *A Time to Keep*, p. 101.

Archives

Anon., *Duties and Emoluments of Police Surgeon*, Edinburgh: Pamphlet Collection of the Royal College of Physicians, c. 1847, 1–4.
Forensic Medicine: Volume of Notes on Forensic Medicine from Lectures Delivered, C. 1906 by Sir Henry Duncan Littlejohn, Physician, While Professor of Forensic Medicine at Edinburgh University, 1897–1906, Edinburgh: National Library of Scotland, 1906, GB 233/MS.19321.
Precognition Against Ann McQue for the Crime of Child Murder at York Place, Edinburgh, Edinburgh: National Records of Scotland, 1860, GB234/ AD14/60/260.
Precognition Against Edward Pratt Evatt for the Crime of Rape and Assault with Intent to Ravish, Edinburgh: National Records of Scotland, 1882, GB234/ AD14/82/41.

Precognition Against Jessie Peattie for the Crime of Child Murder, Edinburgh, National Records of Scotland, 1882, GB234/AD14/82/47.

Precognition Against John Adamson for the Crime of Murder at 39 Potterrow, Edinburgh, Edinburgh: National Records of Scotland, 1902, GB234/AD15/02/22.

Precognition Against John Walker for the Crime of Rape and Assault with Intent to Ravish at Torphichen Village, Linlithgow, Edinburgh: National Records of Scotland, 1874, GB234/AD14/74/307.

Precognition Against John Webster, John Webster for the Crime of Murder at Newtown Hotel, Southmuir of Kirriemuir, Forfarshire, Edinburgh: National Records of Scotland, 1891, GB234/AD14/91/154.

Print of Declarations and Reports of Experts in the Trial of Eugene Marie Chantrelle for Murder in *Trial Papers Relating to Eugene Marie Chantrelle for the Crime of Murder at 81a George Street, Edinburgh. Tried at High Court, Edinburgh*, Edinburgh: National Records of Scotland, 1878, GB234/JC26/1878/296/15.

Trial Papers Relating to Edward Pratt Evatt for the Crime of Rape and Assault with Intent to Ravish. Tried at High Court, Edinburgh, Edinburgh: National Records of Scotland, 1882, GB234/JC26/1882/316.

Trial Papers Relating to John Walker for the Crime of Rape and Assault with Intent to Ravish at Torphichen Village, Linlithgow. Tried at High Court, Edinburgh, Edinburgh: National Records of Scotland, 1874, GB234/JC26/1874/400.

Trial Papers Relating to William King for the Crime of Rape and Assault with Intent to Ravish. Tried at High Court, Edinburgh, Edinburgh: National Records of Scotland, 1876, GB234/JC26/1876/313.

Bibliography

Bates, V., '"So far as I can define without a microscopical examination": Venereal disease diagnosis in English courts, 1850–1914', *Social History of Medicine*, 2012, 26(1): 38–55.

Bourke, J., 'Police surgeons and sexual violence: A history', *The Lancet*, 2017, 390(10094): 548–549.

Bourke, J., 'Police surgeons and victims of rape: Cultures of harm and care', *Social History of Medicine*, 2018, 31(4): 711–731.

Bradshaw, Y., Savage, S.P., Moon, G. and Kelly, K., 'A different sort of doctor: The police surgeon in England and Wales', *Social Policy & Administration*, 1995, 29(2):122–134.

Brown-May, A. and Cooke, S., 'Death, decency and the dead-house: The city morgue in colonial Melbourne', *Provenance: The Journal of Public Record Office Victoria*, 2004, 3: 25–36.

Couzens, K.A., *Medicine on Trial: Medical Testimony & Forensic Expertise in the Scottish High Court of Justiciary, C. 1822–1906*, Unpublished Doctoral dissertation, University of Western Australia, Perth, 2019.

Couzens, K.-A., '"Upon my word, I do not see the use of medical evidence here": Persuasion, authority and medical expertise in the Edinburgh High Court of Justiciary', *History*, 2019, 104(359): 42–62.

Crowther, M.A., 'Criminal precognitions and their value for historians', *Scottish Archives*, 1995, 1: 75–84.

Crowther, M.A., 'Crime, prosecution and mercy: English influence and Scottish practice in the early nineteenth century', in S.J. Connolly (ed.), *Kingdoms United? Great Britain and Ireland since 1500: Integration and Diversity*, Dublin & Portland: Four Courts Press, 1999, 225–238.

Crowther, M.A., 'Forensic medicine and medical ethics in nineteenth-century Britain', in R. Baker (ed.), *The Codification of Medical Morality*, Dordrecht, Boston and London: Kluwer Academic Publishers, 1995, 173–190.

Crozier, I. and G. Rees, 'Making a space for medical expertise: Medical knowledge of sexual assault and the construction of boundaries between forensic medicine and the law in late nineteenth-century England', *Law, Culture and the Humanities*, 2012, 8(2): 285–304.

Digby, A., *Making a Medical Living: Doctors and Patients in the English Market for Medicine, 1720–1911*, Cambridge and New York: Cambridge University Press, 1994.

'High Court of Justiciary', *The Scotsman*, Edinburgh, 5 December 1876, 3.

'High Court of Justiciary—The Queen's Park Murder Case', *The Scotsman*, Edinburgh, 3 June 1872, 6–7.

'High Court of Justiciary: Charge of Child Murder', *The Scotsman*, Edinburgh, 11 May 1860, 4.

'High Court of Justiciary: Concealment of Pregnancy', *The Scotsman*, Edinburgh, 25 July 1882, 3.

'High Court of Justiciary: The Potterow Case', *The Scotsman*, Edinburgh, 20 September 1902, 11.

'High Court of Justiciary: The York Place Child-Murder', *The Scotsman*, Edinburgh, 13 March 1860, 4.

Jackson, L.A., *Child Sexual Abuse in Victorian England*, London and New York: Routledge, 2000.

Kalifa, D., 'Crime scenes: Criminal topography and social imaginary in nineteenth-century Paris', *French Historical Studies*, 2004, 27(1): 175–194.

Lacqueur, T.W., 'Bodies, details, and the humanitarian narrative', in L. Hunt (ed.), *The New Cultural History*, Berkeley: University of California Press, 1989, 176–204.

'The Late Sir Henry D. Littlejohn, M.D.: A Distinguished Public Official and Medical Jurist', *The Scotsman*, Edinburgh, 2 October 1914, 5.

Laxton, P. and Rodger, R. *Insanitary City: Henry Littlejohn and the Condition of Edinburgh*, Lancaster: Carnegie Publishing Limited, 2013.

Levitt, I., 'Henry Littlejohn and Scottish health policy, 1859–1908', *Scottish Archives*, 1996, 2: 63–77.

Littlejohn, H.D., 'A case of poisoning with nitrate of potash, with hints as to the conduct of medical practitioners in cases of suspected poisoning', *Transactions of the Medico-Chirurgical Society of Edinburgh*, 1885, 4: 23–32.

Littlejohn, H.D., 'On the practice of medical jurisprudence: No IV post-mortem examination. B. Internal examination', *Edinburgh Medical Journal*, 1876, XXI(VIII): 1112–1124.

'Littlejohn, Thomas', *Post Office Annual Directory*, Edinburgh: Postmaster General, 1828–1829, 103.

Miller, W.I., *The Anatomy of Disgust*, Cambridge, MA and London: Harvard University Press, 1997.

'Police Commission', *The Scotsman*, Edinburgh, 16 August 1854, 3.

'Professor Sir Henry Littlejohn's opening lecture', *The Scotsman*, Edinburgh, 5 May 1897, 12.

'Resignation of Sir Henry D Littlejohn', *The Scotsman*, Edinburgh, 16 March 1908, 7.

Riggs, P.T., 'Prosecutors, juries, judges and punishment in early nineteenth-century Scotland', *Journal of Scottish Historical Studies*, 2012, 32(2): 166–189.

Robins, J., *The Magnificent Spilsbury and the Case of the Brides in the Bath*, London: John Murray, 2010.

Savage, S.P., Moon, G., Kelly, K. and Bradshaw, Y., 'Divided loyalties? The police surgeon and criminal justice', *Policing and Society*, 1997, 7(2): 79–98.

The Scotsman, 1817–1955: Scotland's National Newspaper, Edinburgh: The Scotsman Publications Limited, 1955.

Shpayer-Makov, H., 'Journalists and police detectives in Victorian and Edwardian England: An uneasy reciprocal relationship', *Journal of Social History*, 2009, 42(4): 963–987.

Shpayer-Makov, H., *The Ascent of the Detective: Police Sleuths in Victorian and Edwardian England*, Oxford and New York: Oxford University Press, 2011.

Smith, A.D. (ed.), *Trial of Eugene Marie Chantrelle*, Glasgow and Edinburgh: William Hodge & Company, 1906.

Summers, R.D., *History of the Police Surgeon*, London: Association of Police Surgeons of Great Britain, 1988.

'The Suspected Murder in the Queen's Park', *The Scotsman*, Edinburgh, 26 March 1872, 3.

Sutherland, H., *A Time to Keep*, London: Geoffrey Bles, 1934.

Tait, H.P., 'Sir Henry Duncan Littlejohn: Great Scottish sanitarian and medical jurist', *The Medical Officer*, 21 September 1962, 108: 183–190.

'United Kingdom Police Surgeons' Association', *British Medical Journal*, London, 20 August 1897, 492–493.

White, B.M., 'The police surgeon as Medical Officer of Health in Scotland 1862–1897', *The Police Surgeon*, 1989, 35: 29–37.

7

'13 Yards Off the Big Gate and 37 Yards Up the West Walls'. Crime Scene Investigation in Mid-nineteenth Century Newcastle upon Tyne

Clare Sandford-Couch and Helen Rutherford

Introduction

All too often, the weakest link in the chain of criminal justice is the crime scene investigation. Improper collection of evidence blocks the finding of truth.[1]

The foundation of all crime scene investigations is the ability of the crime scene investigator to recognize the potential and importance of physical evidence, large and small, at the crime scene…Proper crime scene investigation is the starting point for the process of establishing what happened and who did it.[2]

C. Sandford-Couch (✉)
Newcastle University, Newcastle upon Tyne, UK
e-mail: clare@sandford-couch.com

H. Rutherford
Northumbria University, Newcastle upon Tyne, UK
e-mail: helen.rutherford@northumbria.ac.uk

© The Author(s) 2020
A. Adam (ed.), *Crime and the Construction of Forensic Objectivity from 1850*, Palgrave Histories of Policing, Punishment and Justice,
https://doi.org/10.1007/978-3-030-28837-2_7

161

On 27 February 1863, at the Newcastle Assizes, George Vass was convicted of the wilful murder of Margaret Docherty. The murder took place
in the early hours of New Year's Day and there was little doubt of Vass's
guilt: witnesses gave evidence at the trial that they saw Vass assaulting a
woman around 2 a.m. in the alleyway where the body was found, behind
the West Walls of the town (see Fig. 7.1). Vass was arrested at his home,
close to the murder scene, twelve hours later, on 1 January. Detailed
descriptions of the careful and methodical examination of the crime
scene and collection of material evidence by uniformed constables and
sergeants of the Newcastle Police Force survive in newspaper reports of
the proceedings at the inquest and the trial. This chapter will consider the
duties and actions of the Newcastle upon Tyne Police Force in this case to
reconstruct the approach to the processes of evidence gathering and crime
scene investigation in a nineteenth-century provincial force.

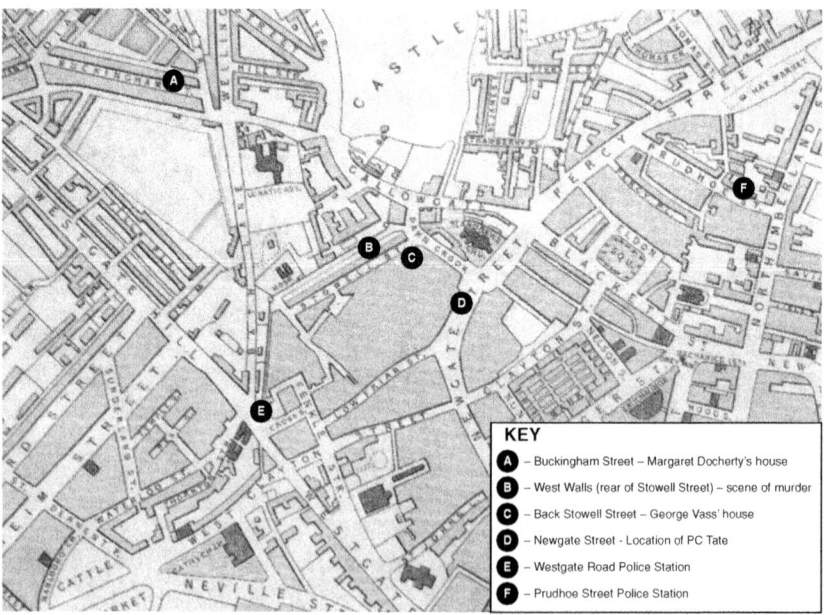

Fig. 7.1 Map of Newcastle upon Tyne, copyright © H.J. Rutherford and
C. Sandford-Couch, reproduced with kind permission of Newcastle City Library,
Local Studies and Family History Centre

The role of the police, in the mid-nineteenth century, has traditionally been perceived as one of crime prevention rather than detection. This may be as a result of the parameters set out for the first police: 'The Metropolitan Police Act of 1829 specifically precluded Robert Peel's New Police from any involvement in the investigation and detection of crime'.[3] However, what is evident from the way that constables of the police force in Newcastle approached the Vass case in 1863 is a recognition of the need to gather evidence for the legal process. This in itself suggests a level of professionalism and sophistication and a methodical approach to crime scene analysis in the provinces in the mid-nineteenth century that has not previously been appreciated.[4]

A micro-historical investigation of the role of the police in connection with this crime offers an opportunity to challenge the London-centric focus of much research into Victorian policing, and to gain an understanding of the early development of scientific investigation of the crime scene. Drawing on the limited official records, newspaper reports of the murder of Margaret Docherty and the National Archives file of the proceedings at the trial of George Vass, we will question what the Vass case can tell us about how knowledge of a crime scene was constructed in Newcastle in the 1860s. In particular, we consider how ordinary witnesses and the police contributed to the making of that knowledge, and how this evidence led to the conviction of Vass. To enable a contextualized analysis of the police actions and investigation into the murder, we first briefly outline the historical background to the formation and function of the Newcastle police force, in the context of policing in the provinces and in England more generally in the nineteenth century.

The 'New Police' in Newcastle

Surprisingly little has been written on the early years of the Newcastle upon Tyne Police. Save for two short pamphlets, Newcastle policing remains ripe for research.[5] Much research into nineteenth-century policing has focused on London and the Metropolitan Force, and while some historians have addressed policing in the provinces, care must be taken not to over-generalize; not all 'new police' forces were the same.[6] To an extent, the scope of this enterprise is restricted by the survival of records. The National Archives holds records relating to the Metropolitan Police, the Royal Irish Constabulary and the Transport Police.[7] Surviving records of other police forces are held either by local archives or by the relevant force and there are significant gaps. The archives of Northumbria Police, into which the Newcastle Force was amalgamated in 1969, contain mainly twentieth-century material. The holdings of the Tyne and Wear archives on the Newcastle Police, contain little beyond the Watch Committee records that form part of the City Council archives.[8] However, careful reading of the minutes of the Newcastle Watch Committee has proved informative on the early years of the force.

The Municipal Corporations Act 1835 empowered town councils to form subcommittees, which assumed responsibility for forming a 'new police' force for the borough. The first report of the first Committee in Newcastle was 11 February 1836. The Watch Committees were to appoint 'a sufficient number of fit men' to be sworn in to act as constables for 'Preserving the Peace by Day and by Night, and preventing Robberies and other Felonies, and apprehending Offenders against the Peace'.[9] Emsley noted: 'much of the history of the English police has been written from the assumption of the Metropolitan Police model spreading from London into the provinces'.[10] This was likely to be the case in Newcastle, which followed many other provincial forces by contacting the Metropolitan Police for a recommendation for its first senior officer in 1836.[11]

John Stephens from the Metropolitan Police was engaged as first Superintendent in Newcastle, a position he held from 1836 until 1854.[12] Although the activities to be undertaken by the 'new police' in Newcastle were largely under the control of the local Watch Committee, Stephens would have had a significant impact upon the nature of policing in the town as it stood in 1863. Interestingly, Stephens had been valet to Sir Robert Peel before he joined the Metropolitan Police.[13] As a result of this close relationship, it is logical to surmise that policing in Newcastle would have been directly influenced by the approach taken by Peel, the 'architect' of the new police. One aspect of this might have been the adoption of guidance along the lines of the *General Instruction Book* (often termed 'Peel's Principles'), issued to all members of the newly formed Metropolitan Police in September 1829, which set out the theoretical duties of policemen and their legal powers under common law.[14] There is no reference to any form of crime scene investigation or detection of crime in these principles. This would suggest that detection and crime scene analysis were not regarded as tasks required or expected to be undertaken by the 'new police'.

However, it is apparent that such activities were not reserved for a separate branch of what we may think of now as a detective force. The Metropolitan Police established a separate Detective Branch in 1842, and by the 1850s some provincial towns had detective forces.[15] Newcastle too established a small detective force; although it is not recorded when precisely, a local newspaper refers in December 1846 to a detective force being active in Newcastle.[16] The role of these early detectives was intended to be distinct from that of the uniformed officers, and it is significant that it was only uniformed officers who were involved in investigating the murder of Margaret Docherty. For this reason, we will not address the detective force of Newcastle police in this chapter.

By the early 1860s, the police force in Newcastle was under the command of John Sabbage. An 1863 guide to Newcastle confirms that the force then comprised 140 men 'formed into four divisions, each being provided with an inspector and sub-inspector'.[17] However, this was short of the target set, and there was an increase of six men to 146 in the official 1863–1864 report.[18] In October 1861, the population of Newcastle was 109,291.[19] The ratio of inhabitants to police officers compared favourably to other areas of the country.[20]

Most men joining the Newcastle force conform to the view that 'a high proportion of recruits were always drawn from the unskilled and semi-skilled working class'.[21] From the Watch Committee minutes, we collated statistics of recruits to the Newcastle force in 1862: of the thirty-four appointees, twenty-two were listed as 'labourer'. Although Emsley cautions, '"labourer" was a general term used by the unskilled in Victorian society and not simply by those who worked on the land', of the 1862 Newcastle recruits, more than half came from Northumberland or other rural locations.[22] Recruits also included three men who had been police constables in other forces. This picture of diverse recruitment is confirmed in broader analyses of the occupational background of police recruits in England from 1840 to 1900.[23] In age, the Newcastle recruits also conform to national patterns, being men in their twenties. Despite Emsley's observation that interest in attracting rural labourers as recruits to the urban forces may have stemmed from a belief that 'agricultural labourers were thought to be fitter and healthier than the urban working class and more willing to take orders and to fit in with the hierarchical structure of the police', we found no difference in height between those recruited from urban or rural locations.[24] All (bar one recruit) were 5 feet 10 inches to 6 feet tall. Only one of the 1862 recruits had his appointment made subject to being passed fit by the doctor; presumably, the others were suitably physically strong and in evident good health. Emsley suggested nineteenth-century policemen needed a certain physicality and toughness: 'in many working class districts…men continued to gain and maintain a reputation by physical strength and aggression, if police officers were to survive in these areas…they had to be as hard as the local hard men'.[25] This may well have been true, but a different aspect of nineteenth-century policing is evident in the Vass case. We can now turn to an analysis of the police actions and investigation into the murder of Margaret Docherty in 1863.

Crime Scene Investigation in the Docherty Murder

Crime scene investigation is both the collection and interpretation of evidence and information for identification and apprehension of criminals and the process of reconstructing past events.[26] Crime scene processing can consist of:

> an examination and evaluation of the scene for the express purpose of recovering physical evidence and documenting the scene's condition in situ, or as found. The end goal of crime scene processing is the collection of the evidence and scene context in as pristine a condition as possible.[27]

We will examine the actions of the Newcastle force in the Vass case in this light. Consider, for example, the detailed evidence given by the police constable (PC) William Tate to the Inquest on Friday, 2 January, the day after the crime:

On Thursday morning, about half past three o'clock, I was on duty in Newgate Street, when a man, named Parker, came to me and said that a woman was lying dead in the West Walls. I said, 'Nonsense, she will only be drunk!', but he told me he had lifted her up, and felt her, and she was dead. I went with him and found that the woman was lying there quite dead. I found Archbold and PC Hepple standing there. We all arrived about the same time. The woman's clothes were all torn off her; she was bare legged, and her breast was bare. Her face was covered with blood and mud, and her legs with mud. Her hair was all covered with the mud also. There was blood on the ground; and about twelve or fourteen yards further up the lane I found the woman's stockings and cap. There were pieces of her dress lying about. There were marks of a struggle at the place where I found the stockings. It looked as if someone had been trailed about. The West Walls are not paved, and there had been a shower of rain a short time before. The struggle appeared to have taken place about thirteen yards above where I found the body. There was an appearance as if someone had been dragged along from where the struggle took place to the spot where the body was. We found that some of the woman's teeth had been knocked out. I went with the body to the Westgate Station, and afterwards took it to the Dead House. The same body was shown to the jury today.[28]

He was the last witness called before the Coroner adjourned the inquest to allow for the post-mortem examination.[29] At the resumed inquest, Sergeant Thomas Watson gave evidence:

I produce the pair of shoes, an apron, and part of a dress which was shown to the witness Docherty just now. I found them at the West Walls last Thursday morning, about half-past four o'clock. One shoe was lying on the ground, and about seven yards nearer to the Darn Crook, another shoe, and the apron and the piece of dress, and a tumbler glass belonging to the Adelaide Hotel. The words 'Adelaide Hotel' are engraved upon it. The body part of the dress was found about half way between the first shoe and the second. The West Walls is a narrow lane which is not paved. The road-way is formed of a sort of black ash. When I saw the place that morning, it was soft on the surface. Some rain had fallen lately. Between the first shoe and the second the ground had the appearance of something having been trailed along. At the place where the second shoe and the apron were found lying, the ground was paddled round, as though a scuffle had taken place.

There was some blood on the ground at the last place; and on the town wall there were several spots of blood just opposite. I have measured the spot where the body was found this morning; it is 13 yards nearer Stowell Street; and when I saw the ground about that spot on Thursday morning it was also all paddled, as if a scuffle had taken place. The marks were chiefly where the apron was found.[30]

Sub-Inspector Thomas Scott gave evidence to the coroner's inquest and material evidence was produced at the inquest, including the trousers Vass had worn on the night of 1 January. Scott stated: 'On Friday, the 2nd inst., I took the prisoner's trousers off, and now produce them. I found marks of blood in the pockets'. After the police surgeon confirmed that the marks were of recent blood, Scott continued: 'The marks on the pockets are outside, not inside, and there are no corresponding marks on the cloth of the trousers. I asked the prisoner how he accounted for having blood on his coat. He said he could not tell'.

Ross Gardner and Tom Bevel define crime scene processing as involving six steps: assessing, observing, documenting, searching, collecting, and analysing scenes.[31] We suggest that in the reports from this case, and the evidence, at the inquest and at the trial, we can identify the six steps outlined by Garner and Bevel, as follows:

Assessing

The first police at the scene carried out this work. PCs Tate and Hepple examined Margaret Docherty's body and ascertained that she was dead. They removed her body on a stretcher. Unlike modern crime scenes, it appears that there was no attempt, or even an expectation, that the scene would be cordoned off or secured.

Observing

The constables noted the appearance of the crime scene, including the position of the streetlight, the weather, and the position of the body; the state of Margaret Docherty's clothing and the attitude of her limbs; the ground was 'paddled' and there were drag marks. The need to be vigilant extended to the work of the arresting officer, Sub-Inspector Scott. He made specific observations in Vass's house and as a result confiscated Vass's clothing for analysis by the police surgeon.

Documenting

Sadly, there is no surviving contemporaneous documentation prepared by the police officers; however, the detail in the written record of their oral evidence suggests strongly that the constables kept a written record of their activities; evidently a degree of literacy was expected of uniformed officers, as Emsley noted, 'each man had his personal notebook'.[32] The officers carried out detailed measurements to document their observations. These included the distance of the body from the end of the road, and from the gate together with the location of bloodstains and the position of Margaret Docherty's shoes and stockings. They took statements from witnesses, including one from Vass himself. It is likely that they produced a detailed plan of the crime scene, as one is referred to in the court reports.

Searching

The scene was carefully searched. This is particularly apparent from the evidence of Sergeant Thomas Watson, which resulted in the finding of a glass from the Adelaide pub, where Margaret Docherty had been drinking, and the blood spots on the wall.

Collecting

The discarded clothing, scraps of dress, apron, shoes, stockings, and bonnet were collected. The glass was picked up, and Vass's coat and trousers were preserved. Sub-Inspector Scott produced these as evidence at the inquest.

Analysing Scenes

It is difficult to assess the extent to which the evidence from the crime scene investigation was analysed, and how or whether the information obtained at the crime scene was brought together. Indeed, it is questionable whether this alone would have led the police to identifying Margaret Docherty and George Vass. The evidence of other witnesses was to prove crucial in this regard—we will return to this later. However, it is clear that the police drew some conclusions from what they observed at the crime scene. For example, PC Tate's evidence at the inquest includes statements indicating some form of analysis of the evidence at the crime scene: 'It looked as if…', '…struggle appeared to have taken place…', 'there was an appearance as if…'.

Against this background, and evidence of a careful and skilful approach to examining a crime scene, we want to address a number of questions: Why did they do this? Was it for clues or deduction? Was crime scene investigation part of the force's *modus operandi* for detection? And would this make detection a function of 'ordinary' policing in Newcastle? How did the policemen learn these skills? What does this type of process tell us about how the police force in Newcastle perceived its role?

The Personnel of Crime Scene Investigation

Emsley has suggested that 'uniformed patrolmen have never been much concerned with the detection of crime'.[33] However, the actions identified above would indicate that the Newcastle force expected ordinary uniformed constables to engage in investigative aspects of police work. It is notable that no one seemed surprised that the police had carried out a detailed survey of the crime scene. When this was described in court, prosecution counsel stated explicitly: '…the evidence of the policemen, Hepple and Watson, who, *as their duty called upon them to do*, made a most careful examination of the body of the deceased, and of the ground around it'.[34] Thus, the barrister referred to it as part of their duty as police constables: it is clearly assumed to be part of the job. This suggests it was the standard and expected response in that place and at that time, to the most serious of crimes. That such activities were part of the identity of the regular police constable in Newcastle in the 1860s appears to challenge commonly held assumptions about the role and function of uniformed police at this time.

It is instructive to identify and establish a little more about the policemen involved in the Vass case, and their activities. The area in which the crime took place formed part of the beat of B Division, based at Westgate Road Police Station. The 'new police' forces were divided into Divisions, each with a hierarchy: a superintendent, inspectors, sub-inspectors, sergeants, and then constables. Turnover of constables was high in most forces in England, and police recruits often served no more than a year. Taylor noted in his study of Middlesbrough in the 1850s, at least 30% of recruits served less than one year and 55% served less than five years.[35] Many men resigned, but it is clear that a large number were dismissed. The Newcastle Watch Committee minutes reveal a similar picture, with almost every meeting of the Committee receiving notice of resignations from the force. However, the three constables and the senior officers involved in the investigation of the Docherty murder were not recent appointees and had unusually long careers in the force.

The first policeman at the crime scene was PC John Hepple. He joined the Newcastle police in 1855.[36] At the inquest he stated that he and PC Galbraith had found the body after two witnesses, Archbold and Shearer, came to the Westgate Station about twenty minutes past three o'clock on Thursday morning, to report a woman lying dead drunk in the West Walls. His evidence was a detailed description of the position and condition of the body as they found it. He made no comments as to the crime scene more widely. His evidence at the trial was brief and factual.[37] PC Galbraith, who had joined the force in 1861, was not called to give evidence at either the inquest or trial.

We have referred above to the detailed crime scene evidence given at the inquest by PC Tate. We cannot know exactly when Tate was appointed; sadly, a volume of Watch Committee minutes covering 24 October 1851–3 February 1860 has been lost. We assume Tate's appointment must be in this period, as he does not appear in entries for 1846–1851 and February 1860 to January 1863. We can therefore assume that he had at least three years' experience and possibly up to twelve years, by the time of the Vass murder. His evidence reveals in part the more expected actions of a nineteenth-century police constable. He was patrolling his beat. He reported passing along the West Walls at 1 a.m., and again at 1.45 a.m., when he 'went 13 to 14 yards down the West Walls but saw nothing then'.[38] He said that he had then walked to Stowell Street and from there to the Westgate Station and then to Prudhoe Street to deliver some dispatches (see Fig. 7.1). At 3.30 a.m., Tate was in Newgate Street when he was approached by the witness Parker and told that there was a dead woman in the West Walls.[39] Clearly, the crime scene was on Tate's regular beat, and this is interesting. The evidence indicates that rather than going direct to a police station, at least seven witnesses (including, strangely, Vass himself) had sought a policeman on his beat around 2–2.30 a.m. and had been unable to find one. This suggests that, despite a failure to do so, they expected to find a policeman passing. Indeed, the witness William Gillespie's evidence referred to looking for 'the police-man' and being unable to find 'him', suggesting perhaps that he was familiar with the policeman who usually walked that beat.[40]

Witnesses suggested that PC Tate was not around the West Walls at 2–2.30 a.m. The Watch Committee records frequently reveal policemen cautioned for being absent from their beats; this was a common problem. The hours policemen spent on duty were usually long, and they covered many miles on each beat. We have not found any detailed information on shift or beat patterns in Newcastle, and it seems there were wide variations across the country. Men may have been tired or needed shelter from inclement weather. The addition of waterproof leggings to the police-man's uniform gives some indication of the conditions policemen might face. However, none of the reports to the Watch Committee from 1 January 1863 of policemen being absent from their beat related to offi-cers from B Division.

In addition to constables, senior officers were involved in the crime scene investigation. Sergeant Watson was a long-serving member of the force, appointed in 1853; he was promoted to sergeant in 1861. Scott was to be appointed inspector in May 1863, after 15 years' service. At 4.30 a.m., Watson went to the West Walls and undertook a detailed search of the crime scene: he gave evidence to the inquest, as set out above. Sub-Inspector Scott apprehended Vass and wrote down his statement. At the inquest he produced the trousers he had removed from Vass on 2 January, and gave evidence that he had observed marks of blood on the outside of the pockets; he made clear that there were no such marks on the inside, nor corresponding marks on the cloth of the trousers.[41] Again, this indicates a detailed approach to examining the material evidence.

'Scientific' Investigative Methodologies

Can we see in the approach of B Division in the Vass case evidence of a professional ethos? At the very least, the case would suggest that the role of an ordinary PC in Newcastle in 1863 routinely included duties and activities that went far beyond those envisaged in 'Peel's Principles'. How did they learn the investigative methodologies we see in this case? Bob Morris has noted 'So far as investigative methodologies were concerned… pragmatism ruled. There was no formal training'.[42] This might suggest policemen were expected to 'learn on the job', but this is problematic. Several members of B Division were involved in examining the crime scene, and all had relatively long service records, yet it is likely that few local police officers would have much experience of dealing with such a serious crime, or of preparing to give evidence at a murder trial. Murder was a rare occurrence in Newcastle. The judicial statistics show that for the year to September 1862 there were only three cases of homicide reported to the police and for the year to September 1863 there was only one reported homicide in Newcastle.[43] Despite limited opportunities to acquire relevant experience, the actions of those involved in the Docherty case are thorough, and in many respects, surprisingly modern.

We believe that the Newcastle police force may have received guidance, if not actual training, in some investigative aspects of their role. A *Police Officers Catechism or Handbook* written by Major A. Browne and Samuel James Nichols gives explicit instruction on how a police officer should respond to certain situations.[44] The *Catechism* was written and revised by Chief Constables of Northumberland and Newcastle and therefore reflects the practice and procedure of the North East England

Forces.[45] It refers constables to *Snowden's Magistrates Assistant and Police Officers and Constables Guide* for further advice and advises police officers to spend their spare time studying its rules.[46] Thus, police officers had a framework and guidance for their everyday conduct. Indeed, the *Newcastle Courant* on 23 December 1842 published a guide to the duties of constables for the consumption of the public.

Consider paragraph 44 of the *Catechism*, which indicates that the duties of police constables included the 'detection of crime':

> Paragraph 44:
> Q.—What are the most important duties of a constable?
> A.—The preservation of life and property, the prevention and detection of crime, the speedy capture of criminals, secrecy, and strict discipline, to protect and not to oppress the public.

Rather than reserving such activities to a specific detective force, which Newcastle undoubtedly had at this time, ordinary constables were not merely encouraged but specifically required to take action to detect crime. Several further recommendations in the *Catechism* could relate directly to the actions of the police in the Docherty case. For example, advice also covered how they should act in a case of murder:

> Paragraph 135:
> Q.—What is the duty of a constable in cases of murder…?
> A.—He must immediately repair to the spot, and take such means as he thinks may lead to the apprehension of the offenders.

> Paragraph 137:
> Q.—What should be done in cases of murder?
> A.—Find out what instrument, or how the murder has been committed and the cause. Ascertain if any person or persons be suspected or have been seen about; make a close examination of the premises and call in a surgeon to examine the body.

Guidance in the *Catechism* also seems to cover some of the crime scene processing activities undertaken following the discovery of Margaret Docherty's body:

Paragraph 143:
Q.—If foot-prints or other marks be found, what should be done?
A.—A correct measure of the length and width of the prints should be taken, and a drawing of the same…The foot-prints or other marks must then be carefully covered up so as to preserve the impression.

Snowden's Guide, published in 1859, offered further advice:

> The officer should take charge of, and produce on the inquest, any papers or other property that may be found on searching the body of any one unknown, that may be found dead in the street, highway, or other by-place.[47]

Again, we see evidence of such police activity in the Docherty case. The *Newcastle Daily Chronicle* on 3 January 1863 praised the 'active endeavours of the police' in being 'successful in unravelling to a great extent the mystery' of Margaret Docherty's murder. The notion of constables in a provincial police force in the mid-nineteenth century being involved in a form of policing requiring mysteries to be unravelled seems far removed from the traditional view of the role of the 'new police' as 'a patrolling, preventative police who went looking for offences'.[48] And yet, this behaviour appeared to be expected, and appreciated, in Newcastle in 1863.

In the nineteenth century, we see the influence of scientific methodologies, with the police starting to take a rational and scientific approach to the investigation of crime. This may be due in part to a wider appreciation of scientific discoveries, and perhaps a public acceptance or awareness of the importance and possibilities of scientific method. The evolutionary theory of Charles Darwin, forensic science, fingerprint technology, etc. all helped to make the general population aware or, arguably, accepting of the possibility of applying scientific methodologies to police work.[49] The first recorded case of a successful investigation of a murder, applying what could be termed 'scientific' processes of careful observation, rational thinking, and awareness of surrounding circumstances, was in 1835, when a Bow Street runner, Henry Goddard, solved a murder by identification of the source of a fatal shot. In this case, much as in that of Vass 30 or so years later, we see a systematic approach to the investigation of a crime.

What is striking in the Vass case is that the techniques involved rely primarily on the human senses, largely unaided by technology. This distinguishes the police activity from what today would be recognized as forensic science, in other words, the application of scientific techniques to the evidence in a criminal investigation.[50] What we see is rather the application of a scientific, or forensic, approach to investigating a crime: the uniformed police constables had been encouraged to develop 'on the job' their skills of crime scene investigation and their understanding of the possibilities offered by close attention to the collection and analysis of material evidence. An example from literature serves to indicate the contemporary awareness of the possibilities promised by the 'science of detection'. In 1862 Mary Elizabeth Braddon's *Lady Audley's Secret*, one of the most widely read novels in the Victorian period, expressly linked the evidence-gathering activities of a 'detective officer' to the subsequent execution of a criminal:

> Circumstantial evidence…Upon what infinitesimal trifles may sometimes hang the whole secret of some wicked mystery, inexplicable heretofore to the wisest of mankind! A scrap of paper; a shred of some torn garment; the button off a coat…a thousand circumstances so slight as to be forgotten by the criminal, but links of steel in the wonderful chain forged by the science of the detective officer; and lo! the gallows is built up.[51]

This contemporary awareness of the importance of material evidence in securing a conviction may offer some indication why the Newcastle force adopted such a painstaking approach to the crime scene, taking care to secure material evidence found in the alleyway, taking detailed measurements, and recording the state of the ground, before their evidence was brought before a court. It is also clear that work was carried out which has not survived or been documented. For example, counsel for the prosecution at the trial referred to a plan, which he used to point out the locations of the various places referred to in the case. Although not stated explicitly in the accounts, it is likely that this was prepared by the police. Sadly, we have been unable to find the plan, which is referred to in the trial accounts in *The Newcastle Chronicle and Northern Counties Advertiser* and the *Newcastle Courant*. Such a plan would depend upon the police making detailed measurements at the crime scene and recording precisely the location of material evidence. It is clear that these measurements were taken and recorded. However, far from Braddon's statement that such approaches were the province of the 'detective officer', the Newcastle police evidently expected members of its uniformed force to apply a methodical, 'scientific' approach to investigating a crime, and this tells us much about how the police force in Newcastle perceived the role of its uniformed officers in 1863. This phrase may suggest a lack of understanding by Braddon, or a possibly wider lack of clarity over respective roles, or that the terminology was elastic or used imprecisely at this time.

When we see the police in the Docherty murder case involved in the collection of material evidence—items of Margaret Docherty's clothing, a glass from a public house, a bloodstained pair of trousers—and making accurate documentary records of these details, we can question: why did they do this? What were they intending the evidence would be used for? Was the evidence for the coroner, to identify the victim? Or to be used at trial, to help secure a conviction? Or, both?

'Expert' Evidence at Trial

Gardner and Bevel suggest that the express purpose of crime scene processing is 'to document the context of the scene and collect any physical evidence present in a usable form'.[52] We must therefore consider how and when the evidence gathered from the crime scene by the Newcastle police force was used in the Vass case. The trial of George Vass took place at the Newcastle Spring Assizes on 27 February 1863. The prosecution called a total of sixteen witnesses, including ten witnesses to aspects of the lead-up to the crime, the crime itself, or Vass's behaviour thereafter. The evidence of these lay witnesses served to link Vass to the assault on Margaret Docherty. Four police witnesses and the police surgeon also gave evidence at the trial and it is important to consider how their evidence was used alongside that of the other prosecution witnesses, and how their evidence was utilized by the prosecution to construct the case against Vass.

Two policemen gave evidence at the trial of examining the crime scene. It is helpful to set out in full some of the evidence. Consider, for example, PC Tate's evidence at the trial:

> I am a police constable, and was on duty on New Year's morning in Newgate Street. Parker came up to me about half-past three o'clock, and said there was a woman lying dead in the West Walls. I went with Parker and Rutherford (police constable) [This is the only mention of PC Rutherford. He was an officer in the force at the time but Tate may have given his name in error.], and found the dead body of a woman lying about 37 yards up the West Walls, from Elliott's corner, at the end of Darn Crook. It was thirteen yards off the big gates. The body was lying on the back, in the carriage way. The clothes were all torn off her. Her legs were quite exposed and bare, and all mud and dirt. Her breast was all bare. She had nothing on her head. Her face was covered with blood. Round about blood was lying where the head was lying, the place was all 'paddled', as if a struggle had taken place where the big gates are, about thirteen yards from where the body was. There was a quantity of blood lying there. The marks were newly done there had been a shower about one o'clock that morning. The West Walls is a wet place anyhow. About one o'clock there was nothing there, and I was about thirteen yards up the Walls at a quarter before two o'clock, and saw nothing.[53]

The manner in which he presented his evidence at the trial is rather different in tone to the evidence that he gave at the inquest where, in his account, he drew far fewer conclusions from what he had seen. This is not unexpected. The function of the inquest, as an inquiry into a death, is different from the purpose of the criminal trial to decide guilt beyond reasonable doubt. However, we still see attention to detail, in the measurements of distance where evidence was found, for example.

In response to a question from Mr Seymour, counsel for the prosecution (again, not set out in the newspaper account), Tate clarified, 'The blood was at the gates'. There are frequent references to bloodstains in the newspaper reports of the crime and its investigation. Evidently, the importance of bloodstains was recognized, although there were limits to what could be drawn from them. Material evidence was produced at the trial including the coat Vass had worn on the night of 1 January, for example, by Sub-Inspector Scott:

> He was wearing this coat. I examined it, and found various marks of blood upon the sleeve and the chest. I asked him how he accounted for any blood on his coat, and he said he could not tell. I could not say whether they were recent stains or not. I observed on the trousers he had on some blood on the front part of the pockets, outside. I did not direct his attention to these marks and did not say anything to him about it.[54]

The significance of bloodstains was becoming of scientific interest. Bloodstains on a pair of trousers featured in a case in 1866, when a Scotland Yard detective asked a Professor of Chemistry and Medical Jurisprudence at Guy's Hospital to analyse the stains.[55] Similarly, in the Vass case, the presence of the bloodstains was described by prosecuting counsel, Mr Seymour, as 'another link' to be 'taken together with other facts'.[56] There was, of course, as yet no means of establishing that the blood was human, let alone who might have shed it. The police surgeon was quite circumspect in his conclusions regarding the bloodstains, stating at the trial: 'I was shown a coat and trousers, and saw some stains which I thought were blood, as far as my experience goes'.[57] This was all that he was prepared to say on oath.

The Newcastle police surgeon, Septimus William Rayne, had been admitted to the Royal College of Surgeons in London in 1839.[58] He was appointed as surgeon to the Newcastle Police in 1845.[59] By the mid-nineteenth century, the role of a police surgeon was predominantly to carry out post-mortem examinations of the deceased victims of crime to assist the coroner and to enable medical evidence to be presented at trial.[60] In his evidence at Vass's trial, Rayne specifically referred to his experience. We think it significant that Rayne described himself in court as 'formerly a pupil of Liston', to give added weight or authority to his evidence. Liston was a famous surgeon, noted for his expertise in the operating theatre and his knowledge of anatomy.[61] Much of Rayne's testimony at the Vass trial dealt with the mechanics of the crime. Rayne dissected and analysed Margaret Docherty's body.[62] He described in court how the marks on her buttocks suggested that she was 'dragged along the

ground or that she had had a scuffle'.[63] This evidence, together with witness accounts that asserted that Vass was seen dragging a woman towards
the West Walls, and the evidence from the police officers about the state
of the 'paddled' ground, developed a compelling picture of the crime.
Rayne's description, in detached medical language, of the damage to
Margaret Docherty's face and internal organs made clear the brutality of
the attack: she had been punched and kicked to death. No weapon was
involved. Rayne expressed his professional opinion that a number of the
injuries would have proved fatal.

The trial jury had no doubt of the guilt of George Vass and, after hearing a day of evidence from ten eye-witnesses, five police witnesses, and
the police surgeon, returned their verdict after only 18 minutes of discussion. What 'proved' Vass's guilt so conclusively to the jury?

We suggest that the Vass trial needs to be considered in light of the
changing nature of the jury trial in the nineteenth century, which led to
a greater emphasis being placed upon the importance of material evidence. The nineteenth century saw new focus on the 'science of proof',
for example, Bentham's *Treatise on Judicial Evidence* in 1825 which arguably led to the probative force of circumstantial evidence over direct testimony.[64] In addition, it has been argued that that following the Prisoners'
Counsel Act 1836, the role of lawyers meant that the trial became a
forum in which evidence would be weighed and contested, making the
gathering, presentation, and use of evidence more important. Such developments served to enhance the importance attached to close observations
of physical evidence at the crime scene. In such circumstances, the role of
the policeman in both gathering such evidence and subsequently presenting it at trial could have led to their being perceived as some form of
'expert witnesses'.[65] As part of an increasingly 'scientific' approach to
police work, the use of the 'expert witness' brought authority to testimony regarding, for example, medical matters, or forensic science.

However, it is wrong to suggest that these members of the Newcastle
force were acting as 'expert witnesses', as we would understand the term
today. The role of the expert witness is to draw on expertise to offer an
opinion as part of their evidence at trial; however, as noted above, it is
noticeable that the police witnesses in the Vass trial offered fewer opinions in their evidence than they had done at the inquest.[66] Rather, the

police witnesses at the trial offered evidence based upon their experience and knowledge of investigative aspects of police work at crime scenes. This form of 'expert' testimony was utilized by prosecutors, probably in the belief that police evidence derived from such processes would have an enhanced impact on juries when considering their verdict. Arguably, a rational and scientific approach to detection increased the importance attached to evidence of the police witnesses. In effect, the weight attached to the police evidence depended upon their expertise in crime scene investigation and their professionalism in investigating crimes.

Conclusion

It is reasonable to suggest that there would be little requirement for 'forensic' work in the majority of cases the men of the Newcastle force were likely to encounter in the 1860s. Indeed, it could be questioned how much 'detection' was needed to secure the evidence leading to the arrest, trial, and conviction of George Vass. However, our research into the police investigation into the murder of Margaret Docherty suggests that the Newcastle police sought to take a rational and scientific approach to investigating crime, and recognizes that the officers, including 'regular' police constables, had an important role to play in that process. In revealing and examining the processes and procedures of a provincial force in the latter half of the nineteenth century, researching the Vass case tells us much about how knowledge of a crime scene was constructed in Newcastle in 1863. Further, it demonstrates how the police, via the meticulous gathering of evidence, were vital to the process of building knowledge that led to the conviction of Vass for the murder of Margaret Docherty.

What is evident from the way that ordinary constables approached the Vass case is a recognition of the need to gather evidence for the legal process, which in itself suggests a level of professionalism and sophistication, and a 'scientific' approach to crime scene analysis in the Newcastle police force in the 1860s that has not previously been appreciated. It is arguable that we can discern in this case a methodical and structured approach to the crime scene that would eventually develop into the modern techniques of crime scene examination.

Notes

1. R.M. Gardner and T. Bevel, *Practical Crime Scene Analysis and Reconstruction*, London: CRC Press, 2009: Rear cover.
2. M.T. Miller and P. Massey, *The Crime Scene a Visual Guide*, London: Elsevier, 2016.
3. L.T. Roach, 'Detecting crime: Part I—Detection and the police', *Criminal Law Review*, May 2002: 379–390.
4. It was the observation of Alison Adam in response to our paper at the British Crime Historians Symposium 2016 that made us aware of how unusual our findings in the case of *Regina v George Vass* might be and sparked our deeper research into the police investigation. Our thanks are recorded here.
5. J. Evans, 'The Newcastle upon Tyne City Police 1836–1969', *Journal of the Police History Society*, 1988, 3: 74–79.
6. For an overview, see C. Steedman, *Policing and the Victorian Community: The Formation of English Provincial Police Forces, 1856–80*, London: Routledge and Kegan Paul, 1984. Studies addressing policing in major provincial towns and cities include: R. Swift, *Police Reform in Early Victorian York, 1835–1856*, York: University of York, 1988; D. Taylor, 'Crime and policing in early Victorian Middlesbrough, 1835–55', *Journal of Local and Regional Studies*, 11, 1991; M. Weaver, 'The new science of policing: Crime and the Birmingham Police Force, 1839–1842', *Albion* 1994, 26: 289–308.
7. I. Bridgeman and C. Emsley, *A Guide to the Archives of the Police Forces of England and Wales*, Bodmin and King's Lynn: Police History Society, 1991. The question of records of provincial forces is discussed in C. Emsley, *The English Police a Political and Social History*, London: Longman, 1996, p. 276.
8. Emsley's *Guide* states that the Northumbria Police Archive includes 'Guidance and Government of the Police Force. Newcastle upon Tyne. 1836' but we have been unable to trace this item.
9. Municipal Corporations Act 1835 (5 and 6 William IV, chap. 76). The first report of the first Committee in Newcastle was 11 February 1836.
10. Emsley, *The English Police*, p. 276.
11. *Newcastle Daily Journal*, 13 February 1836.
12. The Watch Committee minutes refer to 'Superintendent', although the terms Chief Officer, Chief Constable or Chief Inspector may also be

used, which suggests the nomenclature might have been inconsistent. This variation in terminology is considered in M. Stallion and D.S. Wall, *The British Police: Forces and Chief Officers 1829–2012*, Braintree: The Police History Society, 2011, p. 48.

13. R. Cowley, *A History of the British Police: From its Earliest Beginnings to the Present Day*, Stroud: The History Press, 2011, p. 157.
14. Cowley, *History of the British Police*, p. 28.
15. S. Wade, *Plain Clothes and Sleuths*, Stroud: The History Press, 2007, p. 42.
16. *Newcastle Courant*, 11 December 1846.
17. J. Collingwood Bruce, *Reid's Handbook to Newcastle upon Tyne*, London: Longman, Green, Longman, Roberts and Green, 1863, p. 132.
18. Reports of Commissioner, Police (Counties and Boroughs), *Reports of the inspectors of constabulary for the year ended 29th September 1864, made to Her Majesty's principal secretary of state, under the provisions of the Statute 19 & 20 Vict. c. 69*, 1864, p. 90.
19. House of Commons Papers, *Reports of Inspectors of Constabulary to the Secretary of State 1861–62*, 1863.
20. *Cardiff and Merthyr Guardian*, 7 December 1861.
21. C. Emsley, *The Great British Bobby*, London and New York: Quercus, 2009, p. 143. On recruitment, see C. Emsley and M. Clapson, 'Recruiting the English Policeman c. 1840–1940', in D. Taylor (ed.), *The New Police in the Nineteenth Century*, Manchester: Manchester University Press, 1997, pp. 161–177.
22. Emsley, *The English Police*, p. 192.
23. Emsley, *The English Police*, Table 9.1. See also Taylor, *New Police*, p. 48.
24. Emsley, *Great British Bobby*, pp. 142–143; see also Emsley, *English Police*, p. 191. Taylor similarly noted: 'In the eyes of many chief constables and recruiting sergeants, the ideal recruit was an agricultural labourer', Emsley, *New Police*, p. 47.
25. Emsley, *Great British Bobby*, p. 143, quotation at p. 149.
26. J.W. Osterburg and R.H. Ward, *Criminal investigation: A Method for Reconstructing the Past: A Study Guide*, Newark, NJ: LexisNexis and Matthew Bender, 2007.
27. Gardner and Bevel, *Practical Crime Scene Analysis*, p. 1.
28. TNA: ASSI 44/180.
29. *Newcastle Courant*, 9 January 1863.
30. *Newcastle Daily Journal*, 6 January 1863; reported in identical words in *Newcastle Courant*, 9 January 1863.

31. Gardner and Bevel, *Practical Crime Scene Analysis*, pp. 1–2.

32. Emsley, *Great British Bobby*, p. 118.

33. C. Emsley, 'The origins of the modern police', *History Today*, 49(4): 8–14, p. 11.

34. *Newcastle Courant*, 6 March 1863—our emphasis.

35. Taylor, *New Police*, Table 3.3.

36. Tyne and Wear Archives, MD.NC/274/2, Watch Committee reports, February 1860–June 1867, p. 408.

37. *Newcastle Courant* , 6 March 1863.

38. *Newcastle Daily Journal*, 28 February 1863.

39. *Newcastle Daily Journal*, 28 February 1863.

40. *Newcastle Courant*, 9 January 1863.

41. *Newcastle Courant*, 9 January 1863.

42. B. Morris, 'History of criminal investigation', in T. Newburn, T. Williamson and A. Wright (eds.), *Handbook of Criminal Investigation*, Abingdon: Willan, 2007, pp. 15–40, with reference to the 'heroic period' 1829–1878, p. 19.

43. Table 4 in Return of Judicial Statistics of England and Wales, 1862 and 1863.

44. A. Browne and S. J. Nichols, *The Police Officers Catechism or Handbook*, 5th ed., London: Shaw & Sons, 1877, p. 11.

45. We have been able to locate only the fifth edition of the Catechism. This is a revised edition and therefore it may be assumed that the original edition was produced in the 1860s.

46. J. F. Archbold, *Archbold's Snowden's Magistrates Assistant and Police Officers and Constables*, Guide 4th ed., London: Shaw and Sons, 1859.

47. Ibid.

48. Cowley, *History of the British Police*, p. 59.

49. For example, Alfred Swaine Taylor (1806–1880), professor of medical jurisprudence at Guy's Hospital Medical School in 1834, wrote *Principles and Practice of Medical Jurisprudence*, first published in 1865.

50. W.J. Tilstone and K.A. Savage, *Forensic Science: An Encyclopedia of History, Methods, and Techniques*, Santa Barbara and Oxford: ABC-CLIO, 2006, p. 5.

51. For a discussion of this point, see C.J. Rzepka, *Detective Fiction*, Cambridge: Polity Press, 2005, p. 29.

52. Gardner and Bevel, *Practical Crime Scene Analysis*, pp. 1–2.

53. *Newcastle Courant*, 9 January 1863.

54. *Newcastle Courant*, 9 January 1863.
55. A. Moss and K. Skinner, *The Victorian Detective*, Oxford: Shire Publications, 2013, p. 27.
56. *Newcastle Courant*, 6 March 1863.
57. *Newcastle Courant*, 6 March 1863.
58. Royal College of surgeon's website https://livesonline.rcseng.ac.uk/biogs/E003052b.htm, Accessed 31 May 2018.
59. *Newcastle Daily Journal*, 25 January 1845.
60. A complete historical account of the police surgeon does not appear to have been produced, but on the role of the police surgeon, see R.D. Summers, 'History of the police surgeon', *The Practitioner*, 1978, 22(1): 383–387.
61. See Liston's entry in the Oxford Dictionary of National Biography, www.oxforddnb.com.libproxy.ncl.ac.uk/view/10.1093/ref:odnb/9780198614128.001.0001/odnb-9780198614128-e-16772?rskey=YOEIrH&result=6, Accessed 31 May 2018.
62. C. Sandford-Couch, and H.J. Rutherford, 'From the 'Death of a female unknown' to the life of Margaret Dockerty: Rediscovering a nineteenth century victim of crime', *Law, Crime and History*, 2018, 8(1): 21–37.
63. TNA, ASSI 45/74.
64. J. Bentham, *A Treatise on Judicial Evidence*, London: J. W. Paget, 1825.
65. D. Cox has considered their role as prosecution witnesses in trials at the Old Bailey. He examined the extent to which their professionalism in investigating often complex and complicated crimes was utilized by prosecutors as 'expert' testimony. He argued that far from being regarded as incompetent and untrustworthy, they were often respected for their competence and composure both whilst investigating and in the court: see, D. Cox, 'The use of Bow Street Runners as prosecution witnesses, 1792–1839', Union and Disunion in the Nineteenth Century Conference, University of Plymouth, July 2017.
66. The Expert Witness Institute website advises: 'An expert offers special expertise in a particular field. As an expert witness, however, he or she needs to offer additional skills and abilities....When in court, the expert witness methodically presents opinion evidence based on evidence of fact'. www.ewi.org.uk/membership_directory_why_join_ewi/whatisan-expertwitness, Accessed 10 June 2018.

Archives

The National Archives ASSI 41/17; ASSI 44/180; ASSI 45/74; ASSI 47/47
Tyne and Wear Archives Watch Committee reports, MD.NC/274/2, February
1860–June 1867

Legislation

Municipal Corporations Act 1835.

Newspapers

Cardiff and Merthyr Guardian
Glamorgan, Monmouth, and Brecon Gazette
The Newcastle Chronicle and Northern Counties Advertiser
The Newcastle Courant
The Newcastle Daily Journal

Websites

Expert Witness Institute: www.ewi.org.uk/membership_directory_why_join_
ewi/whatisanexpertwitness
Royal College of Surgeons England website: www.rcseng.ac.uk/

Bibliography

Anon., *The Newcastle upon Tyne City Police 1836–1969*, Newcastle upon Tyne:
Reid & Co., 1988.
Archbold, J.F., *Archbold's Snowden's Magistrates Assistant and Police Officers and
Constables Guide*, London: Shaw & Sons, 1859.
Bentham, J., *A Treatise on Judicial Evidence*, London: J. W. Paget, 1825.
Braddon, M.E., *Lady Audley's Secret*, London: Tinsley, 1862.
Bridgeman, I. and Emsley, C., *A Guide to the Archives of the Police Forces of
England and Wales*, Bodmin and King's Lynn: Police History Society, 1991.
Browne, A. and Nichols, S.J, *The Police Officers Catechism or Handbook*, London:
Shaw & Sons, 1877.

Collingwood Bruce, J., *Reid's Handbook to Newcastle upon Tyne*, London: Longman, Roberts and Green, 1863.

Cowley, R., *A History of the British Police: From Its Earliest Beginnings to the Present Day*, Stroud: The History Press, 2011.

Cox, D., 'The use of Bow Street Runners as prosecution witnesses, 1792–1839', Union and Disunion in the Nineteenth Century Conference, University of Plymouth, July 2017.

Crawford, C., 'Legal medicine in history. Legalizing medicine: Early modern legal systems and the growth of medico-legal knowledge', in M. Clark and C. Crawford (eds.), *Legal Medicine in History*, Cambridge: Cambridge University Press, 1994, 89–116.

Critchley, T.A., *A History of Police in England and Wales*, Edinburgh: Constable, 1967.

Emsley, C., *Policing and its Context 1750–1870*, London: Macmillan, 1983.

Emsley, C., *The English Police a Political and Social History*, London: Longman, 1996.

Emsley, C., 'The origins of the modern police', *History Today*, 1999, 49(4): 8–14.

Emsley, C., *Great British Bobby*, London and New York: Quercus, 2009.

Emsley, C. and Clapson, M. 'Recruiting the English policeman c. 1840–1940', in D. Taylor (ed.), *The New Police in the Nineteenth Century*, Manchester: Manchester University Press, 1997, 161–177.

Evans, J., 'The Newcastle upon Tyne City Police 1836–1969', *Journal of the Police History Society*, 1988, 3: 74–79.

Gardner, R.M. and Bevel, T., *Practical Crime Scene Analysis and Reconstruction*, London: CRC Press, 2009.

Miller, M.T. and Massey, P., *The Crime Scene a Visual Guide*, London: Elsevier, 2016.

Morris, B., 'History of criminal investigation', in T. Newburn, T. Williamson and A. Wright, (eds.) *Handbook of Criminal Investigation*, Abingdon: Willan, 2007, 15–40.

Moss, A. and Skinner, K., *The Victorian Detective*, Oxford: Shire Publications, 2013.

Osterburg, J.W. and Ward, R.H., *Criminal Investigation: A Method for Reconstructing the Past: A Study Guide*, Newark, NJ: LexisNexis and Matthew Bender, 2007.

Payne-James, J. and Busuttil, A., et al., *Forensic Medicine, Clinical and Pathological Aspects*, London: Greenwich Medical Media, 2003.

Reports of Commissioner *Police (Counties and Boroughs). Reports of the inspectors of constabulary for the year ended 29th September 1864, made to Her Majesty's principal secretary of state, under the provisions of the Statute 19 & 20 Vict. c. 69.*, 1864.

Roach, L.T., 'Detecting crime: Part I—Detection and the police', *Criminal Law Review*, May 2002: 379–390.

Rutherford, H.J. and Sandford-Couch, C., 'From the 'Death of a female unknown' to the life of Margaret Dockerty: Rediscovering a nineteenth century victim of crime', *Law, Crime and History*, 2018, 8(1): 21–37.

Rzepka, C.J., *Detective Fiction*, Cambridge: Polity Press, 2005.

Stallion, M. and Wall, D.S., *The British Police: Forces and Chief Officers 1829–2012*, Braintree: The Police History Society, 2011.

Steedman, C., *Policing and the Victorian Community: The Formation of English Provincial Police Forces, 1856–80*, London: Routledge and Kegan Paul, 1984.

Summers, R.D., 'History of the police surgeon', *The Practitioner*, 1978, 221: 383–387.

Swaine Taylor, A., *Principles and Practice of Medical Jurisprudence*, Philadelphia: Henry C. Lea, 1865.

Swift, R., *Police Reform in Early Victorian York, 1835–1856*, York: University of York, 1988.

Taylor, D., *Crime, Policing and Punishment in England, 1750–1914*, London: Palgrave, 1998.

Taylor, D., *The New Police in Nineteenth-Century England; Crime, Conflict and Control*, Manchester: Manchester University Press, 1997.

Taylor, D., 'Crime and policing in early Victorian Middlesbrough, 1835–55', *Journal of Local and Regional Studies*, 1991, 11: 48–66.

Tilstone, W.J. and Savage, K.A., et al., *Forensic Science: An Encyclopedia of History, Methods, and Techniques*, Santa Barbara and Oxford: ABC-CLIO, 2006.

Wade, S., *Plain Clothes and Sleuths*, Stroud: The History Press, 2007.

Weaver, M., 'The new science of policing: Crime and the Birmingham Police Force, 1839–1842', *Albion*, 1994: 26, 289–308.

8

The Construction of Forensic Knowledge in Victorian Yorkshire: Dr Thomas Scattergood and His Casebooks, 1856–1897

Laura M. Sellers and Katherine D. Watson

'13 May 1856. Received by railway a box from Mr Allanson of Watford, in which was a jar closed with a bladder, and containing a stomach (which might be of a dog) with contents, and two portions of intestine.'[1] The box was accompanied by a letter requesting a chemical analysis of the enclosed samples, marking the start of what became the extensive medico-legal practice of the Leeds-based doctor, toxicologist, and lecturer Thomas Scattergood (1826–1900). He carefully documented his forensic work in two casebooks compiled over the course of forty years, providing a record of the mainly criminal cases for which he acted as a consultant, together with his experiments, sketches, annotations, conclusions, and many associated newspaper clippings. This chapter uses Scattergood's casebooks and media reportage of the inquiries he was involved in to examine the

L. M. Sellers
University of Leeds, Leeds, UK

K. D. Watson (✉)
Oxford Brookes University, Oxford, UK
e-mail: kwatson@brookes.ac.uk

© The Author(s) 2020
A. Adam (ed.), *Crime and the Construction of Forensic Objectivity from 1850*, Palgrave
Histories of Policing, Punishment and Justice,
https://doi.org/10.1007/978-3-030-28837-2_8

development of forensic techniques and the construction and circulation of forensic knowledge in the second half of the nineteenth century.

Scattergood was one of a small number of medically trained toxicologists whose forensic practice was correspondingly wide, taking in a range of suspicious deaths and injuries of both humans and animals. The casebooks reveal that as he grew in experience, repute, and confidence, Scattergood was asked to carry out a wider range of investigations, though poisonings formed the majority of his practice. Forensic examinations were undertaken at the request of coroners, police officers, other doctors, farmers, lawyers, and landowners, hinting at the wider networks that Scattergood's status as a regional expert witness connected him to.

The chapter thus addresses three broad areas of historiographical and historical interest. Firstly, we consider the medico-scientific content of the notebooks, to show that, iceberg-like, the detailed work that underpinned even relatively uncomplicated forensic cases lies largely hidden; criminal depositions, court proceedings, and media reportage had little need for or interest in such detail, even in capital cases. Secondly, the cross-referencing and multiple types of tests that Scattergood conducted are considered as a means of constructing forensic knowledge, adopted as part of his routine forensic practice. We ask whether this knowledge was truly objective or whether it was subtly oriented towards the expectations of his clients. This is linked to our final point: Scattergood's role as an expert witness, in precisely the period when this special type of witness was gaining public recognition, adds to our understanding of the historical development and professionalization of forensic investigation.

Introducing Thomas Scattergood

Thomas Scattergood was born on 14 February 1826 in Huddersfield, where his father worked as a Methodist minister. He studied medicine in Newcastle upon Tyne and Leeds before being appointed to the post of assistant apothecary at the Leeds General Infirmary in 1846; he subsequently qualified Member of the Royal College of Surgeons (MRCS) and Licentiate of the Society of Apothecaries (LSA) in 1850 and entered general practice in Leeds. In 1851 he became a lecturer in chemistry at the

Leeds School of Medicine (founded in 1831), and from 1869 to June 1888 he lectured in forensic medicine and toxicology, subjects in which he gained a regional reputation as an expert. Alongside his other commitments, in 1863 he took up the post of honorary surgeon to the Hospital for Women and Children, becoming consultant surgeon in 1889; an obituary reported that he had a 'vast and varied experience of the diseases peculiar to women' and that although he never claimed to be a specialist, his advice was often sought.[2] He was instrumental in the amalgamation of the Medical School with the Yorkshire College (established 1874) and became the first Dean of the new Faculty of Medicine in 1884, a post he held until his death in February 1900, four years before the University of Leeds was established as the modern successor to the Leeds School of Medicine. Scattergood died aged seventy-four of cardiac arrest following a bout of influenza and was buried in Lawnswood Cemetery, Leeds.[3] Unlike many Victorians of his profession, Scattergood published very little during his career: he contributed one brief article and a letter to the *British Medical Journal* but nothing at all to *The Lancet*,[4] and he did not publish his lectures on forensic medicine as a textbook. But he gave talks outside the medical school on a range of subjects including minerals,[5] warmth and life,[6] 'monsters,'[7] and disease,[8] and he was an active member of the Leeds Musical Festival Committee, the Leeds Sanitary Aid Society, and other philanthropic bodies.[9]

During his lifetime Scattergood was extremely well known as a forensic expert in the North of England: he was sent work from across the country and appeared in numerous court cases. In a newspaper cutting of a murder trial in 1877, Scattergood is reported saying of himself 'I am a surgeon, living at Leeds, and am lecturer at Leeds School of Medicine. I have also had considerable experience as an analytical chemist.'[10] We are fortunate that, given the dearth of published work by Thomas Scattergood, he compiled three manuscript casebooks and a set of lecture notes which span his career. His notebooks record the cases he dealt with in some detail, including experiments and speculations on how to detect cause and manner of death. These rich sources allow us to explore the work of one forensic expert based in an area of the United Kingdom so far unexplored in the existing historiography,[11] and to examine how his expertise reflected changes in nineteenth-century science and medicine. Scattergood's work gives us an insight into the types of crimes committed against both humans and animals—the latter have never before been included in histories of forensic practice—and how one expert in particular conducted medico-legal investigations. We begin by presenting an overview of the medico-scientific content of the casebooks, before considering in more detail his work as the main forensic expert witness in the trials of two notorious murderesses, Elizabeth Pearson (1875) and Mary Ann Cotton (1872), as a means of explicating our three main points of analysis.

Practising Forensic Medicine in Leeds: Case Studies and Clues

Although Scattergood had an interesting and extensive lecturing career and ran a successful medical practice, our research focuses primarily on his forensic work. His experience and interest in forensic medicine and science were wide-ranging, as the index compiled at the end of his first casebook confirms,[12] but his lasting legacy is as a toxicologist. Together with psychiatry, toxicology was the main area of medico-legal expert practice in the Victorian period, and historians have shown the potential that existed for controversy arising from scientific disagreements between experts.[13] It is however to Scattergood's credit that he was never embroiled in professional arguments of the type that his more famous contemporary, Alfred Swaine Taylor of Guy's Hospital in London, experienced.[14] Taylor was a pioneer of nineteenth-century medico-legal practice and teaching, however, and Scattergood's lecture notes contain frequent references to him, particularly his *Principles and Practice of Medical Jurisprudence*, published in 1865.[15] Scattergood also owned a copy of the second edition of the textbook by another London expert, William Guy of King's College,[16] demonstrating both the importance of the expanded volume of research and teaching in forensic medicine during the period and Scattergood's commitment to ensuring that he kept abreast of developments in what was still a relatively new field.

At the start of the nineteenth century forensic medicine was neither systematically practised nor taught to medical men, although there was a growing recognition that a surgeon might well have to give evidence at an inquest or a trial, prompting the publication of the earliest textbooks in

English on the subject, those by Samuel Farr (1788) and William Dease (1793). But it was in the mid-nineteenth century that modern forensic medicine came into its own. The earliest lectures delivered in Britain were those by Andrew Duncan in Edinburgh, in 1789, but although it became an important part of the Scottish curriculum, and one of Duncan's English students, G. E. Male was inspired to write a textbook in 1816, forensic medicine was untaught in London until the 1820s.[17] However, from January 1831 formal teaching in forensic medicine expanded quickly because the Society of Apothecaries introduced a new requirement for students seeking its Licence, the main qualification for medical practitioners in England and Wales between 1815 and 1886. Henceforth, all students had to take a compulsory course of lectures in forensic medicine, and medical schools had therefore to offer suitable courses. Given that he qualified in 1850, Scattergood would certainly have studied forensic medicine as part of his training, probably in Newcastle where it was taught by Dr Robert Mortimer Glover, a gifted chemist, pharmacologist, and physician.[18] Scattergood was evidently so interested in the subject that he became one of the first to teach extensive courses on toxicology and forensic medicine in Leeds. As well as teaching, Scattergood also practised and consulted on numerous cases during his career.

Of the three casebooks held by the Brotherton Library at the University of Leeds, volumes one and two focus primarily on Scattergood's forensic work. They are well organized and mostly chronological: volume one covers from 1856 to 1876 and volume two goes from 1875 to 1897, although the entries tail off quickly after 1885 as, presumably, Scattergood began to wind up his forensic practice once he became Dean of the Medical School. Almost every case in both volumes has a title and date, includes detailed notes about the case, and records the specimens Scattergood worked with, his actions and thought process, and the results of his findings and the court case if there was one. Some of the case entries have marginal annotations, sketches, or newspaper clippings relating to the work.

The newspaper clippings from court cases are often carefully annotated and grammar-checked. He was obviously a pedantic man and wanted all of the details to be correct, at least in his own records. He was described in an obituary as having 'sound and ready judgement,' a 'strong will,' and a 'sense of justice.' It was noted that his 'strict uprightness' made him well suited to preside over the Medical Board at the College. He was known for his 'honesty of purpose'; his 'apparent brusqueness was simply directness of purpose and love of truth.'[19] But Scattergood's records are not particularly attentive to people: he wasted few words on facts about patients, victims, or killers, restricting details to a few words or a line or two at most. He was not concerned particularly by the psychology of murder.[20]

The third volume is less organized than the first two. It contains some forensic cases and patient notes but also includes Scattergood's speculative thoughts on the way in which medical men could ascertain causes of death, in what seem to be a series of memos related most probably to his teaching. A fourth notebook records a partial lecture course on forensic medicine. It is so incomplete that it is impossible to determine how many lectures there were or how the contents changed over the years, but the material seems to have been compiled between 1869 and the mid-1880s and did not change much, if insertions and deletions can be taken as indicators of change. Through these notes and the other three casebooks we know that Scattergood advised his students they needed to be aware of a huge range of topics including decomposition of bodies in the earth; age of bodies; circumstances of death; blood stains, clotting, and splatters; human versus animal distinctions; internal examinations; wounds and injuries as causes of death; time of injury; weapons that caused injury; injuries due to accident, suicide, or homicide; injuries caused in life or death; chemical injuries; death by fire/burning, lightening, cold, and strangulation; amputations; assault; police work; adulteration of food; and abortions.[21] His work included cases of human and animal death or injury, and he dealt with patients and 'clients' from amongst the living and the dead; he appears to have wanted his students to take note of it all.

Scattergood's notes are often quite concise, hiding the sheer amount of work he must have undertaken, but the summaries of his experiments and observations suggest the high level of analysis that supported his conclusions. One of the best examples of this phenomenon occurred in 1876 when Scattergood testified at the inquest on Jessie Fitzakerly, whose case is discussed below. He summarized his testimony in forty words, but this conclusion was based on work carried out with four other men: a Dr

Hollingsworth; Scattergood's son Oliver, who did not qualify in medicine until 1884; and two others whom we have not yet identified. The work involved a full post-mortem examination and a visit to the site of Fitzakerly's death, all of which was recounted in three pages of closely written notes that included a sketch of her head injury.[22]

In every case, even the most straightforward expertise and time was required but Scattergood, the media, and the courts summarized such work simply. Even in capital cases, it does not seem that Scattergood was required to present his findings in minute detail: it was the conclusions to be drawn from them that were considered most important. But even though the outside world was rarely able to access the detail of Scattergood's work many people would have come across him in newspapers as he built up his reputation in the courts. It seems likely that there were also verbal networks of recommendation: Scattergood was well known as an active member of the Leeds medical and social community. There were also professional networks, both medical and legal, which included his colleagues, the police, coroners, lawyers and judges, and an as yet unexplored network of other people, many of whom worked with or had some professional interest in animals.

This chapter opened with Scattergood's first recorded case, when in May 1856 a letter from Mr Allanson of Watford, Hertfordshire arrived by railway accompanying a box in which there was a jar closed with a bladder, containing a stomach with contents and two portions of intestines from a dog. This case required extensive and detailed work from Scattergood. As with his human cases, he did a range of tests, all of which were time-consuming to prepare and perform. He recorded that the stomach was of 'unusual appearance' and was examined for traces of strychnine. In order to carry out his tests, one-third of the stomach was 'cut small [and] mixed with water and acidulated with [acetic acid], boiled for 15 min[utes] and filtered'—an accident meant some of the liquid was lost. The rest was sent to a steam bath with alcohol: the extract, Scattergood reported, had a 'bitter taste' but there was no conclusive result to prove the presence of strychnine. Another third of the liquid was heated with water and acetic acid, boiled, and filtered. It was then mixed with animal charcoal, boiled, and filtered again. Scattergood noted it tasted only of acid. The liquid was then dried with boiling alcohol and mixed with sulphuric acid and potassium dichromate and filtered after which the 'usual reaction of strychnine was clearly and abundantly exhibited.' To corroborate his results the final third of the liquid was tested for metallic poisons—which were found not to be present. On 22 May, Scattergood undertook physiological testing when a sample was found to be poisonous to a newt. He left the newt in the substance for 24 hours; compared to one in water, the newt was dead but not rigid. On 24 May, a sample was made into pills and fed to a young rabbit which died 53 minutes later, its symptoms carefully documented. Following these extensive tests, Scattergood concluded that strychnine was definitely the cause of the dog's death.[23]

This dog was by no means the only animal to appear in Scattergood's casebooks. Animals could be worth a great deal of money and intentional (or unintentional) poisonings had to be investigated. One such example was the poisoning of horses by arsenic at Goole in 1859, a case investigated by a senior police officer, Supt Green. Scattergood was sent a bottle of water, a bag (like a small pillowcase) containing chopped hay, oats and leaves and a hamper containing parts of two horses (1—stomach, small intestines, large intestines, 2—stomach no contents, part of rectum, left kidney, part oesophagus, tongue, bits of small intestines). He studied all body parts for appearance, weight, and traces of arsenic.[24] On the strength of his evidence, John Dodsworth and Thompson Bullas were charged with killing five horses with arsenic. Bullas was later released for lack of evidence and Dodsworth was eventually acquitted at the summer assizes; Scattergood was not mentioned at all in the trial report.[25]

It is interesting that the range of animal cases Scattergood dealt with was perhaps wider than the human cases. More research needs to be done on why this was the case and how his reputation spread to those who owned animals or investigated crimes relating to animals. At least two of the animal poisoning cases recorded in his casebooks came through a Mr Wilson, whom we have not yet managed to identify, and others from a company called Hirst, Brooke and Hirst, a Leeds-based chemical retail company which made a variety of products, including tonic wine that was advertised extensively in Yorkshire during the 1880s.[26] Still others came via the police, or directly from landowners and farmers. What is unclear is who was paying for this service, and why they felt it was necessary to go to such effort and expense, although the objective was presumably to obtain justice in court and/or an insurance claim. We should note that the casebooks do not include references to charges levied for Scattergood's services, but such work was not undertaken free of charge. Under the terms of the Medical Witnesses Act of 1836 coroners could pay doctors two guineas to perform a post-mortem examination and toxicological analysis, and magistrates could authorize additional fees for expert evidence—Alfred Swaine Taylor charged two guineas per sample in the 1840s,[27] but the statutory provision did not include animal victims and the coroner's fee of two guineas was unlikely to cover the cost of time and reagents.

One of the key changes to Victorian Britain that facilitated forensic practice was the expansion of the road and most importantly railway networks. It was these transport links which allowed Mr Allanson to send the samples to Scattergood. Katherine Watson's work on poisoning crimes has shown that it became fairly common for forensic samples taken by a local medical practitioner to be sent from the scene of a suspected murder to a toxicologist by post, or sometimes via a police officer who travelled by train.[28] By the time Scattergood became active as a toxicologist in the 1850s, the railway network was connecting towns and cities across the country, and it only continued to grow.[29] Leeds was particularly well placed at the centre of the country to form part of a wider network: the increasing size and wealth of the city made it an industrial hub and supported the need for the Medical School and later Yorkshire College.

The number of cases that Scattergood recorded shows that his services were in demand; the level of detail demonstrates that he was aware of contemporary techniques and was thorough in his work. He needed his findings to be able to stand up in court. The range of places, from County Durham to Hertfordshire, Lincolnshire, and Shropshire, as well as Yorkshire begs the question of how people became aware of his services, particularly as he published so little. It would also be interesting to know how much and why they paid for the travel and his expertise. More work needs to be done on the economy of this industry. Geographically, Scattergood was clearly a regional expert whose sphere of influence was extended by the power of the news media, one suspects, as well as his institutional, professional location in a major regional centre.

Multiple Organs, Multiple Testing

Scattergood theorized, researched, and worked on a wide range of causes of death, but the majority of his cases involved poisoning. There are examples of poisoning by strychnine, arsenic, lead, croton oil, opium and laudanum, cyanide, aconite, phosphorus, zinc sulphate, silver nitrate, oxalic acid, sulphuric acid, morphine, chloral, and potassium bromide in his work. These poisonings were a combination of accidental and intentional; many formed parts of formal crime investigations. Cases involving strychnine and arsenic were the most common as these poisons were readily available in household products, particularly vermin-killers, via over-the-counter sales.[30] Both substances could be identified and isolated using careful chemical techniques. For arsenic, there was the Marsh test, developed in 1836 and the Reinsch test of 1841. For strychnine toxicologists relied on colour reactions, microscopic examination of its crystalline form and physiological tests.[31] Scattergood's casebooks record a great deal of detail regarding his toxicological analysis and give some insight into his thought processes and use of cutting-edge techniques.

In cases which involved strychnine Scattergood on two occasions made sketches of the crystals he obtained. In 1862 he received samples of a human stomach, intestines, and their contents via the police from Epworth, Lincolnshire. It was a suspected strychnine poisoning and Scattergood outlined a number of ways he tested the specimens. These included colour tests, observation under the microscope, a taste test (it was bitter), a physiological test, and a negative test for arsenic. With respect to the crystalline form obtained from reaction with bichloride of mercury, he noted that 'crystals were formed resembling the accompanying sketch, which may be taken as like the figure given by Dr Guy (62 No. 3), which he states to be very characteristic.' This was a reference to William Guy's 1861 book *Principles of Forensic Medicine*. At the inquest, he announced that the stomach contained Battle's Vermin Killer, and more than enough to kill the individual. Afterwards, he noted the deceased was a middle-aged woman, wife of an innkeeper and that the couple did not get on, but there is no indication that a criminal case ensued; perhaps it was a suicide?[32]

In 1875 Elizabeth Pearson, of Gainford in County Durham, was accused of murdering her elderly uncle, apparently so she could gain possession of his furniture. She had reported that her uncle had been having fits before he died, but this was found to be suspicious. Scattergood was contacted by Thomas Dean, the deputy coroner of Bishop Auckland, and asked to take on the case and samples were then posted to him by the police: 'a glass jar wrapped in brown paper which was gummed & tied up.' He recorded that 'The jar had a glass stopper with cork ring, & was secured by string & sealed with the seal of T. Homfray of Gainford.' Homfray was the victim's doctor and the first to suspect foul play. Careful notes were made about the chain of custody of the samples. The jar contained the stomach, liver, bowel, and stomach contents of the deceased received 8 days after the man's death. Scattergood then set to work preparing the samples for testing. He wrote: 'On March 24th morning I opened the jar. Contents had no particular odour. They consisted of 8½ oz (nearly) of liver, apparently healthy, which I washed with HO distilled, & put in a separate clean jar.' There was also a human stomach with about a foot of colon attached: '…I cut off the latter, wash the outside of it & put it in a separate jar. It was full of solid faeces. Washings of liver & bowel were put together.'[33] He went on to describe the condition and preparation of the stomach and stomach contents. Having undertaken this lengthy and probably unpleasant task of preparing his samples he was ready to start his tests.

In total Scattergood undertook twenty-seven tests, most of which resulted in a chemical analysis. Each was time-consuming. He first recorded: 'The contents of washings [from the stomach] were allowed to stand, then poured off & by repeated washings & decantations, a sediment was obtained.' He then summarized the results of his tests as 'There was no appearance of Calomel or of Arsenic, but a blue powder and some quantity of granules of starch were taken.' The blue powder 'carefully separated & washed weighed 18/1000 of a grain (=1/55 grain about).' For each test he recorded the stages he deemed to be relevant to the investigation and presumably any potential court appearance.

The unsuccessful results were recorded much more briefly. He found no arsenic in his samples and summarized this in one sentence: 'The residues on filters from above process were all treated by Reinsch's process:

the result was entirely negative.'[34] One interesting element of Scattergood's work is his commitment to tasting his samples: after many of the tests during the Gainford investigation, he recorded that he found the taste to be bitter.

As an example of the level of detail he recorded when he felt it was relevant, consider this extract from the notes he made and some of his observations: 'The piece of bowel (about 8 inches) which had been attached to stomach...was detached...It seemed small & thin (as was also the stomach it may be observed) & contained faeces of solid consistence. It was well washed, cut small & digested with S.V.R. & A on water bath, then strained (the liquid had a strong faecal smell). The solid was well pressed, more spirit added & again pressed & then strained mixed liquids evap[orate]d to dryness. Dissolved in water filtered & again evap[orate]d to dryness: redissolved in acidulated water & filtered: alkalized with NH_3 and shaken with chloroform: then liquids separated & more chloroform used. The mixed chloroformic magmas were evapd to dryness over water bath. The residue was considerable. It was redissolved in acidulated water filtered alkalized, shaken with chloroform which came off nearly colourless & evap[orate]d to dryness.'[35] This was just part of the process. After all this work he concluded: 'The chloroform residue was not all crystalline—it was bitter—but it gave no reaction with sulphuric acid + MnO_2 & sulphuric acid $+KO_2CrO_3$. A portion was dissolved in weakly acid[d] water brought to a small drop & a little sol[n] of bichromatic potash added, when dry a few tufts of yellow crystals were found in it: excess of bichromate was dissolved out leaving tufts unchanged: on allowing HSO4 to flow over them the distinct strychnine reaction appeared (1in objective).'[36] Scattergood had got his result. This case note ends with a comment: 'The woman Pearson was convicted of murder at Durham summer assizes, & executed.'[37]

This case is an example of the cross-referencing and multiple types of tests that Scattergood conducted that were hinted at in some of the previous case studies. Together they show the breadth of information required to make a claim about someone's death. This multi-test approach, combined with any relevant circumstantial evidence or observations from other parties, such as the deceased's usual doctor, was adopted as part of his routine forensic practice.

Scattergood also dealt with other types of murder and physical traumas in both theoretical and practical ways. As noted earlier his casebooks and lecture notes allude to all sorts of ways a person might die, and how a medical man might interpret their death. One of Scattergood's interests was the science of blood. When blood was found he needed to find a way to answer the question: Whose blood was it? He noted that if it was on a victim it was usually theirs—but on a suspect, it was much harder to tell. Scattergood was able to tell if the substance he was looking at was blood using a microscope; however, it was difficult to know if it was bird, mammal, or reptile. His techniques improved and it was possible to tell it was mammal, but it was not always clear if it was human or a four-legged creature. In September 1869 Scattergood was asked to examine a pair of corduroy trousers by Inspector Murray of the West Riding police for suspected blood stains on the left knee and cuff. He 'examined this stain [knee] by the microscope and chemically and found it consisted of blood.' But 'the other mark was dark coloured soil. I am of the opinion that the blood is not that of a bird or a fish. There are no means of positively distinguishing between human blood and that of any English quadruped. The appearances of it are consistent with it being human blood.' The inquest returned a verdict that the victim, Richard Kellett, had been murdered by person or persons unknown.[38] As noted above, it was not possible to distinguish human blood from that of other mammals until just after Scattergood's death.

Similarly, when two-and-a-half-year-old Marsh Roebuck was found with his throat slit in Holmfirth in June 1877 Scattergood identified blood splatters on the clothes of the accused, eleven-year-old James Henry Stephenson. Using a spectroscope he concluded that 'their appearance is consistent with human blood stains. It is not the blood of a bird, reptile, or fish, but I cannot say that it is not the blood of a four-footed mammal.'[39] Scattergood might not have been able to work out for certain where blood came from with his microscope but that did not mean that it was not a question worth asking. He advised his students to ask what the blood was on and how it could have got there. In cases where a murder or accident had been concealed blood would normally be found on clothes. This could then be examined, as in Stephenson's case.[40]

The other key clue for the forensic doctor was to identify weapons; could the weapon have produced the injuries or blood patterns found?

One interesting case, which Scattergood illustrated with small drawings in his casebook, occurred in December 1882. Three men in Leeds had had a fight and one of them had died of a fractured skull following a blow to the head. It was ascertained that the other two men had walking sticks and one of them caused the fatal blow. Unfortunately, in this case, Scattergood could not provide sufficient evidence to lay the blame on either one.[41]

In other instances, clues had to be found in the environment or circumstances. Scattergood titled one of his cases 'Remarkable fracture of skull apparently from a fall.' On 26 December 1876, Scattergood noted that Jessie M. Fitzakerly had been found dead 32 hours previously. She had been intoxicated over Christmas and then visited friends and drank more, walked home around 4 or 5 a.m. but was unable to walk steadily; she fell on the doorstep when she got home. At 9 or 9.30 a.m., a neighbour called and the husband answered sleepily, then about 11 a.m. the husband called for the neighbours as he could not find his wife. They found her dead at the bottom of the steps with her head on the bottom step and limbs pointing up the stairs. When Scattergood saw the body it was 'perfectly fresh.' There was blood at the bottom of the cellar steps, a bloody footprint two steps up caused by a woman's boot, two steps higher another boot mark, nine in all. The boots matched that of the friend who had accompanied the Fitzakerly couple home. Some blood marks looked like they had come off a petticoat. The body when examined had a number of scuffs and bruises, but of note were four puncture marks on the right hand, abrasions and black bruises on the left, and marks on the face including something that was not mud or blood. The back of the hair was soaked in blood. The internal organs were examined and found healthy (except the stomach which was thrown away without further examination). Scattergood and his collaborators in this investigation concluded that a violent fall backwards down the stairs would cause the injuries and probably caused her death but a weapon might have produced the same result. An open verdict was returned.[42]

Becoming an Expert Witness

Scattergood wrote that 'The question before the court really is, was the death the result of natural causes…' If, as is usually the case, the answer is that the patient died from natural causes the inquiry into death can stop. Expertise was to be called when 'the court is not satisfied without knowing what those causes were.' This included 'Sudden, violent, [and] premature deaths...'[43] These were the cases Scattergood's knowledge was needed for and what he was preparing his students to deal with. He estimated there were 'something like 25,000 inquests annually in Eng[land] and Wales.'[44] There was a demand for medico-legal expertise and an increasing need for expert witnesses in the courts.[45]

In the North East of England Mary Ann Cotton (1832–1873) remains one of history's most notorious murderers and Scattergood's most famous case. She is believed to have murdered between twelve and twenty-one people, potentially including three husbands, her mother, a lover, her best friend, and at least some of her children and stepchildren. Her motive was money and she carefully claimed life insurance on those around her. Cotton's fourth husband, former lover, and two children passed away in quick succession. She had predicted the death of her last surviving stepson, seven-year-old Charles Edward Cotton to the parish overseer after she had tried unsuccessfully to give the child to his uncle and then the workhouse. When he heard of the child's death the overseer went to the police and reported his suspicions, persuaded the doctor not to certify the death and the case was passed to a coroner. A local doctor examined the body but did not have time to conduct the necessary chemical analysis until after the inquest, at which point the strong suspicions that Mary Ann Cotton was a poisoner led to the exhumation of the body. Samples taken from it were sent to Scattergood in the care of Sgt Hutchinson, who travelled to Leeds from County Durham by train on the instruction of Supt Henderson of Bishop Auckland, where the killing took place. The network of investigators for this case expanded to include Scattergood, and his network of contacts expanded in a corresponding fashion. The way in which the samples were obtained and transported is important too, as it is indicative of the growing concern for maintaining a careful chain of custody for human remains in murder trials.

Scattergood confirmed the presence of arsenic and recorded his work in careful detail. Later the bodies of Cotton's lover and two more children were also examined and found to contain arsenic.[46] At her trial Cotton was found guilty and sentenced to death; the judge noted that poison always left 'complete and incontestable traces of guilt.'[47] About a week after her trial Scattergood followed up a point that had been made by

Cotton's defence counsel, Mr Campbell Foster, that the arsenic might have entered the body accidentally via arsenical wallpaper or soap mixed with arsenic to keep pests at bay. Scattergood was extremely sceptical and dismissed the suggestion because wallpaper 'would not account for the presence of solid AsO_3 in the stomach' and the soap 'could not possibly have been powdered any more than butter could have been powdered.'[48] There was an attempt to secure a reprieve on the grounds that she could not afford an expert witness to challenge Scattergood but this was unsuccessful and Mary Ann Cotton was hanged.[49] The Cotton murders were Scattergood's most famous investigation and show the ultimate power of a forensic expert working within the criminal justice system. The impact of forensic testimony on the processes of criminal justice could be immense: it might help to convict a killer or to undermine the case against an accused person.

The Cotton and Pearson cases also raise an important contextual point. Scattergood was drawn into forensic work apparently because of the prevalence of poisoning crimes in mid-Victorian England. This automatically opened up what we can think of as a market for his scientific and medical abilities, but that market was clearly regional, not national or purely local. His training as a chemist and as a surgeon gave him the necessary skills to conduct both post-mortem examinations and toxicological analyses, uniting two key elements of forensic expertise in one individual. In addition, Scattergood began practising as a forensic expert in the mid-1850s, precisely the time when policing became truly national and subject to the same standards set by central government. County Durham set up a police force in 1840, Leeds in 1836, but the West Riding force was established late in 1856, following government legislation that required all counties to establish an efficient police force.[50] Part of what Scattergood's practice opens to historical research is his links to the various local and regional police forces.

Finally, the investigations discussed in this chapter, and the casebooks in which they were recorded, speak loudly to Scattergood's role as an expert witness in precisely the period, the second half of the nineteenth century, when this special type of witness was gaining public recognition. Scattergood's work helps add to our knowledge of the development of medico-legal practice, the impact of the expert witness in the criminal courts, and the professional links that fostered both.

Conclusion

Thomas Scattergood's casebooks provide us with a wealth of medico-scientific content from the second half of the nineteenth century. Covering almost 40 years of forensic practice, Scattergood was called upon to offer his expertise on a wide range of cases involving both humans and animals. His expertise lay primarily in the science of toxicology and poisoning deaths but he had much to say on other means of death. Every case covered in his casebooks hints at the volume of work which underpinned each conclusion Scattergood reached. The level of work required matched the available tests, and multiple tests were required to ensure the results were accurate and would meet the demands of the courts or his clients. All the evidence to hand suggests that his findings were scrupulously objective, as befit his personality, and there is little evidence that his clients had any expectations other than that they would be given accurate information.

We are at the start of our research into the work of Thomas Scattergood. We are particularly interested in who sought out Scattergood's expertise and how this changed over the course of the late nineteenth century. Changes in travel and communication brought together a wide variety of individuals, many of whom have not yet been acknowledged by historians of crime or forensic medicine and science. We are interested in where, why, how, and at what cost forensic expertise could be sought, and wish to know more about the individuals involved; the casebooks bring a wide variety of people fore. But many of the questions raised by Scattergood's casebooks cannot be answered until they have been fully transcribed and studied in detail. The geography of his forensic practice and the networks that connected Scattergood, the police, coroners, the courts, insurance companies, the media, patients, and clients need to be fully mapped. In doing so, we will be able to situate this regional expert more securely within the history of forensic medicine.

Notes

1. T. Scattergood, *Medical Case Histories: Volume 1, 1856–1876*, MS 534/1, p. 1.

2. 'Thomas Scattergood, MRCS, LSA', *British Medical Journal*, 3 March 1900, p. 547.
3. *The Yorkshire Evening Post*, 23 February 1900, p. 4; *The Yorkshire Post*, 24 February 1900, p. 8; 'Thomas Scattergood, MRCS Eng., LSA', *The Lancet*, 10 March 1900, pp. 737–738.
4. T. Scattergood, 'Morbilli and rubeola', *British Medical Journal*, 29 January 1870, 1: 121; 'A case of poisoning by nitrate of silver', *British Medical Journal*, 20 May 1871, 1: 527.
5. T. Scattergood, 'On minerals', 1867, Wellcome Library, London, MS4407 (Leeds Philosophical and Literary Society).
6. T. Scattergood, 'Warmth and life', 1868, Wellcome Library, London, MS4409 (Working Man's Club, Leeds).
7. T. Scattergood, 'Note on the proper treatment of Monsters', 1876, Wellcome Library, London, MS4411 (Leeds and West Riding Medico-Chirurgical Society).
8. T. Scattergood, 'Instruments and apparatus used in the detection of disease', 1876, Wellcome Library, London, MS4413 (Priestley Club).
9. 'Thomas Scattergood, MRCS, LSA', *British Medical Journal*, 3 March 1900, 1: 547.
10. Cutting pasted into MS 534/2, p. 60.
11. Important studies of the past 30 years include the doctoral theses of Crawford, Duvall, Merry, and Ward.
12. MS 534/1, Index, placed after p. 268.
13. I.A. Burney, *Poison, Detection and the Victorian Imagination*, Manchester: Manchester University Press, 2006, pp. 135–144; T. Ward, 'A mania for suspicion: Poisoning, science, and the law', in J. Rowbotham and K. Stevenson (eds.), *Criminal Conversations: Victorian Crimes, Social Panic, and Moral Outrage*, Columbus: Ohio State University Press, 2005, 140–156; M. Essig, 'Poison murder and expert testimony: Doubting the physician in late nineteenth-century America', *Yale Journal of Law and the Humanities*, 14 (2002): 177–210.
14. N.G. Coley, 'Alfred Swaine Taylor, MD, FRS (1806–1880): Forensic toxicologist', *Medical History*, 1991, 35: 409–427, pp. 425–426.
15. A.S. Taylor, *The Principles and Practice of Medical Jurisprudence*, London: John Churchill & Sons, 1865. See, for example, MS 534/4, pp. 11r, 13v.
16. W.A. Guy, *Principles of Forensic Medicine*, 2nd ed., London: Henry Renshaw, 1861; MS 534/1, p. 81.
17. J. Ward, *Origins and Development of Forensic Medicine and Forensic Science in England, 1823–1946*, Unpublished PhD thesis, The Open

University, 1993, p. 22; C. Crawford, 'A scientific profession: Medical reform and forensic medicine in British periodicals of the early nineteenth century', in R. French and A. Wear (eds.), *British Medicine in an Age of Reform*, London and New York: Routledge, 1991, pp. 203–230.

18. R.J. Defalque and A.J. Wright, 'The short, tragic life of Robert M. Glover', *Anaesthesia*, 2004, 59: 394–400.

19. 'Thomas Scattergood, MRCS, LSA', *British Medical Journal*, 3 March 1900, 1: 547.

20. For the key Victorian developments in forensic psychiatry, see J.P. Eigen, *Mad-Doctors in the Dock: Defending the Diagnosis, 1760–1913*, Baltimore: Johns Hopkins University Press, 2016.

21. MSS 534/1-4—List compiled from across the four manuscripts.

22. MS 534/2, pp. 43–45. For Oliver Scattergood, see *The Medical Register for 1887*, London: General Medical Council, 1887, p. 916.

23. MS 534/1, pp. 1–3.

24. MS 534/1, pp. 16–25.

25. *Hull Packet*, 13 May 1859, p. 8; *Huddersfield Chronicle*, 23 July 1859, p. 6.

26. See, for example, numerous advertisements in the *Knaresborough Post*, accessed via The British Newspaper Archive, https://www.britishnewspaperarchive.co.uk; Grace's Guide to British Industrial History, https://www.gracesguide.co.uk/Hirst,_Brooke_and_Hirst, Accessed 9 June 2019.

27. K.D. Watson, 'Medical and chemical expertise in English trials for criminal poisoning, 1750–1914', *Medical History*, 2006, 50: 373–390, p. 387.

28. Ibid., p. 386.

29. E. Alvarez, X. Franch, and J. Martí-Henneberg, 'Evolution of the territorial coverage of the railway network and its influence on population growth: The case of England and Wales, 1871–1931', *Historical Methods: A Journal of Quantitative and Interdisciplinary History*, 2013, 46(3): 175–191, pp. 177–178.

30. K.D. Watson, *Poisoned Lives, English Poisoners and their Victims*, London: Hambledon and London, 2004; Coley, 'Alfred Swaine Taylor', p. 410.

31. Watson, *Poisoned Lives*, pp. 16–30.

32. MS 534/1, pp. 79–84.

33. All quotations taken from MS 534/2, pp. 4–10.

34. Ibid., p. 5.

35. Ibid., p. 9. We have not yet deciphered what S.V.R. & A stands for, although A is possibly acetic acid.

36. Ibid. The objective refers to the microscope he used to observe the crystals.

37. Ibid., p. 10.

38. MS 534/1, p. 148; a full account of the inquest appeared in *The Leeds Mercury*, 29 September 1869, p. 4.

39. MS 534/2, pp. 57–60.

40. See also *Huddersfield Chronicle*, 16 June 1877, p. 6; *The Leeds Times*, 4 August 1877, p. 3. Stephenson was convicted of manslaughter and sentenced to two weeks in prison and five years in a reformatory school.

41. MS 534/2, p. 128.

42. MS 534/2, pp. 43–45.

43. MS 534/4, p. 4.

44. Ibid.

45. I.A. Burney, *Bodies of Evidence: Medicine and the Politics of the English Inquest, 1830–1926*, Baltimore and London: Johns Hopkins University Press, 2000, pp. 107–136; C.A.G. Jones, *Expert Witnesses: Science, Medicine, and the Practice of Law*, Oxford: Clarendon Press, 1994, pp. 76–86.

46. Watson, *Poisoned Lives*, pp. 212–217.

47. Quoted in ibid., p. 216.

48. MS 534/1, p. 188.

49. Watson, *Poisoned Lives*, p. 217.

50. R. Cowley, *A History of the British Police: From its Earliest Beginnings to the Present Day*, Stroud: The History Press, 2011.

Archive

The British Newspaper Archive, https://www.britishnewspaperarchive.co.uk.

Brotherton Library, Special Collections, University of Leeds:

Scattergood, T., *Medical Case Histories: Volume 1, 1856–1876*, MS 534/1.

Scattergood, T., *Medical Case Histories: Volume 2, 1875–1897*, MS 534/2.

Scattergood, T., *Medical Case Histories: Volume 3, 1846–1885*, MS 534/3.

Scattergood, T., *Notes for Lectures on Forensic Medicine, c.1860s–c.1890s*, MS 534/4.

Archives and Manuscripts, Wellcome Library, London:

Scattergood, T. '*On Minerals*', 1867, MS4407.
Scattergood, T., '*Warmth and Life*', 1868, MS4409.
Scattergood, T., '*Note on the Proper Treatment of Monsters*', 1876, MS4411.
Scattergood, T., '*Instruments and Apparatus used in the Detection of Disease*', 1876, MS4413.

Bibliography

Alvarez, E., Franch, X. and Martí-Henneberg, J., 'Evolution of the territorial coverage of the railway network and its influence on population growth: The case of England and Wales, 1871–1931', *Historical Methods: A Journal of Quantitative and Interdisciplinary History*, 2013, 46(3): 175–191.
Anon., *Huddersfield Chronicle*, 23 July 1859a, 6.
Anon., *Huddersfield Chronicle*, 16 June 1877a, 6.
Anon., *Hull Packet*, 13 May 1859b, 8.
Anon., *The Leeds Mercury*, 29 September 1869, 4.
Anon., *The Leeds Times*, 4 August 1877b, 3.
Anon., (Obituary notice), *The Yorkshire Evening Post*, 23 February 1900a, 4.
Anon., (Obituary notice), *The Yorkshire Post*, 24 February 1900b, 8.
Anon., 'Thomas Scattergood, MRCS, LSA', *British Medical Journal*, 3 March 1900a, 547.
Anon., 'Thomas Scattergood, MRCS Eng., LSA', *The Lancet*, 10 March 1900b, 737–738.
Brownlie, A.R., 'Blood and the blood groups: A developing field for expert evidence', *Journal of the Forensic Science Society*, 1965, 5: 124–174.
Burney, I.A., *Bodies of Evidence: Medicine and the Politics of the English Inquest, 1830–1926*, Baltimore and London: Johns Hopkins University Press, 2000.
Burney, I.A., *Poison, Detection and the Victorian Imagination*, Manchester: Manchester University Press, 2006.
Coley, N.G., 'Alfred Swaine Taylor, MD, FRS (1806–1880): Forensic toxicologist', *Medical History*, 1991, 35: 409–427.
Cowley, R., *A History of the British Police: From Its Earliest Beginnings to the Present Day*, Stroud: The History Press, 2011.
Crawford, C., *The Emergence of English Forensic Medicine: Medical Evidence in Common-Law Courts, 1730–1830*, Unpublished DPhil thesis, University of Oxford, 1987.

Crawford, C., 'A scientific profession: Medical reform and forensic medicine in British periodicals of the early nineteenth century', in R. French and A. Wear (eds.), *British Medicine in an Age of Reform*, London and New York: Routledge, 1991, 203–230.

Defalque, R.J. and Wright, A.J., 'The short, tragic life of Robert M. Glover', *Anaesthesia*, 2004, 59: 394–400.

Duvall, N., *Forensic Medicine in Scotland, 1914–39*, Unpublished PhD thesis, University of Manchester, 2013.

Eigen, J.P., *Mad-Doctors in the Dock: Defending the Diagnosis, 1760–1913*, Baltimore: Johns Hopkins University Press, 2016.

Essig, M., 'Poison murder and expert testimony: Doubting the physician in late nineteenth-century America', *Yale Journal of Law and the Humanities*, 2002, 14: 177–210.

Guy, W.A., *Principles of Forensic Medicine*, 2nd ed., London: Henry Renshaw, 1861.

'Hirst, Brooke and Hirst', *Grace's Guide to British Industrial History*, https://www.gracesguide.co.uk/Hirst,_Brooke_and_Hirst.

Jones, C.A.G., *Expert Witnesses: Science, Medicine, and the Practice of Law*, Oxford: Clarendon Press, 1994.

Merry, K.J., *Murder by Poison in Scotland during the Nineteenth and Early Twentieth Centuries*, Unpublished PhD thesis, University of Glasgow, 2010.

Scattergood, T., 'A case of poisoning by nitrate of silver', *British Medical Journal*, 20 May 1871, 1: 527.

Scattergood, T., 'Morbilli and rubeola', *British Medical Journal*, 29 January 1870, 1: 121.

Taylor, A.S., *The Principles and Practice of Medical Jurisprudence*, London: John Churchill & Sons, 1865.

The Medical Register for 1887, London: General Medical Council, 1887.

Ward, J., *Origins and Development of Forensic Medicine and Forensic Science in England, 1823–1946*, Unpublished PhD thesis, The Open University, 1993.

Ward, T., 'A mania for suspicion: Poisoning, science, and the law', in J. Rowbotham and K. Stevenson (eds.), *Criminal Conversations: Victorian Crimes, Social Panic, and Moral Outrage*, Columbus: Ohio State University Press, 2005, 140–156.

Watson, K.D., *Poisoned Lives, English Poisoners and their Victims*, London: Hambledon and London, 2004.

Watson, K.D., 'Medical and chemical expertise in English trials for criminal poisoning, 1750–1914', *Medical History*, 2006, 50: 373–390.

9

Reporting Violent Death: Networks of Expertise and the Scottish Post-mortem

Nicholas Duvall

On 19 January 1933, the town of Dumfries, in south-west Scotland, was rocked by what the local newspaper described as a 'tremendous sensation'.[1] Lena Muir, of Cameron Place, was found in her home by her brother, dead with serious head wounds. The only suspect in her violent killing was her husband, John Maxwell Muir, an unemployed coach-painter. The pair had been married for around twelve years in what appears to have been an unhappy and abusive relationship. Mrs Muir, previously a waitress at the Imperial Restaurant in the town, had complained to her family that her husband was untrustworthy, on several occasions absconding with money, including the previous year to a hotel in Carlisle with another woman. When the couple lived in Coventry, some years before, she had complained, in letters, that her husband had struck her.[2]

This chapter is adapted from research from the Economic and Social Research Council-funded PhD project 'Forensic Medicine in Scotland 1914–1939', University of Manchester 2013.

N. Duvall (✉)
Edinburgh, UK

© The Author(s) 2020
A. Adam (ed.), *Crime and the Construction of Forensic Objectivity from 1850*, Palgrave Histories of Policing, Punishment and Justice,
https://doi.org/10.1007/978-3-030-28837-2_9

211

On the day of Mrs Muir's death, her brother, Charles Dudson, had met his brother-in-law coming home from the pub, drunk, and watched him entering his home, a room and kitchen in a tenement, a neighbour helping him with the key. Worried, he started to look for his sister, first trying their mother's house, then returning to the Muirs' house. The door was answered by his eleven-year-old nephew, who was in tears. Asked what was wrong, the boy replied that his father had returned home drunk. Growing anxious, Dudson went home to fetch his wife, then returned. There was no immediate sign of Mrs Muir, so he checked with John Maxwell Muir's parents, but his sister was not with them. He returned again to the tenement in Cameron Place. After conferring with his wife and a neighbour, he checked the bedroom. There he saw Muir in bed, asleep. Under the bed was Mrs Muir, dead. Dudson called out, 'Come quick, she is here'. Muir woke, and Dudson asked him what he had done with his sister. They struggled, and Muir attempted to escape via the bedroom window, but Dudson ran outside and pushed him back inside. Muir then successfully exited via the kitchen window, but was apprehended by another neighbour, who held him until the police arrived.[3] Lena Muir's body was later removed from the house, and a post-mortem examination was carried out by the local police surgeon and another doctor.

Although there are several dramatic and historically interesting aspects of this case, including an example of popular attitudes to capital punishment, in this chapter the case is used to examine a feature of the medico-legal post-mortem in Scotland in this period. As the Muir case and two others cited here demonstrate, the mandatory Scottish post-mortem report, not a feature of practice in the rest of Britain at this time, facilitated a system whereby additional medical expertise could be brought to bear in the investigation of a suspicious death after an autopsy had been carried out.

The post-mortem examination was the central feature of the medical examination of death. It was the primary means of finding out why someone had died. In Scotland, a particular feature of the post-mortem was the report written by the doctors who carried it out (a report was a requirement of all expert witnesses in Scottish legal procedure). It contained details of their observations and their opinion on the cause of death. These reports are of historical significance, first because they offer insight into the practice of the post-mortem, albeit with limitations, and second because they facilitated communication between medical experts. More than one doctor could pass opinion on the cause of death, from a geographic distance, without having attended the original autopsy. For example, while a general practitioner in a town in a geographic periphery might have performed the post-mortem, by reading the observations from the report and examining samples taken from the body, a forensic medicine specialist in a major city could offer additional expert opinion. Likewise, in a court action, different sides might hire experts who might come to different conclusions based on observations contained in the same original post-mortem report.

This gives nuance to existing writing about the post-mortem report. Although these reports have not really been considered from a historical point of view, Stefan Timmermans has written about their use in his ethnographic study of an early twenty-first-century mortuary in the United States. He characterizes the report as primarily being an instrument of medical authority. Rather than being a descriptive narrative of the post-mortem procedure, he argues that the report forms an argument for a particular interpretation of the body, namely what the cause of the death was. The report has to be thorough and tightly argued, to prevent it from being picked apart by hostile stakeholders. As such, the report represents a Latourian 'black box' (concealed process), within which the uncertainties of the autopsy's performance are masked. This presents a grim prospect for the historian since any 'study of death investigators that relies only on the final products misses the gradual construction of a cause of death'.[4] This was, for him, the reason for a direct observational study. This is impossible for a historical study.

The report does have limitations as a source for post-mortem practice; they were written concisely. More detailed, if idealized, accounts of how autopsies were performed may be found in textbooks. The report's real value for the historian is in its status as a means of communication among experts. It reflects Shapin and Schaffer's concept of 'virtual witnessing', 'the production in a reader's mind of such an image of an experimental scene as obviates the necessity for either direct witness or replication'.[5]

The carefully structured medical report communicated essential findings to other experts (and investigating authorities), who had not attended the autopsy. It allowed them to visualize what the dissector had seen and interpret these observations to form their own opinions on the death. In some cases, these professional readers challenged the report's conclusions, which complicates Timmermans's notion of the report as a citadel of medico-legal authority, although users retained a necessary degree of trust in the first doctor's skills of observation.

Legal Framework of the Post-Mortem

In Scotland, the dissection of a dead body for legal purposes was overseen by the procurator fiscal, a lawyer responsible in a geographical area for prosecutions and investigations of suspicious and unexplained deaths. He would direct police inquiries. The police, discovering a dead body, would send for the divisional police surgeon, often a general practitioner.[6] The police surgeon would make preliminary observations about the body, and the *locus* where it had been found. When the procurator fiscal had obtained a warrant from a sheriff (lower court judge), the doctor would examine the body at a suitable location. If the death was suspicious, two doctors would carry out the examination, to corroborate each other, as required by Scots criminal procedure. In addition to the post-mortem, the procurator fiscal could instruct the medical witnesses to examine any other relevant articles, such as items of stained clothing, and to perform any necessary laboratory tests.[7] These examinations would also be documented in report form. These reports were then returned to the procurator fiscal, who in serious cases would forward them, along with his own report, to his superiors at the Crown Office in Edinburgh, for instructions as to how to proceed.[8]

Overall, the investigation of deaths in Scotland was quite structured. Decisions about major prosecutions were taken by the Crown Office in Edinburgh, rather than locally. This resulted in a flow of reporting from regional legal officers to the centre, with decisions returning in the opposite direction. This was mirrored by the system of medico-legal expertise.

Post-mortem Procedure

Source material on the actual conduct of the post-mortem is quite limited. The end report was not a blow-by-blow account of the procedure. Some photographs exist, but these do not depict the examination underway. Instead, the most complete picture has to be drawn in reverse, using instructional textbook accounts of how best to perform an examination, in the hope that practitioners followed these directions sufficiently closely for them to represent a reliable account of post-mortem procedures. While the authors, including many who practised in Scotland, would themselves have conducted many autopsies and been very familiar with them, the texts represent a practical ideal. That various possible pitfalls were outlined in the texts suggests that some autopsies were carried out less proficiently, necessitating the authors detail mistakes to avoid.

The frameworks of examination set out in the textbooks follow a general pattern. The first step was to identify the body, to ensure that the correct one was being examined. This would be carried out by a family member, or if the identity of the deceased was not known, by the police officer who had discovered the remains, or been the first to arrive after discovery. Once this had taken place, a thorough external examination of the body was made. According to John Glaister Sr., Professor of Forensic Medicine at Glasgow from 1899 to 1931, this included noting 'appearances indicative of the time of death and the position in which the body has lain for some time after death', as well as any 'marks of violence, or any other marks, from any cause whatever, pointing to the cause of death'.[9] Items of clothing would also be examined, where relevant, 'and described as regards its nature and condition, noting any tears, loss of buttons, or disarrangement indicating a struggle'. Also, 'any ligatures found on the body, and the method of tying should be described before removing them'.[10] If the identity of the cadaver had not been established already, characteristics likely to aid identification, such as weight, height and any distinguishing marks, were noted in detail.[11]

The length of time since death would be determined by taking the rectal temperature, assessing the states of rigor mortis (the temporary stiffening of a body after death), lividity (characteristic red marks caused by the pooling of blood in the parts of a dead body closest to the ground) and the extent of putrefaction.[12] Any injuries or wounds would also be noted. Glaister pointed out the importance of making incisions to confirm the status of any bruises, because 'questions may arise in Court regarding their possible confusion with post-mortem lividity'.[13] The survey of wounds was intended to be extremely thorough, including their number, position direction, depth, the presence of any foreign bodies and the degree of any bleeding.[14] Sydney Smith, Regius Professor of Forensic Medicine at the University of Edinburgh, suggested making sketches and diagrams of the wounds, and indeed, such drawings can be found among the surviving case notes of a number of practitioners. Finally, once the body had been examined, it was washed and its scalp shaved, to reveal any small wounds or marks which had been obscured by blood, dirt or hair, 'especially about the neck and mouth'.[15] After this second external examination had taken place, the body was ready to be opened, and the internal cavities and organs inspected.

The internal examination had to be very thorough, with no organs omitted. This was not only because failing to do so might cause an important detail pertaining to the cause of death to be missed, but because an incomplete report would attract adverse attention in court. On the first point, Douglas Kerr, an Edinburgh police surgeon, reminded readers that while a partial internal examination might reveal disease which could account for death, often 'on opening the skull and examining the brain the real cause of death may appear'.[16] Likewise, Glaister advised that even if the main cause of death had been found, fuller examination could reveal contributory evidence.[17] Missing a potentially pertinent part of the body could cause others, at a later date, to question the validity of the examination. Smith advised that the viscera, where evidence of poisoning was likely to be found, be examined in every case, otherwise, the omission might be the subject of questioning at a future trial.[18] Glaister raised the possibility of an incomplete examination having very serious consequences for a medical witness. Close cross-examination could lead him to 'make statements which a re-examination of the body will disprove, and thus, very properly, make him the victim of a charge of perjury'. He gave an example of a doctor missing the dislocation of the first and second vertebrae and a fractured odontoid process and ruptured lateral ligaments, a very grave injury, instead attributing the cause of death to 'failure of the heart's action, due to shock'.[19]

The textbook authors also emphasized the paramount importance of preventing evidence about the cause of death, which could have crucial bearing on a future trial, from being destroyed before it could be properly recorded. As Ian Burney has noted with reference to nineteenth- and early twentieth-century England, the ability to 'maintain the integrity of death as displayed on and in the body even as [the dissector] cut, sawed and hammered' was a prized skill, the mark of a true expert.[20] Authors advised following a specific order to ensure nothing was missed since incisions could not be reversed. For example, upon opening the abdomen, Smith advised noting the presence of any blood, fluids or damage before continuing, so that there could be no doubt about whether any damage had been there already or had been caused during the examination.[21] Wounds had to be treated especially carefully. Incisions had to be made around them so that they could be examined in their entirety, and their depth gauged.[22] Doctors also had to resist the temptation of evaluating whether a particular blade had caused the wound by fitting it into the wound, as this could enlarge the wound and contaminate the weapon with blood from the body, thus destroying evidence.[23] Finally, in cases of suspected poisoning, great care had to be taken to ensure any samples taken for further, toxicological examination, did not become contaminated. Chemical preservatives were not to be used, although exceptions could be made for very hot climates.[24] Care also had to be taken to prevent the stomach contents leaking into the other viscera, as this would complicate an attempt to estimate the time since the ingestion of the poison.[25]

The solemnity of the medical witness's duty weighed heavily. The practitioner always had to have an eye to a future courtroom appearance. Thus, the examination had to be thorough, to avoid a charge of perjury, and careful, to avoid the loss of vital evidence. Of course, once the examination was complete, it could not really be performed again, at least not to the same degree with the remains in their pristine state. Though samples were often taken and kept for future reference, the major solution to this problem was the production of the written report describing the observations, findings and opinions of the doctors who had carried out the original examination. As mentioned above, for the historian the report has caveats as a source. Timmermans demonstrates that the report is not a transparent account of an autopsy's performance in contemporary practice, as it can obscure the uncertainties pathologists encounter during dissection.[26] Neither was it in the early twentieth century. Textbook authors emphasized the need for writing the report carefully. Smith stated that 'the same care should be taken in connection with the report as is advised in connection with the giving of oral evidence'.[27]

The report was expected to conform to a clear, rhetorical structure. A preamble containing background information about the identity of the deceased and the presence of witnesses was followed by the main part of the report, containing a description of the internal and external examination of the body. Precision was very important for this section. Smith recommended that, although every part of the body should be covered here, 'the system or part affected should be given prominence and treated first'.[28] This would provide rhetorical support to the final section, the conclusions and deductions. As Glaister made clear, this could only be founded on facts included in the earlier sections of the report, not on anything not included in the description of the organs.[29] He also emphasized the importance of concise, lucid writing and the avoidance of jargon. The intended audience included not just fellow doctors who might carry out further work on the case, but also jurors and lawyers. Care had to be taken to cater for this last audience, otherwise the report's conclusions might be misconstrued, or called into question:

> This conciseness, brevity, and clearness of language are of greatest value in the statement of opinion, for, otherwise, the issues become confused, and the report will probably give rise to much unnecessary dubiety, and, perhaps, cross-examination.[30]

Deflecting scepticism and scrutiny was a primary consideration when writing the report.

Nevertheless, despite the care which was taken to construct an argument within the report, as the cases discussed below demonstrate, other doctors were able to use them to gain information about what had been found at the post-mortem, which helped them to form conclusions of their own about a death (although they might also draw upon other forms of evidence where available, or argue for an exhumation to allow further evidence to be gathered). The medical element of the investigation of the Muir case offers an example of how this worked in practice. When additional expertise, beyond that of the doctors who carried out the initial post-mortem, was required, the post-mortem report, in this case along with select samples taken at the autopsy and the crime scene, allowed a university-based medico-legal expert in Edinburgh to contribute. The case also illustrates the hierarchy of expertise which existed within the Scottish system, with the university expert able to undertake a wider range of tests than the local police surgeon.

John Donnan, the Dumfries police surgeon, was called to the scene of the crime at around 22.00 hours on the day of the incident. Giving his evidence in court at Muir's trial in April, he recounted finding a woman's body lying under the bed, fully clothed. There was a pool of blood under her head, her face was bloodstained and her hair was clotted with blood from a wound on the top of her head. On examining the body where it lay in the bedroom, at about 22.30, he estimated death had occurred between five and eight hours earlier. He moved into the kitchen, where he found Muir in custody. He observed he had a large cut on his lower lip, which Donnan later sutured, had blood on his face and smelled of alcohol. Muir was watching everyone keenly. Donnan recalled that when he asked for a cigarette, and a constable said he could not have one, he replied, 'I am not convicted yet'. Donnan also examined the house that evening. He found that the linoleum in front of the bed was damp. The police showed him an axe found on the premises by police. He observed that there was hair on the blunt end and bloodstains on the head and shaft. He paid another visit to the house, to examine the kitchen and bedroom, in February.[31]

The next morning, Donnan performed the post-mortem examination with Dr Gordon Hunter in the mortuary of the Dumfries Infirmary. Death had been caused by 'fracture of the vault of the skull, haemorrhage, and surgical shock'. They found marks on the neck like fingers, as if from the grip of a hand. It was their opinion that the head wounds could have been caused by an axe wielded with moderate violence. At least four blows had been struck, any of which could have caused death.[32]

In addition to Donnan and Hunter's examination, a number of items relating to the case were sent to the forensic medicine department at the University of Edinburgh, where Sydney Smith examined them. Some of the items were pieces of physical evidence from the scene of the crime, such as linoleum flooring, the axe alleged to have been the murder weapon and items of clothing worn by the accused and the deceased. These items were subjected to tests the facilities for which Dumfries apparently lacked, such as blood grouping tests, which were carried out to determine whether blood on the coat of the accused had come from him or the victim. However, the work of Smith and the Dumfries doctors overlapped somewhat when Smith was asked to give his opinion about sections of the victim's skull and scalp, which had been removed at autopsy. In his report, he described the wounds present on the samples, and speculated as to whether the axe could have caused them:

> The Skull shows comminution of bone over the whole of the right side and back of the head with fissured fractures running to the left side. Evidence of separate blows can be seen at the back of the head, the front of the head, and the top of the head, all on the right side, and correspond to the injuries of the scalp which have already been described. The injuries of scalp and skull were caused by several severe blows from an instrument of [a] fairly heavy nature which has a cutting and also a blunt surface. The axe sent to me for examination (Label I) could cause all the injuries found.[33]

By describing the wounds and giving an opinion as to what might have produced them, Smith was reproducing work which would have been done in Dumfries at the post-mortem. During the autopsy Donnan and Hunter had examined and described the wound, and their testimonies in court make it clear they had examined the axe and considered whether it had caused the injuries, although they did not refer to the alleged weapon itself in their joint report on the post-mortem. During the trial, Smith and Donnan were both questioned about the level of force which would have been required to cause the injuries suffered by Mrs Muir. They were in agreement that a moderate level of force had been used since, despite considerable wounding, the damage to the brain had been more minimal. As Smith testified:

The first blow that was struck might have been used with considerable violence, but, if the skull was once broken, I think the other blows, if any great violence had been used, would have gone right into the brain, but the brain was not pulped up, so that I think they must have been of average violence.[34]

The reason for Smith's scrutiny of the skull and scalp fragments is not specified in the documents; however, it is most likely to have been to add further corroboration to the post-mortem findings. Given the serious nature of the case, the Crown wanted the opinion of a more specialized forensic expert than the doctors in Dumfries, who would have had much less experience of violent crime than Smith, who had practised in Egypt during a volatile time in that country's history. From the Crown's point of view, Smith, a prominent figure, would have been a highly credible witness. This suggests the existence of a hierarchy of the expertise called upon by the Crown.

This hierarchy is further confirmed by the broad range of expertise which Smith displayed in this case. Not only was he able to comment on matters relating to the physical body, in the form of the skull and scalp samples, but also to employ techniques of the laboratory to help construct a narrative of what occurred in the Muir's home. This is illustrated by his interpretation of the piece of linoleum flooring, removed from the room in which Mrs Muir was allegedly attacked. The piece of flooring was heavily stained with blood, and was dented 'due to a blow from a rectangular object striking on the corner'.[35] Prompted by the prosecution advocate, he combined his medical findings with what he had observed on the linoleum to construct a narrative of the attack, which he relayed in court:

Q.   From the indication you found on the linoleum, label no. 6, did you form the opinion that one blow at least had been struck whilst the victim was on the ground?

A.   I think it is quite probable three or four were struck whilst she was on the ground. I think probably the first blow knocked her down, and when the fell she probably fell forward on to the side of her face, owing to the incised wound over the left eye, and then three or four blows were struck on the right side.[36]

This demonstrates the breadth of expertise and oversight which forensic specialists had. University medico-legal experts scrutinized not just
the body, or parts of it, but material evidence from the scene of the crime,
such as clothing and flooring samples. Information from the two sets of
knowledge, medical and non-medical, was integrated to create a whole.

In the Muir case, the participation of Smith, the non-local expert, was
facilitated not just by his reading of the original report, but by his scrutiny of samples taken during the post-mortem examination. This combination of samples and report to allow another medical expert to participate
in the investigation after the autopsy was not uncommon. However, this
was not always possible. Sometimes, samples had not been taken, and the
report was all a doctor, called in for a second opinion, had to go on.
Nevertheless, even with the first doctor's report on its own, the second
doctor could come to a diverging opinion.

The investigation of the death of a woman in Biggar, South Lanarkshire,
in 1921 is an example of this. The woman had died as a result of multiple
cut wounds. The conclusion of an initial post-mortem by one Dr Marshall
was that she had died by suicide. Her body was buried after the post-
mortem. However, Harvey Littlejohn, Sydney Smith's predecessor as
Regius Professor of Forensic Medicine at Edinburgh, was asked by the
Crown Office to review the post-mortem report and other documents in
the case. In a letter to the Crown Agent, the Crown Office's chief legal
adviser, Littlejohn advised that the body be exhumed. He justified his
opinion based on the documents which he had been sent and set out
three reasons for his decision. The second and third concerned the general circumstances of the case, including the suspicious behaviour of
another member of the household. However, Littlejohn's primary point
concerned the woman's body and her wounds. For this, he relied on
Marshall's report.

Although he disagreed with Marshall's conclusions, Littlejohn utilized
his description of the character of the woman's injuries:

> In the report of Dr Marshall at least ten separate injuries of a more or less
> severe nature are enumerated. Some of these are comparatively slight, such
> as the bruise on the right side of the face and abrasions and bruises on the
> front of the neck and shoulder, but the others are incised wounds, varying

in length from one to six inches, and embrace the scalp, the face and the neck. The wound on the right side of the neck is consistent with self-infliction, but the other wounds, more especially the wound on the scalp behind the left ear which passed down to the bone, and that on the cheek which penetrated the mouth, are inconsistent with self infliction.

In Littlejohn's opinion, these injuries were more likely to have been the result of 'a homicidal attack with a sharp instrument, such as a razor'.[37] This example demonstrates the way in which the structured post-mortem report worked as a means of communication between medical witnesses. Littlejohn had not attended the original autopsy, but the detail provided in Marshall's account of his examinations allowed Littlejohn to form a view about how the woman had died, which dissented from the original medical opinion. The report allowed Littlejohn's experience and expertise to be brought to bear beyond his own physical geographical confines into a more provincial area.

Nevertheless, this use of the report was a preliminary. Although it allowed Littlejohn to form his opinion, this opinion was merely an initial one. The information from Marshall's report did not satisfy him fully. The previous doctor might have missed certain things; Littlejohn thus advised an exhumation and second autopsy be carried out:

> I am of opinion that an exhumation of the body would enable a complete examination to be made, and that although decomposition may be expected to have advanced considerably, yet it may still be possible to make out whether there are injuries other than those referred to by Dr Marshall, and whether [the deceased] suffered from disease of any of her important organs.[38]

Medical experts did not only give opinion in cases of suspicious death. An accidental death might give rise to a civil action, for example. It might be months or even years after any official autopsy that either side in a dispute might seek additional medical expertise. In such cases, exhumation might not be possible, or particularly necessary. Instead, further medical opinion would be based solely on the observations contained in the original post-mortem report. For example, in 1934 and 1935, Sydney Smith was asked to provide medical opinion for two civil actions which arose from a road accident in Glasgow, in which a lorry driver had died behind the wheel, causing his vehicle to swerve and hit people and property. In the two actions, the people injured sued the late driver's employers, arguing that the crash had been caused by their driver's negligence. The defenders, on the other hand, argued that the driver had suffered heart failure, causing him to lose control of his vehicle. The accident could not have been prevented, and so they were not liable. Medical evidence was crucial to the case, since death caused by trauma, rather than heart failure, would point towards liability.

The post-mortem had been carried out by John Glaister Jr., Professor of Forensic Medicine at the University of Glasgow. He had suggested that the driver had suffered a spontaneous, and fatal, rupture of the aorta, which caused him to swerve. Trauma injuries were sustained at, or just after, death. Smith was instructed to make reports on the death by the pursuers of the two actions, in 1934 and 1935. His findings were based on information in Glaister's report, eyewitness accounts and his own medical knowledge. He dissented from Glaister regarding the rupture, which he thought had been brought about by trauma from the collision, not spontaneously. Witnesses had observed signs of life from the driver after the impact; he may have swerved to avoid children in his vehicle's path. Medically, Smith thought a spontaneous rupture unlikely, because it had been so complete. This could only really be attributed to trauma. 'With such a history [of trauma] it seems to me to be most improper to suggest that the rupture must be spontaneous', Smith wrote.[39] He had found Glaister's medical interpretation of the incident unconvincing. Smith's information came from indirect evidence, and he stated this at the beginning of his reports. He had not examined the body itself, but relied on the observations as to its appearance recorded by Glaister. Smith's use of the report in this manner reflected a demarcation between Glaister's observations, which Smith was prepared to trust as competent, and his opinions, with which he disagreed.

Although not necessarily utilized in isolation, the post-mortem report was an important means of communicating vital information observed by the doctor performing an autopsy to a forensic specialist, allowing the latter expert to employ their experience and give an expert on a case without having attended the post mortem. As in the Muir case, the geographical reach of an expert witness's knowledge and skill was expanded, creating a network of expertise which allowed peripheries to benefit from the facilities of the centres. While contemporary textbook discussion of post-mortem reports did emphasize careful writing to avoid their contents being pulled apart under cross-examination, their content was not so opaque that other expert witnesses could not use their contents, and other available sources of information such as samples and eyewitnesses accounts, to arrive at conclusions of their own.

At Muir's trial, the defence contended that Muir had been suffering from temporary insanity, exacerbated by alcohol consumption, at the time of the attack, and so could not be held wholly responsible for his actions, and guilty of murder. They did not seriously pursue the possibility that Lena Muir was not killed by her husband. The root cause of Muir's supposed condition had been a childhood head injury. However, the weight of the medical testimony about Muir's mental state was not particularly favourable to this hypothesis. The defence did call two doctors, including a doctor from Glasgow who had attended Muir at the time of his childhood injury in 1903. In his experience, such an injury could make 'a man exceedingly irritable' in later life. Likewise, Andrew Wyllie, assistant physician and clinical pathologist at the Crichton Royal Institution, the local psychiatric hospital in Dumfries, argued that a brain injury might have been a factor in the crime, making it harder for Muir to control his behaviour, and be easier upset by a little alcohol. However, David Kennedy Henderson, Professor of Psychiatry at the University of Edinburgh, called by the Crown, had also examined him and found no evidence of mental disorder, and no reason to suspect that any had existed at the 'material time' in the case. Likewise, William McAlister, the Medical Superintendent at Bangour Hospital in Edinburgh, testified that while Muir had been known to commit violent acts while drunk, this did not indicate mental disorder. The jury appeared to be convinced by this and returned a verdict of guilty of murder. Muir was duly sentenced to death by hanging.[40]

This was not the end of the matter. An appeal was launched against the verdict and sentence, on the grounds that the judge had not properly instructed the jury that they were entitled to return a verdict of guilty of the lesser crime of culpable homicide and that the jury's verdict of guilty of murder, rather than culpable homicide, was 'contrary to the weight of the evidence'. In the meantime, as the appeal was being prepared, a petition to the Secretary of State, asking for a reprieve, was signed 3700 times in Dumfries in the two days after sentencing.[41] The leader column of the local newspaper seemed to reflect the sentiments of the petitioners. It said, 'It would, indeed, have been a sad reflection on Dumfries had this man been allowed to go to his doom without a sign that anybody care for him or his', and noted that many believed the death penalty ought to be reserved for the perpetrators of premeditated murders, the implication being that Lena Muir's was not.[42]

Muir's appeal was heard on 12 May and was upheld on the ground that the judge should have instructed the jury on the culpable homicide verdict. A verdict of guilty of culpable homicide and a sentence of life imprisonment were therefore substituted. The editorial of the Standard stated that there would be a 'general feeling of relief and thankfulness' in the town at this, and that 'No one will be more relieved than the Secretary for Scotland, who has escaped the difficult and delicate task of deciding as to whether clemency should be extended in this case'.[43]

Notes

1. 'Dumfries tragedy: Young married woman found dead: Husband arrested', *Dumfries and Galloway Standard*, 21 January 1933.
2. 'Dumfries murder trial: Special plea of temporary insanity: Dramatic story at High Court: Brother's tragic discovery: Extracts from dead woman's diary: Judge and child witnesses', *Dumfries and Galloway Standard*, 12 April 1933.
3. Ibid.
4. S. Timmermans, *Postmortem: How Medical Examiners Explain Suspicious Deaths*, Chicago: University of Chicago Press, 2006, pp. 63–70, 294, n. 60.
5. S. Shapin and S. Schaffer, *Leviathan and the Air-Pump: Hobbes, Boyle, and the Experimental Life*, Princeton, NJ: Princeton University Press, 1985, pp. 60–61.

6. M.A. Crowther and B. White, *On Soul and Conscience: The Medical Expert and Crime: 150 Years of Forensic Medicine in Glasgow*, Aberdeen: Aberdeen University Press, 1988, p. 84.
7. J. Glaister, Sr., *A Text-Book of Medical Jurisprudence and Toxicology*, 3rd ed., Edinburgh: E. & S. Livingstone, 1915, pp. 32–34.
8. D. Dewar, *Criminal Procedure in England and Scotland*, Edinburgh: W Green, 1913, pp. 31–34.
9. Glaister, *Medical Jurisprudence and Toxicology*, p. 34.
10. S.A. Smith, *Forensic Medicine: A Textbook for Students and Practitioners*, London: J. & A. Churchill, 1925, p. 32.
11. The process by which a range of individual characteristics was used to identify human remains has been discussed by Fraser Joyce with reference to the 1910 Crippen case in London. F. Joyce, 'Experts, laymen, and the identification of Cora Crippen: An exercise in medicolegal cooperation', *Medico-Legal Journal*, 2011, 79(2): 58–63.
12. D.J.A. Kerr, *Forensic Medicine: A Text-Book for Students and a Guide for the Practitioner*, London: A & C Black, 1936, pp. 45–54.
13. Glaister, *Medical Jurisprudence and Toxicology*, p. 35.
14. Smith, *Forensic Medicine*, p. 81.
15. Ibid., p. 33.
16. Kerr, *Forensic Medicine*, p. 23.
17. Glaister, *Medical Jurisprudence and Toxicology*, p. 36.
18. Smith, *Forensic Medicine*, p. 33.
19. Glaister, *Medical Jurisprudence and Toxicology*, p. 36.
20. I. Burney, *Bodies of Evidence: Medicine and the Politics of the English Inquest, 1830–1926*, Baltimore, Johns Hopkins University Press, 2000, p. 121.
21. Smith, *Forensic Medicine*, pp. 33–34.
22. Glaister, *Medical Jurisprudence and Toxicology*, p. 35.
23. Smith, *Forensic Medicine*, p. 81.
24. Kerr, *Forensic Medicine*, p. 25; Smith, *Forensic Medicine*, p. 36.
25. Smith, *Forensic Medicine*, pp. 35–36.
26. Timmermans, *Postmortem*, pp. 63–69, 294, n. 59.
27. Smith, *Forensic Medicine*, p. 4.
28. Ibid.
29. Glaister, *Medical Jurisprudence and Toxicology*, p. 38.
30. Ibid.

31. 'Sentenced to death: Dumfries man guilty of murder: Unanimous verdict by jury: Closing scenes in High Court trial: Execution fixed for May 4', *Dumfries and Galloway Standard*, 15 April 1933.
32. Ibid.
33. Report by Sydney Smith (Production no. 3) on Productions nos. 33 & 34 in case of John Maxwell Muir, 27 February 1933, Trial papers in case of John Maxwell Muir, NRS JC26/1933/98.
34. Testimony of Sydney Smith, Report of proceedings at trial of John Maxwell Muir, 11 April 1933, in papers relating to Appeal against conviction of John Maxwell Muir, NRS JC34/1/135, pp. 149–150.
35. Report by Sydney Smith (Production no. 4), 27 February 1933, Trial papers in case of John Maxwell Muir, NRS JC26/1933/98.
36. Testimony of Sydney Smith, Report of proceedings at trial of John Maxwell Muir, 11 April 1933, NRS JC34/1/135, p. 150.
37. Letter from Harvey Littlejohn to the Crown Agent, 30 September 1921, Post-mortem notebooks of Professor Henry Harvey Littlejohn, Edinburgh University Library Special Collections, EUA IN1/ACU/F1/2, Vol. XIII (April 1919–August 1923), p. 77.
38. Ibid., p. 78.
39. Letter from Sydney Smith, 18 October 1934, Smith (Sir Sydney) Papers and photographs on forensic medicine, Edinburgh University Library Special Collections, MS. 2753; Sydney Smith medical report, 7 March 1935, Smith (Sir Sydney) Papers and photographs on forensic medicine, Edinburgh University Library Special Collections, MS. 2753.
40. 'Sentenced to death: Dumfries man guilty of murder: Unanimous verdict by jury: Closing scenes in High Court trial: Execution fixed for May 4', *Dumfries and Galloway Standard*, 15 April 1933.
41. For context, according to the *Standard*, the burgh contained approximately 5000 homes.
42. 'The Reprieve petition', *Dumfries and Galloway Standard*, 29 April 1933.
43. 'Reprieved', *Dumfries and Galloway Standard*, 13 May 1933.

Archives

Littlejohn, H.H., Post-mortem notebooks, Edinburgh University Library Special Collections, EUA IN1/ACU/F1/2.
National Records of Scotland, Papers relating to Appeal against conviction of John Maxwell Muir, NRS JC34/1/135.

National Records of Scotland, Trial papers in case of John Maxwell Muir, National Records of Scotland, JC26/1933/98.

Smith, S.A., Papers and photographs on forensic medicine, Edinburgh University Library Special Collections, MS. 2753.

Bibliography

Burney, I., *Bodies of Evidence: Medicine and the Politics of the English Inquest, 1830–1926*, Baltimore: Johns Hopkins University Press, 2000.

Crowther, M.A. and White, B., *On Soul and Conscience: The Medical Expert and Crime: 150 Years of Forensic Medicine in Glasgow*, Aberdeen: Aberdeen University Press, 1988.

Dewar, D., *Criminal Procedure in England and Scotland*, Edinburgh: W Green, 1913.

'Dumfries murder trial: Special plea of temporary insanity: Dramatic story at High Court: Brother's tragic discovery: Extracts from dead woman's diary: Judge and child witnesses', *Dumfries and Galloway Standard*, 12 April 1933.

'Dumfries Tragedy: Young married woman found dead: Husband arrested', *Dumfries and Galloway Standard*, 21 January 1933.

Glaister, J., Sr., *A Text-Book of Medical Jurisprudence and Toxicology*, 3rd ed., Edinburgh: E. & S. Livingstone, 1915.

Joyce, F., 'Experts, laymen, and the identification of Cora Crippen: An exercise in medicolegal cooperation', *Medico-Legal Journal*, 2011, 79(2): 58–63.

Kerr, D.J.A., *Forensic Medicine: A Text-Book for Students and a Guide for the Practitioner*, London: A & C Black, 1936.

'Reprieved', *Dumfries and Galloway Standard*, 13 May 1933.

'Sentenced to death: Dumfries man guilty of murder: Unanimous verdict by jury: Closing scenes in High Court trial: Execution fixed for May 4', *Dumfries and Galloway Standard*, 15 April 1933.

Shapin, S. and Schaffer, S., *Leviathan and the Air-Pump: Hobbes, Boyle, and the Experimental Life*, Princeton, NJ: Princeton University Press, 1985.

Smith, S.A., *Forensic Medicine: A Textbook for Students and Practitioners*, London: J. & A. Churchill, 1925.

'The Reprieve petition', *Dumfries and Galloway Standard*, 29 April 1933.

Timmermans, S., *Postmortem: How Medical Examiners Explain Suspicious Deaths*, Chicago: University of Chicago Press, 2006.

Part III

The Media and Ethics in Constructing Forensic Objectivity

10

Detecting the Murderess: Newspaper Representations of Women Convicted of Murder in New York City, London, and Ireland, 1880–1914

Rian Sutton and Lynsey Black

Introduction

This chapter examines the figure of the 'murderess' , drawing on cases of women convicted of the murder of an adult in New York City, London, and Ireland, from 1880 to 1914. Through analysis of these cases, the chapter explores how the appearance, demeanour, and emotion of the accused women, as interpreted by the press, both contributed to and assuaged anxieties about women's lethal violence. Contributing to the literature on women who kill,[1] the chapter engages with the idea of 'detecting the murderess'—the question of whether women who killed could be identified through some outward sign. Bridget Walsh has argued that there was seeming acceptance through the Victorian period that the

R. Sutton
University of Edinburgh, Edinburgh, UK

L. Black (✉)
Maynooth University, Maynooth, Ireland
e-mail: Lynsey.Black@mu.ie

© The Author(s) 2020
A. Adam (ed.), *Crime and the Construction of Forensic Objectivity from 1850*, Palgrave Histories of Policing, Punishment and Justice,
https://doi.org/10.1007/978-3-030-28837-2_10

233

murderess could be anyone, and has suggested that this prompted public unease.[2] Particularly in this period, women on trial for the murder of an adult were viewed as aberrant, and consequently, as dangerous—to the individual, the family, and society. The chapter engages with press attempts to wrangle expectations of how such women should appear and their attempts to resolve the fears associated with women's lethal violence.

The chapter, therefore, engages with the concept of the murderess. Kirsten Saxton employed this term, stating that because her work was 'concerned primarily with the effects of femininity on murder; it is exactly the nonneutral haunting and titillating feminine associations of the term *murderess* in which I am interested.'[3] Likewise, Annie Cossins noted in her work on women who kill that, 'the real evil was Woman, the archetypal figure against whom nothing could protect a man.'[4] Cossins also noted, as does Judith Knelman, that the term 'murderess' conveyed more than the term 'murderer.'[5] The term murderess is thus used here because it recurs in the archival newspaper sample across the jurisdictions, and because it implies a gendered concept of lethal violence.

The period 1880–1914 saw a new language of criminality emerging through the science of criminal anthropology, which gifted a terminology of physical signification by which to identify the 'born criminal,' including the 'female born criminal.' Further, the analysis herein is drawn from press depictions of the women on trial; the rise of New Journalism in this period ensured that this was an era of increasingly sensational content in which criminal trials were often reported at length. These influences are explored further below. Following this 'scene setting,' the chapter turns to examine the 'testifying body,' and the extent to which women's criminality was viewed as detectable from their outward appearance. Discussion is then presented of how women were judged to 'feel their position,' as press accounts gauged how sensible the accused were to the peril in which they found themselves. Finally, the chapter explores the use of redemption arcs, as a means of assuaging public fears and resolving the tension of the murderess figure.

Table 10.1 outlines the cases of the sixteen women sentenced to death for the murder of an adult across three jurisdictions—New York City, London, and Ireland.

Table 10.1 Women convicted for the murder of an adult in New York City, London, and Ireland, 1880–1914

Name	Location	Victim	Method	Tried	Outcome
Chiara Cignarale	New York City	Husband	Shooting	1887–1888	Reprieved
Maria Barberi	New York City	Partner	Razor	1895–1896	Reprieved
Martha Place	New York City	Stepdaughter	Acid/ suffocating	1898–1899	Executed
Louisa Jane Taylor	London	Friend	Poison	1883	Executed
Elizabeth Gibbons	London	Husband	Shooting	1884	Reprieved
Mary Eleanor Pearcey[6]	London	Friend	Stabbing/ beating	1890	Executed
Kate Marshall	London	Sister	Stabbing	1898	Reprieved
Emma 'Kitty' Byron	London	Partner	Stabbing	1902	Reprieved
Marion Seddon	London	Husband	Poison	1905	Reprieved
Elizabeth Buchanan	Ireland	Husband	Hatchet	1881	Reprieved
Catherine Dooley	Ireland	Cousin	Hatchet	1884	Reprieved
Catherine Delaney	Ireland	Husband	Poison	1885	Reprieved
Mary Brophy	Ireland	Brother	Hatchet/ knife	1886	Reprieved
Isabella McIlwaine	Ireland	Neighbour	Beating/ burning	1888	Reprieved
Mary Daly	Ireland	Husband	Stabbing	1902	Executed
Sarah Anne Pearson	Ireland	Mother-in-law	Poison	1905	Reprieved

Scene Setting

In the late nineteenth century, two discourses emerged that influenced how the popular conception of the murderess was constructed and communicated to the public; these were the archetype of the 'born criminal' and the narrative style of New Journalism. Both emerged from a culture of anxiety about the changing nature of class and gender relations, which in turn stoked fears about crime and the criminal.[7] As Lisa Downing has noted, middle-class notions of public hygiene framed crime as a contagious social disease linked primarily to the sick and disorderly bodies of the lower classes.[8] Furthermore, the changing socioeconomic context of the period prompted middle-class fears of the 'lower class' as a group whose members were perceived to be foreign, unintelligible, and a threat to the social order.[9] It was within this context that Cesare Lombroso's idea of the 'born criminal' was developed and found popular reception. Lombroso's theory used emerging ideas of evolution, social heredity, and eugenics to present the criminal as an atavistic throwback whose hereditary degeneracy could be read on the body, thereby visually distinguishing him or her from other 'normal' members of society. The figure of the 'born criminal' was reassuring in that it made an invisible threat visible and intelligible in a way that fitted with already accepted understandings of the proper order of society, especially in terms of race, ethnicity, class, gender, and health—both physical and mental.[10]

This reassurance was undercut by the fact that few criminals perfectly embodied the 'born criminal.'[11] This proved to be especially problematic with respect to the 'female born criminal' as Lombroso struggled to reconcile his assertion that women were less evolved than men with the fact that women committed significantly less crime than men.[12] However, the foundational contradictions inherent in the way women were viewed bolstered the 'logic' of Lombroso's views on women. Over the course of the nineteenth century, middle-class values of women as guardians of morality and domestic purity became firmly entrenched.[13] Contrarily, women were believed to possess a natural affinity for duplicity and immorality.[14] Female criminals were believed to be a greater social threat than male criminals as a result of their 'double deviance' in not only breaking the law but also failing to conform to narrowly defined notions of acceptable feminine behaviour.[15] As Downing described it, Lombroso's 'female born criminal' was a strange hybrid that was both excessively feminine in her deviousness but also masculinised in her appearance—although, as Lombroso noted, women could disguise the signs of their innate criminality with make-up and clothing, making the 'female born criminal' even harder to detect.[16] In this way, Lombroso's 'female born criminal' was both masculine and feminine, both 'Other' and an everywoman, visible and invisible. As Mary Gibson and Nicole Hahn Rafter argued, the figure gained cultural currency because it was founded on accepted myths of women's nature and offered the assurance that female criminals could be identified and brought to justice.[17]

The image of the 'born criminal' in the public imagination coincided with the emergence of a new style of press reporting which was both influenced by and a challenge to that image. The sensationalist style of New Journalism dominated press reporting on both sides of the Atlantic in this period.[18] This marked a turning point in press culture from an obligation to inform to a desire to entertain readers as a means to generate profits in an increasingly competitive market.[19] The foundation of sensational press reporting was compelling human interest stories, ideally with a narrative thread that could stretch over the course of days or weeks and captivating characters about whom such narratives could be told.[20] Trials offered all the necessary components to attract and retain readers and women's murder trials added an extra layer of fascination due to their comparative rarity. Reporters attempting to describe women on trial would focus on physical appearance, emotional expression, and general demeanour, endeavouring to glean meaning from even the slightest gesture. In her article on modern-day courtroom sketches, Charlotte Barlow argued that such sketches are a product of the context in which they are created, 'influenced by [the artist's] own subjectivities and the cultural scripts they were taught.'[21] The same was true of press descriptions of women on trial in the late nineteenth and early twentieth century. Reporters relied on what Barlow refers to as 'ideological codes of meaning' that their readership could easily understand and interpret, of which the figure of the 'female born criminal' was one. This figure offered a collective cultural focal point against which the accused could be assessed as to how and to what extent she either conformed to or flouted shared cultural expectations. Often, as outlined below, press reports revealed the ways real female criminals failed to embody the expectations inscribed on the murderess, demonstrating that despite its staying power the figure was inherently unreliable, thereby intensifying the very anxiety it was created to quell.

It should be noted that the categories of appearance, demeanour, and emotionality are inevitably interlinked; the tears of a 'beautiful' woman could be construed very differently from those of a woman who was perceived to be 'unattractive.' The interpretation of these factors was imbricated with wider markers of identity such as ethnicity, race, and class. Walsh argued that both criminal justice outcomes and press depictions of women must be considered in light of how various facets of identity were negotiated.[22] The cultural boundary between what made a woman worthy or unworthy of sympathy was not immutable but was instead the product of a negotiation conducted on a case-by-case basis. For example, Marlin Shipman noted that nationality and race substantially changed how some women were represented by the press.[23] Naturally, also, many women were made intelligible through their location within a certain class, and Mary S. Hartman has argued that middle-class women could get away with murder.[24]

The interconnectivity of these various identity markers and the role they played in determining the innate criminality of the accused is most strikingly evident in the case of Chiara Cignarale, an Italian woman who shot her abusive husband. Cignarale's 'Italianness' featured heavily in the press coverage and functioned as an ethnic filter on the already gendered lens through which the press viewed her. This is most clearly expressed in an article in the *Sun* which placed Cignarale firmly within her ethnic group when describing her hair as 'black and glossy with the peculiar greasy appearance characteristic of her race.'[25] In contrast, however, she was elevated within that group with the assertion that she was 'better looking, brighter, and much neater than the average Italian woman of the lower-class.'[26] Evidently, in order to make Cignarale intelligible to their readership, the press had to assess her in terms of her ethnicity, class, appearance, cleanliness, and intelligence, set against a backdrop of preconceived notions of how these characteristics would present in an Italian woman. Collectively, this prompted the conclusion that 'if she were placed among a thousand women of her own class she would be the last one that an acute observer would pick out for a murderess.'[27] Tellingly, this reveals both that there was a popularly conceived notion of a 'murderess' and that Cignarale did not conform to it despite her factual guilt. The preoccupation with this evident disconnect is indicative of larger social anxieties about the difficulty of detecting the murderess and may explain the attempts by clemency campaigners to rationalize Cignarale's crime in a way that removed her moral guilt. In their eyes, she was not a threat to society, a 'born criminal,' but a normal, perhaps marginally superior, Italian woman who had been forced to act by circumstances beyond her control.

The Testifying Body

Lombroso's idea of criminality as something that could be seen on the body took root in fertile ground as it echoed the same basic reasoning as physiognomy, a popular pseudo-science.[28] The theory of physiognomy was developed by Johann Lavater, an eighteenth-century pastor who believed that a person's nature was inscribed on their physical body leaving tell-tale signs of repeated immoral thoughts or behaviour. Simply put, a person of moral purity would be more attractive than a person who indulged in immorality.[29] Sarah Lennox found that such ideas were commonly expressed in Victorian beauty manuals and Katie Barclay, commenting on Ireland, noted that the works of Lavater were frequently promoted in the press.[30] As such, Lombroso's theory that criminals looked different from 'decent' people, fit with long-held and widely shared beliefs. According to David Horn, the popular thinking of the time, especially in physiological research, was that the body actively testified against itself revealing deep truths of the inner self that could be read by those with the necessary knowledge.[31]

When faced with an unsympathetic case, press reports often seem to have drawn on such theories. In Ireland, Catherine Dooley was accused of murdering her cousin with a hatchet, an act that resulted in her disparaging treatment by the press. An article in the *Leinster Express* described her as a woman 'whose appearance is the reverse of prepossessing. She emigrated to America when she was about fifteen years of age, and evidence of a long residence in that country are apparent in her aspect.'[32] The idea that an extended stay in a country could be seen on the body, and evidently reflect poorly on Dooley's character, was directly in keeping with the theory of physiognomy. Martha Place received similar negative treatment in the New York City press after the brutal murder of her stepdaughter whom she allegedly burned with acid and then suffocated. While the murder of a young woman was already enough to raise public ire, Place was also depicted as a class interloper who originally entered the family as the housekeeper before seducing William Place and successfully marrying above her station. In keeping with the general tone, the *New York Times* described Place as a rat:

> She is rather tall and spare, with a pale sharp face. Her nose is long and pointed, her chin sharp and prominent, her lips thin and her forehead retreating. There is something about her face that reminds one of a rat's and the bright but changeless eyes somehow strengthen the impression. She looks like a woman of great strength of mind and relentless determination.[33]

This, and other similar descriptions, reinforced the idea of Place as inherently immoral and likely contributed to the lacklustre clemency campaign mounted on her behalf which failed to prevent her execution in 1899, making her the first woman in the United States to die in the electric chair.

In some situations where the sympathy felt for the accused ran counter to physiognomic expectations, the press endeavoured to find other aspects of the accused that could be described as appealing. One such case was that of Mary Eleanor Pearcey, who was tried in London for the murder of Phoebe Hogg and Hogg's infant child. Generally, such a crime would not garner favourable treatment in the press. However, in this case, public disapproval was primarily directed at William Hogg, husband and father to the victims respectively, who had been engaged in an extra-marital affair with the accused. It was suggested that if not for his behaviour, his wife and child would not be dead, and Pearcey would not be a murderess. Press reports wavered on whether Pearcey could be deemed attractive. One article stated that while she could not be said to be good looking, her 'face may be said to be an interesting and expressive one and character-ized by great gentleness admirably in keeping with her soft, low, musical voice.'[34] Similarly, a female correspondent for the *Pall Mall Gazette* insisted that 'there is nothing of the murderess in her appearance; in fact she is a mild, harmless-looking woman,' yet went on to describe Pearcey as having 'not a single good feature in her face. Her eyes are dark and bright, but of no size; her mouth is large and badly formed, and her chin is weak.'[35] The coverage of Pearcey demonstrates the connection between the murderess and a certain visible, physical aspect; but it also reveals the instability and amorphous nature of this figure in that Pearcey can be seen to meet the physiognomic requirements of being unattractive and yet still not fully embody the murderess in light of the broader context of her crime.

Sympathy for the accused could, therefore, discourage the reading of the women as murderesses, even if it was factually accurate, as indicated by the coverage of Pearcey. Similarly, when Emma 'Kitty' Byron faced trial before a London court for the murder of her partner, Arthur Reginald Baker, press coverage was generally favourable indicating a reading of her as being just like any other woman. She was described in the *Pall Mall Gazette* as looking 'like a spectator who had drifted in to the grim building out of curiosity and found her way by chance to the dock' seeming 'more like a careworn governess, or the promising young understudy in a problem play.'[36] Despite having stabbed her partner to death in the street in front of witnesses, this coverage echoed the consensus that more important than her crime, Byron was, in fact, the victim of a libertine who ruined her and left her; a fate that could befall any woman if she was not careful. This case also demonstrates a further tactic by which the anxiety regarding the murderess could be resolved, and one which recurs in the sample—the shifting of culpability to a man, even if that man was the victim.

Still, as Walsh identified, there was an increasing awareness that the appearance of the woman on trial was often incongruous with popular notions of the murderess. In commenting on this incongruity, the press contributed to undermining the collective sense of security afforded by the idea that social dangers could be seen and thereby easily combatted.[37] This inconsistency between women on trial and the mythic murderess was evident in every jurisdiction of this study. In an Irish context, when Mary Daly stood trial for the murder of her husband, an article in the *Leinster Leader* asserted that the accused was 'quiet looking, and certainly does not present the appearance of one who would be guilty of such a desperate and brutal crime,'[38] a description that likely tapped into unease that the angel of the house was secretly its greatest threat.

Press coverage, especially in Ireland and London, also indicated that embodying or failing to embody the figure of the murderess was about more than the physical features of the accused. A woman's general demeanour, particularly the extent to which it denoted respectability, could prevent the reading of her as a murderess. When Sarah Anne Pearson, an Irish woman, faced extradition from Montreal, an article published in the *Anglo-Celt* asserted that 'her conduct and general bearing certainly did not suggest that the woman had become or was likely to be a murderess even in thought.'[39] The favourable way Pearson presented herself proved endearing to the audience and was said to have prompted a general wish that her extradition might fail.[40] This desire that an accused woman of appropriate demeanour might escape justice was not unique to Pearson or Ireland. In 1905 Marion Seddon stood trial in London for the murder of her husband. At the inquest, Seddon testified that she and her husband, an elderly couple, had fallen on hard times and had decided to commit suicide together—she survived but he did not. An article in *Reynolds's Newspaper* described her as 'a strongly built gray-haired woman of refined speech' while in the *Pall Mall Gazette* she was said to be 'dignified-looking.'[41] In response, the coroner's jury ruled her husband's death a suicide and despite the insistence of the Coroner, refused to make any mention of her in their verdict. Seddon was eventually convicted of murder and faced a death sentence, but her status as a respectable matron combined with the pathetic circumstances that led to her husband's death meant that the commutation of her sentence was hardly in doubt.

In its reporting on Chiara Cignarale, the *New York Tribune* asserted that the 'frail body and delicate face were far different from the popular conception of a murderess.'[42] The figure of the murderess was therefore compelling enough that reporters could use the term and trust that their collective readership held some image in their mind of what the term entailed. Yet, despite this, the majority of women on trial failed to conform to such a neat classification, repeatedly demonstrating that the murderess of the popular imagination was a myth. On a case-by-case basis, this may have offered some reassurance. Women on trial could be seen as ordinary women placed in extreme circumstances that compelled them to act, drawing an imaginary line between the 'born murderess'—a threat to the very fabric of society—and a woman who committed murder under adverse circumstances, but who had not completely abandoned her femininity. But more broadly these contradictions contributed to a wider social anxiety by repeatedly demonstrating that, generally, those who would commit murder were wholly undetectable until they had struck. This sentiment was echoed by a comment in the *Times* saying of Mary Pearcey that her 'character, as known from her antecedents, is at variance with such ferocity. But this, perhaps, is only one more proof that no one can tell of what a human being may be capable until actual trial had been made.'[43] Reassurance about the preservation of society in the face of such crimes would need to be sought from some other source.

Feeling Her Position

Assessing the moral purity and respectability of the accused through the signs imprinted on her physical body was not the only way to determine innate criminality. Trials can be viewed as performative spaces in which participants embody particular roles, both consciously and through the interpretative efforts of others, which convey specific meanings to various audiences.[44] Especially for accused women, emotion, and accompanying demeanour were key aspects of this performance. Such performances were enacted before an audience of the judge, jury, public spectators, and press, and through them the wider reading public. In his article on the role of crying in the Victorian courtroom, Thomas Dixon discussed tears as a complex public act, the meaning of which was mediated by the beliefs of both the weeper and their audience.[45] The same is true of all expressions of emotion, and as Victoria Bates asserted, there 'is no single relationship between signifier and its signified meaning.'[46] Rather, the significance of an expression of emotion depends on the viewer's interpretation.

However, these interpretations do occur within the broader framework of a shared cultural context which offers basic parameters from within which meaning can be made. For women on trial in this period, middle-class standards of 'true womanhood' established the broader context through which their emotional performance was assessed.[47] Yet even within this rubric, interpretations depended on the specific features of an individual case and a defendant who failed to display excessive emotion could indicate either a steely but appropriately feminine middle-class resolve or cold and criminal indifference. Consideration of press coverage indicates that these performances were a crucial turning point in a larger narrative arc which required that women on trial be made to feel the gravity of their situation and reflect on the authority and legitimacy of the criminal justice system. This melodramatic trope offered readers a strong moral framework with a simple narrative in which the guilty were made to at least acknowledge what they had done.[48] By presenting the successful completion of this narrative arc to the public, the press not only succeeded in telling a compelling story but also went some way towards calming societal fears about insidious criminal threats by assuring their readers that even if the murderess could not always be identified visually, she would still be found and punished by the criminal justice system.

Pinpointing the moment in which the accused became aware of the true danger of her situation was a central feature of press reporting in all three jurisdictions. Allusions to whether the defendant 'felt her position' were used with frequency. The attentiveness reporters devoted to attempting to read this emotional turning point in the face of the accused is evident in coverage of Mary Pearcey's trial, published in the *Daily News*:

> And through it all the prisoner sat seemingly quite unmoved, though now and again there was, or one fancied there was, a hard, fixed rigidity about the face and a shadow of abject misery about the lines of the eyes which apparently testified to at least a momentary realisation of the dreadful peril of her position.[49]

This raises the question of exactly what reporters were looking for as an indication that the accused 'felt her position' and consideration of press coverage suggests more than one answer. In most cases, reporters were looking for an expression of 'emotion,' a term that was often shorthand for tears, suggesting that weeping was the only appropriately emotive behaviour for women. Elizabeth Gibbons, on trial for the shooting death of her husband in London, was described as appearing 'deeply affected by her position, and frequently sobbed in a piteous manner.'⁵⁰ Tears were also seen as an effective way to cultivate sympathy as in the case of Mary Brophy, on trial in Ireland for the murder of her brother, whose bitter sobbing caused all in the court to be 'visibly affected' to the point that even 'the judge broke down completely.'⁵¹

Dramatic changes in physical appearance were also noted by the press and interpreted as being a result of the physically and emotionally draining nature of the trial experience. This is especially evident in the coverage of the trial of Maria Barberi, an Italian immigrant in New York City, who murdered a man she asserted had raped her multiple times and then refused to marry her. At the time of the murder, it was reported in the *New York Times* that 'In her demeanour she is the personification of vengeance satisfied. She has cut the throat of the man whom she loved temporarily and apparently cares not whether she lives or dies.'⁵² However, by the time of her trial, Barberi's unconcern had abandoned her, and the press tracked her decline. Barberi was described in the *Evening World* as looking miserable, 'her eyes were red with weeping and as she sat by her counsel the tears continuously streamed down her cheeks.'⁵³ The next day it was said that 'the little defendant had apparently passed a sleepless night for her eyes were bloodshot and swollen.'⁵⁴ The phrase 'little defendant' demonstrates the sympathy felt towards Barberi, something that likely would not have occurred if she had remained the embodiment of 'vengeance satisfied.' Her physical, emotional, and later (possible) mental breakdown when faced with the punitive power of the state made it possible to see her as a victim who merited a second trial and eventual acquittal.

Although it is evident that crying was the preferred emotive expression from women standing trial, failure to cry was not automatically equated with an unfeeling and innately criminal nature. In trials where there was already a generous degree of sympathy felt for the accused, lack of emotion could be interpreted favourably. When Emma Byron attended the Mansionhouse police court after stabbing Baker it was reported in *Reynolds's Newspaper* that 'her features were firm set and she entered the dock with deliberate step and stood rigid, mastering her emotion as if getting ready to meet any fate.'⁵⁵ The reporter assumed that, despite appearances, Byron was experiencing a powerful depth of emotion. This suggests that, because Byron was viewed sympathetically, the interpretation of her emotional state by the reporter was influenced, at least in part, by the expectation of what a woman in her situation would be experiencing. Byron's lack of emotion denoted middle-class fortitude and feminine resolve.

Another reading of sympathetic women who failed to perform an appropriate emotive response, or who failed to fulfil the narrative arc of 'feeling their position,' was that they simply lacked the mental capacity to do so. This could take the form of a suggestion that the woman was not intellectually capable of processing the situation, an assertion that was tied to class status. This is evident in the interpretation of Isabella McIlwaine's demeanour who it was said 'did not seem to appreciate or feel her position.'[56] McIlwaine was a very poor woman of the 'labouring class' and spoke Irish as her first language—something generally considered as 'backwards.' Although the fact of a language barrier suggests that her failure to understand was rooted in this basic obstacle to comprehension, it was instead presented in the press as an intellectual barrier. Beyond an intellectual failing, the failure to express appropriate emotion could also be seen to indicate mental instability on the part of the accused. Despite having displayed excessive emotion throughout her trial, on the day her guilty verdict was announced, Maria Barberi 'stopped and it was as if she was carved from stone.' This sudden cessation of weeping caused considerable concern, but when she was returned to her cell and commenced to scream and weep again the matron said 'Thank God … Her reason will be saved.'[57] The matron's relief indicates that the perception of Barberi's sanity was tied directly to her ability to properly emote. Conversely, when giving her testimony, Barberi was described as becoming 'so hysterical she had to be removed from court.'[58] These two incidents in Barberi's trial are indicative of the narrow parameters in which women were expected to perform emotion—crying too much or too little could result in being deemed mentally unfit.

In cases where the woman on trial was not deemed to be worthy of sympathy, a failure to express emotion was not treated to a favourable interpretation. Instead, the passive demeanour of the accused was seen to indicate frigidity and innate immorality that matched Lombroso's idea of the 'female born criminal.' In Ireland, Catherine Dooley's courtroom behaviour was deemed to be highly inappropriate and allowed negative inferences to be made regarding her lack of respect for the process. She was depicted as indifferent to the gravity of the murder trial, but not to her financial interests, which served to reinforce the view that she killed her cousin, John Dooley, for mercenary gain. It was reported in the *Leinster Express* that despite her 'passive demeanour' during the trial:

> In the interval of adjournment for luncheon she was engaged bargaining for the sale of some livestock; and was apparently not rendered indifferent to her financial interests by the perilous position in which she is placed.[59]

In London, Louisa Jane Taylor was also believed to have murdered for mercenary gain. Shortly after Taylor moved in with the Tregellis family, Mary Ann Tregellis became ill and died, leading to the accusation that Taylor poisoned the woman so that she could marry William Tregellis and access his pension. As a woman who took advantage of others for her own personal gain, and used poison to do so, Taylor was the epitome of the feared 'female born killer.' This distaste for Taylor and her crime was evident in the press coverage as little was said of her at trial apart from the fact that she 'did not exhibit the least emotion' upon hearing the death sentence passed.[60] Dooley and Taylor were depicted as unnatural in their lack of emotion and are masculinized by their supposed interest in financial matters. Unlike Emma Byron, they were not given the benefit of the doubt that their stolid demeanour was a cover for the strong emotions they were endeavouring to contain.

Redemption and Reconciliation

Although it was clear that the murderess could not easily be detected from her outward appearance, reassurance could be given that she would be apprehended, and would bow to the power of the state. This narrative arc reached an inevitable conclusion for some of the convicted women through the press framing of their execution. In these cases, the press often favoured a moral fable in which women 'went well' to their deaths. Frequently then, the press narratives on the women changed considerably over the period in which the case was reported, creating redemption arcs which could facilitate the resolution of the tension implicit in the figure of the murderess. These redemption arcs were often framed by women's changing emotional responses through the trial. As noted, in response to the troubling spectre of women's lethal violence, the public could be comforted, and their fears assuaged, by appropriate displays of emotion which redeemed the murderess. The appearance of seemingly genuine emotion was often taken as a reliable marker of inner self, quieting anxieties regarding the implacability of women on trial.[61] As with 'feeling her position,' redemption arcs relied on the accused acknowledging the gravity of her circumstances. However, in the context of execution, redemption arcs were most impactful when the subject demonstrated bravery and moral strength.

Within the Irish sample, the case of Mary Daly offers a clear example of how redemption arcs could function. Daly had been convicted of the murder of her husband. Throughout her trial, she had seemed indifferent to proceedings; saving one dramatic fit of sobbing, she was reported to spend her hours in court gazing out the window, appearing generally 'unnerved.'[62] The fact that Daly had been convicted along with Joseph Taylor, a man with whom she had been having an affair, clearly motivated many negative readings of her throughout. However, the reporting that followed Daly and Taylor's executions took on a different tone, and represented Daly as the submissive figure in her husband's murder. In this framing, Daly's indifference was interpreted positively, and in the moments before her death by hanging, Mary could be said to demonstrate resignation to her fate and reconciliation with her God, sealing the resolution of her problematic character. What was once indifference was now fortitude: 'The woman's fortitude at the last moment was remarkable.'[63] Headlines in the newspapers proclaimed: 'MARVELLOUS COURAGE' and 'EDIFYING REPENTANCE.'[64] Describing her hanging as 'edifying' meant it had pedagogic usefulness. The function of the redemption arc is an example to others, and perhaps holds out the hope that capital punishment is not such a bad thing: 'Such a reclamation of one who had been so debased was really marvelled at.'[65]

The use to which her death was put is clear in the description of her dead body too:

When viewed by the jury, the corpse presented a quiet, calm appearance. The lips were slightly parted, and there was nothing to indicate that the end had been other than a peaceful and painless one. On the breast was a Crucifix, and Rosary beads were laid across the hands.[66]

The widespread newspaper reporting of her final piety, which was largely attributed to her rather than emanating from clear evidence, created a strong rationale for legitimising capital punishment as a cleansing and cathartic, and ultimately redemptive, practice. However, this reclamation of the soul could also be put to work assuaging public fears of monstrous and lethal femininity. In life, Daly had been problematic—she had seemingly conspired with her partner to murder her husband, and throughout her trial had failed to show much concern at her awful deed. In death, however, Daly could be repackaged as a wronged woman. In meeting a 'good death,' and in her reconciliation to piety, the murderess was finally tamed.

Conclusion

The chapter has explored how press accounts wrestled with notions of the murderess, and how this vague archetype crumbled in the face of real-life trials. The analysis has demonstrated that interpretations of women on trial were subject to many competing strands of meaning, related to perceptions of class, respectability, ethnicity, as well as to consideration of the circumstances of their crimes. However, across three disparate jurisdictions, certain commonalities suggest that similar currents of thought were underpinning press discourses. In particular, the shared cultural touchstone of the murderess was invoked and the women on trial were continually considered in light of this figure, as press reports gave judgement on whether such women were readily identifiable as killers. The mixed success of this endeavour ensured that coping mechanisms were used, through which previously undetectable murderesses could be brought low against the immense power of the state. For some women, their eventual execution could represent a final triumph of the state and society, which had won out against an unseeable threat. In the narratives spun around those women who were executed, clear efforts were made to redeem monstrous femininity and to rehabilitate the murderess.

Notes

1. G.M. Bakken and B. Farrington, *Women who Kill Men: California Courts, Gender, and the Press*, Berkeley: University of California Press, 2009; N. Goc, *Women, Infanticide, and the Press, 1822–1922: News Narratives in England and Australia*, Farnham: Ashgate, 2013; J. Knelman, *Twisting in the Wind: The Murderess and the English Press*, Toronto: University of Toronto Press, 1998; L. Seal, *Women, Murder and Femininity: Gender Representations of Women Who Kill*, Basingstoke: Palgrave Macmillan, 2010; M. Shipman, *'The Penalty is Death': US Newspaper Coverage of Women's Executions*, Columbia, MO: University of Missouri Press, 2002; B. Walsh, *Domestic Murder in Nineteenth-Century England: Literary and Cultural Representations*, Farnham: Ashgate, 2014; J.C. Wood, *The Most Remarkable Woman in England: Poison, Celebrity and the Trials of Beatrice Pace*, Manchester: Manchester University Press, 2012.
2. Walsh, *Domestic*.
3. K. Saxton, *Narratives of Women and Murder in England, 1680–1760*, Farnham: Ashgate, 2009, p. 1. Emphasis in original.
4. A. Cossins, *Female Criminality: Infanticide, Moral Panics and the Female Body*, Basingstoke: Palgrave Macmillan, 2015.
5. J. Knelman, *Twisting*.
6. Her birth name was Wheeler, but she was referred to as Pearcy, Piercy, Piercey, or Pearcey, which was used most commonly in the press and official documents and so is used here.
7. A. Linders and A., van Gundy-Yoder, 'Gall, gallantry, and the gallows: Capital punishment and the social construction of gender, 1840–1920', *Gender and Society*, 2008, 22: 324–348.
8. L. Downing, 'Murder in the feminine: Marie Lafarge and the sexualization of the nineteenth-century criminal woman', *Journal of the History of Sexuality*, 2009, 18: 121–137, pp. 122–123.
9. N. Hahn Rafter, 'Criminal anthropology: Its reception in the United States and the nature of its appeal', in P. Becker and R.F. Wetzell (eds.), *Criminals and their Scientists: The History of Criminology in International Perspective*, Cambridge: Cambridge University Press, 2006, p. 160.

10. D. Horn, *The Criminal Body: Lombroso and the Anatomy of Deviance*, Abingdon: Routledge, 2003, pp. 12–15; Rafter, 'Criminal', p. 177; M. Gibson, 'Labelling women deviant: Heterosexual women, prostitutes and lesbians in early criminological discourse', in P. Wilson (ed.), *Gender, Family and Sexuality: The Private Sphere in Italy, 1860–1945*, Basingstoke: Palgrave Macmillan, 2004, p. 90.
11. Horn, *Criminal*, p. 16.
12. Downing, 'Murder', p. 132; Horn, *Criminal*, p. 52; C. Lombroso and G. Ferrero (new translation and Introduction by N. Hahn Rafter, and M. Gibson), *Criminal Woman, the Prostitute, and the Normal Woman*, Durham, NC: Duke University Press, 1895/2004, Introduction, p. 9.
13. V.M. Nagy, 'Narratives in the courtroom: Female poisoners in mid-nineteenth century England', *European Journal of Criminology*, 2013, 11: 213–227, p. 214; C.B. Ramsey, 'Intimate homicide: Gender and crime control, 1880–1920', *University of Colorado Law Review*, 2006, 77: 101–191, p. 116.
14. Downing, 'Murder', pp. 124 and 132.
15. P. Hutchings, *The Criminal Spectre in Law, Literature and Aesthetics: Incriminating Subjects*, Routledge, 2001, p. 110; Gibson, 'Labelling', p. 89; Downing, 'Murder', p. 137
16. Downing, 'Murder', p. 132.
17. Lombroso and Ferrero, *Criminal*, p. 27.
18. Bakken and Farrington, *Women*, p. 7.
19. N. Darby, 'The Hampstead murder: Subversion in press portrayals of a murderess', *Law, Crime & Society*, 2018, 8(1): 5–20, pp. 1 and 6.
20. J. Rowbotham, K. Stevenson and S. Pegg, *Crime News in Modern Britain: Press Reporting and Responsibility, 1880–2010*, Basingstoke: Palgrave Macmillan, 2013, pp. 68–76.
21. C. Barlow, 'Sketching women in court: The visual construction of co-accused women in court drawings', *Feminist Legal Studies*, 2016, 24: 169–192, p. 172.
22. Walsh, *Domestic*.
23. Shipman, '*Penalty*'.
24. M.S. Hartman, *Victorian Murderesses: A True History of Thirteen Respectable French and English Women Accused of Unspeakable Crimes*, London: Robson Books, 1977.
25. 'Mrs. Cignarale's torture', *Sun*, 5 June 1887.
26. Ibid.
27. Ibid.

28. Walsh, *Domestic*, p. 138.
29. 'Attractiveness' was not an objective criterion and was interpreted within a specific context and related to factors such as ethnicity and class.
30. S. Lennox, 'The beautified body: Physiognomy in Victorian beauty manuals', *Victorian Review*, 2016, 42: 9–14, p. 11; K. Barclay, 'Performing emotion and reading the male body in the Irish court, c. 1800–1845', *Journal of Social History*, 2017, 51: 293–312.
31. Horn, *Criminal*, p. 6.
32. 'Murder in the Queen's country', *Leinster Express (LE)*, 25 August 1883.
33. 'Mrs. Place convicted', *New York Times (NYT)*, 9 July 1898.
34. 'The Kentish Town tragedy', *Daily News (DN)*, 4 November 1890.
35. 'Fourth edition', *Pall Mall Gazette (PMG)*, 21 November 1890.
36. 'The City tragedy', *PMG*, 17 December 1902.
37. Walsh, *Domestic*.
38. 'The Clonbrock murder', *Leinster Leader (LL)*, 13 December 1905.
39. 'Poisoning mystery', *Anglo-Celt*, 11 February 1905.
40. Ibid.
41. 'Poison mystery at Richmond', *Reynolds's Newspaper (RN)*, 24 September 1905; 'A tragedy of trade', *PMG*, 28 September 1905.
42. 'A woman to be hanged', *New York Tribune*, 28 May 1887.
43. 'The trial of Mary Eleanor Wheeler, alias', *Times*, 4 December 1890.
44. S. D'Cruze, *Crimes of Outrage: Sex, Violence and Victorian Working Women*, London: UCL Press, 1998; G. Frost, *Promises Broken: Courtship, Class and Gender in Victorian Britain*, Charlottesville: University Press of Virginia, 1995; S. Frigon. 'Mapping scripts and narratives of women who kill their husbands in Canada, 1866–1954: Inscribing the everyday', in A. Burfoot and S. Lord (eds.), *Killing Women: The Visual Culture of Gender and Violence*, Ontario: Wilfrid Laurier University Press, 2006.
45. T. Dixon, 'The tears of Mr Justice Willes', *Journal of Victorian Culture*, 2012, 17: 1–23, p. 4.
46. V. Bates, '"Under cross-examination she fainted": Sexual crime and swooning in the Victorian court', *Journal of Victorian Culture*, 2016, 21: 456–470, p. 457.
47. G. Frost, *Promises Broken: Courtship, Class and Gender in Victorian Britain*, Charlottesville: University Press of Virginia, 1995; Frigon, 'Mapping'; D'Cruze, *Crimes*; Walsh, *Domestic*.
48. Walsh, *Domestic*, p. 13.
49. 'The Kentish-Town murders', *DN*, 12 November 1890.

50. 'The mysterious death at Hayes', *DN*, 9 December 1884.
51. 'The Blackpool murder', *Examiner*, 23 July 1886.
52. 'Maudlin sentiment in parallel', *NYT*, 28 April 1895.
53. 'Cataldo's slayer on trial', *Evening World (EW)*, 8 July 1895.
54. 'Maria Barberi wept', *EW*, 9 July 1895.
55. 'City stockbroker murdered', *RN*, 6 December 1902.
56. 'The murder in Donegal', *Belfast Newsletter*, 8 December 1888.
57. 'Maria Barberi breaks down', *EW*, 17 July 1895.
58. 'Why she killed Cataldo', *Sun*, 13 July 1895.
59. 'The Cardtown murder', *LE*, 8 September 1883.
60. 'The city tragedy', *DN*, 16 December 1882.
61. A. Ballinger, 'Masculinity in the dock: Legal responses to male violence and female retaliation in England and Wales, 1900–1965', *Social and Legal Studies*, 2007, 16: 459–481.
62. 'The Queen's Co. murder', *Nationalist and Leinster Times (NLT)*, 19 July 1902.
63. 'The Clonbrock tragedy', *Examiner*, 10 January 1903.
64. 'Execution of Mary Daly', *LL*, 10 January 1903.
65. 'Mrs Daly executed', *NLT*, 17 January 1903.
66. Ibid.

Newspapers

Anglo-Celt
Belfast Newsletter
Daily News
Examiner
Leinster Express
Leinster Leader
Nationalist and Leinster Times
New York Times
New York Tribune
Pall Mall Gazette
Reynolds's Newspaper
Evening World
Sun
Times

Bibliography

Bakken, G.M. and Farrington, B., *Women Who Kill Men: California Courts, Gender, and the Press*, Berkeley: University of California Press, 2009.

Ballinger, A., 'Masculinity in the dock: Legal responses to male violence and female retaliation in England and Wales, 1900–1965', *Social and Legal Studies*, 2007, 16: 459–481.

Barclay, K., 'Performing emotion and reading the male body in the Irish Court, c. 1800–1845', *Journal of Social History*, 2017, 51: 293–312.

Barlow, C., 'Sketching women in court: The visual construction of co-accused women in court drawings', *Feminist Legal Studies*, 2016, 24: 169–192.

Bates, V., '"Under cross-examination she fainted": Sexual crime and swooning in the Victorian court', *Journal of Victorian Culture*, 2016, 21: 456–470.

Cossins, A., *Female Criminality: Infanticide, Moral Panics and the Female Body*, Basingstoke: Palgrave Macmillan, 2015.

Darby, N., 'The Hampstead murder: Subversion in press portrayals of a murderess', *Law, Crime & Society*, 2018, 8(1): 5–20.

D'Cruze, S., *Crimes of Outrage: Sex, Violence and Victorian Working Women*, London: UCL Press, 1998.

Dixon, T., 'The tears of Mr Justice Willes', *Journal of Victorian Culture*, 2012, 17: 1–23.

Downing, L., 'Murder in the feminine: Marie Lefarge and the sexualization of the nineteenth-century criminal woman', *Journal of the History of Sexuality*, 2009, 18: 121–137.

Frigon, S., 'Mapping scripts and narratives of women who kill their husbands in Canada, 1866–1954: Inscribing the everyday', in A. Burfoot and S. Lord (eds.), *Killing Women: The Visual Culture of Gender and Violence*, Ontario: Wilfrid Laurier University Press, 2006.

Frost, G., *Promises Broken: Courtship, Class and Gender in Victorian Britain*, Charlottesville: University Press of Virginia, 1995.

Gibson, M., 'Labelling women deviant: Heterosexual women, prostitutes and lesbians in early criminological discourse', in P. Wilson (ed.), *Gender, Family and Sexuality: The Private Sphere in Italy, 1860–1945*, Basingstoke: Palgrave Macmillan, 2004.

Goc, N., *Women, Infanticide, and the Press, 1822–1922: News Narratives in England and Australia*, Farnham: Ashgate, 2013.

Hahn Rafter, N., 'Criminal anthropology: Its reception in the United States and the nature of its appeal', in P. Becker and R.F. Wetzell (eds.), *Criminals and their Scientists: The History of Criminology in International Perspective*, Cambridge: Cambridge University Press, 2006.

Hartman, M.S., *Victorian Murderesses: A True History of Thirteen Respectable French and English Women Accused of Unspeakable Crimes*, London: Robson Books, 1977.

Horn, D., *The Criminal Body: Lombroso and the Anatomy of Deviance*, Abingdon: Routledge, 2003.

Hutchings, P., *The Criminal Spectre in Law, Literature and Aesthetics: Incriminating Subjects*, Abingdon: Routledge, 2001.

Knelman, J., *Twisting in the Wind: The Murderess and the English Press*, Toronto: University of Toronto Press, 1998.

Lennox, S., 'The beautified body: Physiognomy in Victorian beauty manuals', *Victorian Review*, 2016, 42: 9–14.

Linders, A. and van Gundy-Yoder, A., 'Gall, gallantry, and the gallows: Capital punishment and the social construction of gender, 1840–1920', *Gender and Society*, 2008, 22: 324–348.

Lombroso, C. and Ferrero, G., (new translation and Introduction by N. Hahn Rafter and M. Gibson), *Criminal Woman, the Prostitute, and the Normal Woman*, Durham, NC: Duke University Press, 1895/2004.

Nagy, V.M., 'Narratives in the courtroom: Female poisoners in mid-nineteenth century England', *European Journal of Criminology*, 2013, 11: 213–227.

Ramsey, C.B., 'Intimate homicide: Gender and crime control, 1880–1920', *University of Colorado Law Review*, 2006, 77: 101–191.

Rowbotham, J., Stevenson, K. and Pegg, S., *Crime News in Modern Britain: Press Reporting and Responsibility, 1880–2010*, Basingstoke: Palgrave Macmillan, 2013.

Saxton, K., *Narratives of Women and Murder in England, 1680–1760*, Farnham: Ashgate, 2009.

Seal, L., *Women, Murder and Femininity: Gender Representations of Women Who Kill*, Basingstoke: Palgrave Macmillan, 2010.

Shipman, M., *'The Penalty is Death': US Newspaper Coverage of Women's Executions*, Columbia, MO: University of Missouri Press, 2002.

Walsh, B., *Domestic Murder in Nineteenth-Century England: Literary and Cultural Representations*, Farnham: Ashgate, 2014.

Wood, J.C., *The Most Remarkable Woman in England: Poison, Celebrity and the Trials of Beatrice Pace*, Manchester: Manchester University Press, 2012.

11

'Children's Lies': The Weimar Press as Psychological Expert in Child Sex Abuse Trials

Heather Wolffram

In November 1930, reflecting on the guilty verdict in the case of a thirty-two-year-old village school teacher accused of seventeen instances of inappropriate conduct with his female pupils, the Magdeburg-based Social Democratic newspaper *Volksstimme* published an article titled 'Meditations about a morality trial. Children's testimony and its credibility—science and lay opinion.'[1] Portraying the outcome of the proceedings as a dreadful miscarriage of justice, which had effectively destroyed the life of a young teacher, the article sought to question the court's faith in the reliability of the young witnesses and to critique the presiding judge for his neglect of expert psychological testimony. 'Meditations about a morality trial' began by stressing that the court's decision about the guilt of the teacher, Erich Polte, was based almost exclusively on the testimony of children, who, at the time of the alleged events in 1925, were nine or ten.[2] It continued by noting that the prosecutor had acknowledged that the sources of error in children's testimony were great,

H. Wolffram (✉)
University of Canterbury, Christchurch, New Zealand
e-mail: heather.wolffram@canterbury.ac.nz

© The Author(s) 2020
A. Adam (ed.), *Crime and the Construction of Forensic Objectivity from 1850*, Palgrave Histories of Policing, Punishment and Justice,
https://doi.org/10.1007/978-3-030-28837-2_11

even if he had sought to mitigate this admission by maintaining that these errors were no worse than those committed by adults. In response to the presiding judge's agonies over finding guilty a defendant who gave all appearances of being a good man, the article's author remonstrated that the court might simply have refrained from giving the children's testimony credence and have paid attention to the expert witnesses.[3] Instead, the article complained, the psychological experts had been deemed superfluous and the court had stubbornly maintained that lay opinion sufficed in deciding whether a witness was credible or not. Pointing to the holes and contradictions in the children's testimony, 'Meditations about a morality trial' closed with a strident criticism of the verdict and the court's decision-making processes, reminding readers not only of the propensity of children to fantasy, but the old dictum of German justice that even one per cent doubt about a defendant's guilt should lead to an acquittal.[4]

The *Volksstimme*'s engagement with the questions of children's credibility in sex crimes trials and appropriate psychological expertise in such cases did not end with Polte's sentence to a year in prison.[5] The teacher's January 1931 appeal, afforded the newspaper the opportunity both to reiterate their critique of the first trial and to express an opinion about the ability of the German justice system more generally to deal with children's accusations.[6] During the second trial, the new presiding judge was praised for appointing the Berlin sexologist Max Marcuse (1877–1963) as the court's expert on juvenile credibility.[7] According to the *Volksstimme*, it was Marcuse's report that provided the basis for the over-turning of the first verdict by maintaining that the key accusatory witnesses should not be considered reliable on typological and individual grounds and that Polte's personality and private circumstances did not support the contention that he was a sexual predator.[8] While the newspaper celebrated the outcome in this trial as a triumph for justice and science, it lamented that the German justice system more generally remained inconsistent in its application and understanding of psychological expertise, relying on judicial experience, rather than medical or scientific knowledge. In particular, it pointed to the 1930 Potsdam-based Frenzel trial, a case of putative incest, in which the respectable middle-class defendant was found guilty in both his first trial and on appeal.[9] Closing its discussion of the

Polte trial, the *Volksstimme* declared, 'Is the world not disgusted by the case of the head official Frenzel? Given the yet to be clarified situation, in this case, we should be glad that the Magdeburg court has not created a second Frenzel case from the Polte (Güsen) case. German justice is already polluted enough by the Frenzel case.'[10] The newspaper's disgust here was not a result of its belief that the defendant, Arthur Frenzel, had, in fact, assaulted his daughters, but of the decision of the presiding and lay judges in the two iterations of this trial to rely both on their own knowledge of children's credibility and the findings of those psychological experts, who in contrast to their colleagues and in defiance of the widespread popular discourse on juvenile testimony, deemed the main accusatory witness reliable.

As the *Volksstimme*'s discussion of the Polte and Frenzel trials tends to suggest, in Weimar Germany, the issue of witness credibility and psychological expertise was highly contentious; nowhere more so than in trials involving accusations of child sexual abuse. Such accusations caused collective horror not only because they highlighted society's failures in terms of child welfare and protection, but also because they had the potential to reverse the power dynamic between adults and children, spurring fears among the middle classes of the damage that might be wrought on the reputations of '*unbescholtene Bürger*' (upright citizens) by the false accusations of suggestible or malicious youths.[11] As the *Volksstimme* stressed in the Polte case, anyone, particularly a teacher, who committed such offences against children could not be punished severely enough, but the risk, given what was widely acknowledged about children's reliability, of unfounded allegations ruining the lives of respectable men, must weigh heavily on the decision-making processes of the courts.[12] While incest and the sexual assault of children appears to have been readily accepted as a problem that occurred among the poor, there was enormous reluctance to believe that bourgeois men like Polte and Frenzel might be guilty of such offences.[13] Instead, in the courts and in the press, there was heavy reliance on a popular discourse, which understood juvenile testimony as unreliable and dangerous; the dominance of which enabled, at least, some newspapers to label young people's accusations as 'Children's lies,' even where physical evidence, such as the presence of venereal disease, tended to suggest the veracity of the children's claims.[14]

This discourse, which emerged around the turn of the century, was moulded not only by experimental findings in the nascent field of forensic psychology but by the professional ambitions of several groups. The experimental work conducted from 1900 onwards by psychologists such as William Stern (1871–1938), Karl Marbe (1869–1953) and Otto Lipmann (1880–1933) on witness credibility was part of a broader attempt to prove the social utility of psychology.[15] In a context in which it was unclear whether psychology would survive within the universities once its differentiation and separation from philosophy was complete, the application of psychological knowledge within institutions like the courts, the military and industry, seemed crucial.[16] Allowing their research to be driven by the questions most significant in real world contexts, psychologists of testimony soon found the exigencies of legal proceedings narrowing their focus to the credibility of juvenile witnesses. Thereafter, they were joined in this endeavour by a number of pedagogues, whose interest in such research was aroused not least because theirs was the profession most frequently accused of inappropriate behaviour with children.[17] Psychologists and pedagogues, who claimed expertise on children's testimony, however, had to compete for space in the courtroom with psychiatrists and forensic specialists (*Gerichtsärzte*), who maintained that it was they who were best equipped to deal with juvenile witnesses.[18] Meanwhile, as a result of the professional freedoms granted to defence lawyers during the late nineteenth century, which enabled them to better defend their clients, late Imperial courtrooms became host to some of the newest theories and findings in both the physical and social sciences.[19] When in the early twentieth century, then, the results of psychologists' and pedagogues' experiments with children became available, it was unsurprising that defence lawyers began to call on psychological experts. They were quick to appreciate the potential of this new field for defending their clients against accusations of child sexual abuse with statistical and typological information that highlighted the errors of perception and memory made by young people.[20] While Stern and his colleagues did not necessarily maintain that children's testimony was any more dangerous than that of adults, stressing instead that the sources of their errors were different, the mobilization of the psychology of testimony by professionalizing defence lawyers meant that the vast majority of expert testimony on children's credibility heard in German courtrooms before the First World War portrayed it as unreliable. It was not until the Weimar period that prosecutors began to call on psychological experts to help them establish the credibility of young accusatory witnesses, by which time the discourse of children's dangerousness as witnesses was well established in the public sphere. This was despite the fact that in the scientific literature and among those with a claim to expertise on children's credibility, including psychologists, pedagogues, psychiatrists and forensic specialists, this understanding of juvenile testimony was by no means universally accepted.

Although it is evident why defence lawyers would have had a vested interest in perpetuating this discourse, as did pedagogues, to some extent, it is less apparent why the press, particularly left-wing newspapers like the *Volksstimme*, might have felt it necessary to push this line, representing their own opinion in such matters as superior not only to that of the public, whose views it attempted to shape, but often to that of professional jurists and psychological experts. This chapter, which will examine the press coverage of several Weimar sex crimes trials involving children's accusations will argue that the press, particularly the socialist and liberal press, which saw Germany's justice system as an anachronistic and reactionary vestige of the Imperial regime, pushed this discourse as a means of protecting individual liberty, modernizing the courts through the application of science and criticizing specific judges, who the press felt interfered with important principles, like open justice.[21]

Recent work on trials of the Weimar era, including that of Benjamin Carter Hett and Henning Grunwald, has demonstrated just how prolific and influential court reporting on both political and non-political trials was in terms of judicial critique and reform.[22] Judges and prosecutors complained frequently that the media scrutiny under which they worked was disruptive, interfering with independent judicial decision-making.[23] This was not just paranoia on their part, press critique of specific judges and courtroom conditions began to be noted by the Justice Ministry from 1927 and impacted upon decisions about court personnel.[24] While this problem was experienced most intensely in political trials, it is clear that the same kinds of pressures might be experienced in sensational non-political trials, where the press focused on the shortcomings of the legal system or of court personnel.[25] Certainly, this seems to have been the case in a number of the sex crimes trials involving juvenile accusatory witnesses during the late 1920s and early 1930s.

While histories of professionalization and expertise in the sciences, including the forensic sciences, have used press reports to establish the dynamics and debates among communities of experts, such analyses can overlook what newspapers might tell us about the communication of expert knowledge beyond circles of experts. There are, naturally, a range of difficulties in trying to gauge public reception of scientific ideas by analysing newspaper texts, but we can, this chapter contends, use them to understand how the press interpreted expert knowledge and the messages they wanted to convey to the public about it.[26] As Ross Bowling has asserted in his work on the Berlin press coverage of several serial murder cases during the Weimar Republic, reporters did not simply repeat the claims of experts in criminal trials, but '…would variously bowdlerise, challenge or expound upon the expertise deployed in a sensational case.'[27] In so doing, they offered themselves up as experts in their own right and pushed a variety of political agendas, such as the retention of social norms or the need for legal reform.[28] The Weimar press' engagement with the issue of juvenile witnesses in sex crimes trials, their advocacy of psychological expertise in the courtroom and their promotion of a highly sceptical view of children's credibility is an excellent example of this.

In order to highlight the operation of the press as psychological expert in Weimar sex crimes trials, this chapter will discuss in more detail the commentary made by the *Volksstimme* about the problems of children's testimony and psychological expertise in the Polte case, pointing to the way in which the arguments put forward here built on those made by the press in several earlier trials; in particular those of Lützow and Frenzel. The growing sense of expertise on the part of the press about children's testimony and psychology in the courtroom from one case to another will become apparent through this discussion as will the positions taken on these issues by newspapers from different parts of the political spectrum. In addition, the chapter will consider the extent to which newspapers' representations of forensic psychology to their readers were accurate portrayals of the findings and state of the field, showing how the press often chose to ignore the debates and methodological differences between experts in order to sustain their own claims to expertise.

Reporting Credibility and Expertise in the Polte Trial

From the first day of the Polte trial, which was held in the town of Burg, the *Volksstimme* was eager to stress for its readers the centrality of children's testimony to the outcome of this trial and to comment on what constituted appropriate psychological expertise. The children, the newspaper emphasized, were testifying to events that only they had witnessed and that had occurred up to five years earlier. This meant that the court's decision about Polte's guilt would be dependent, almost exclusively, on an assessment of the children's veracity, memories and comprehension of events.[29] Both the prosecution and defence certainly understood that these would be the crucial questions, insisting on the presence and participation in this trial of experts in juvenile testimony. As the *Volksstimme* made clear, however, the conflict over which experts to deploy and the priority given to each became so intense on the trial's first day that the presiding judge eventually decided to do without psychological expertise entirely.[30] The cause of this conflict, as the *Volksstimme* represented it, was the prosecution's stubborn insistence on the use of Frau General Superintendent Meyer, head of Magdeburg's youth bureau, as a court-appointed expert on children's credibility. While the newspaper expressed its approval of the nomination of the *Kreisarzt* Dr Jürgens and appeared excited about the defence's invitation to the Berlin sexologist Dr Marcuse, who had recently been involved in the Frenzel trial, they poured scorn on the qualifications of Frau Meyer. In this regard, the newspaper complained,

> According to the original opinion of the court and prosecutor about it, a lay-expert pastor's wife sufficed because throughout nine years she was leader of the municipal youth bureau, Magdeburg, and earlier a teacher; a woman, who on the basis of her strong religious stance, poses a great danger for the objective assessment of the credibility of children, especially in sex crimes trials.[31]

According to the *Volksstimme*, it was only the efforts of the defence lawyer, the renowned Berlin criminal barrister Dr Frey, who had also been a key figure in the sensational 1926 Lützow trial, that had ensured the acceptance of the medical and scientific experts. The priority given to Frau Meyer by the prosecutor, however, led to such hostility from the defence and other experts, who the newspaper claimed were right to feel insulted about the priority given to a lay witness, that Dr Frey suggested that, for the remainder of the trial, the court forego the use of experts. To end the deadlock over this issue, the presiding judge and other parties agreed.

While the dismissal of the experts was not initiated by the court, the *Volksstimme*'s response to the court's decision in the Polte case to rely on its own understanding of children's credibility led to a strident critique both of the first verdict and the presumption of judges, more generally, that they could do without psychological expertise, relying instead on lay opinion. This was clearest in the newspaper's last article about the case, which argued:

> Just as a metalworker should not be allowed to presume to be able to do the work of a goldsmith, if he is not informed, so a judge or state prosecutor, as jurist, cannot make offers to decide medical-scientific questions with judicial knowledge, without being informed.[32]

Although Judge Segall, who presided over the appeal held in Magdeburg in January 1931, was praised for making use of Marcuse's expertise during the pre-trial proceedings, the newspaper argued that this case demonstrated with startling clarity why a psychological expert should be available to the court as early as the judge's initial investigation.[33]

Analysis of this engagement with children's credibility and psychological expertise in the pages of the *Volksstimme* highlights three key themes that the newspaper mobilized in order to present itself as an expert in this field. First, was the promotion of the idea, ostensibly supported by the findings of the psychology of testimony, that juvenile witnesses were innately dangerous. Second, was the question of who was qualified to act as a psychological expert; a clear preference being given to those whose disciplinary backgrounds predisposed them to viewing children and adolescents as highly suggestible and mentally labile. Third, was the problem of the reliance of judges either on their own mastery of witness psychology or on that of experts who gave children's testimony credence. While it was socialist newspapers like the *Volksstimme*, the *Danziger Volksstimme* and *Vorwärts*, which seemed most dedicated to presenting themselves as expert on forensic psychology in the late Weimar period, a survey of the coverage given to similar trials by other newspapers reveals that the themes highlighted by the *Volksstimme* were not exclusive to the Polte case or to the socialist press, having become common features of press engagement with sex crimes trials involving children's testimony by the early 1930s. By the time of Polte's appeal in 1931, it is clear that many newspapers felt equipped to use their own understanding of forensic psychology to challenge that of the courts and some expert witnesses.

From the Lützow Trial to the Frenzel Trial

The trial of Freiherr Kurt von Lützow was one of the largest, longest and most well-publicized sex crimes trials involving children to date, when it took place in 1926. Lützow was a head teacher of a school in Zossen accused of 75 counts of inappropriate behaviour with boys between the ages of ten and sixteen and the use of corporal punishment for the purposes of sexual gratification.[34] Beyond the sensation caused by a respected teacher facing charges of child abuse, the case, which used several experts in children's testimony, was significant for highlighting the potential impact of the new forensic psychology on judicial decision-making processes. This was noted, in particular, by members of the defence team, who pointed to the contest in this trial between conventional means of finding justice through reliance on witness testimony and oaths and the new psychological approach to ascertaining the truth.[35] While the newspapers that covered the case reported such statements and gave considerable space to the experts' testimony on the credibility of the key accusatory witnesses, they did not fully engage with the psychological issues arising from this trial. Liberal newspapers, such as the *Vossische Zeitung* and *Berliner Volks-Zeitung*, for instance, which were some of the leading voices in discussions of the contemporary crisis of confidence in the justice system

(*Vertrauenskrise der Justiz*), all but ignored the psychological issues in the Lützow trial, focusing instead on the enormous cost of the proceedings to taxpayers and the issue of corporal punishment in German schools.[36] The Social Democratic newspaper *Vorwärts*, however, hinted at the detrimental effects of puberty on juvenile testimony in its coverage of the Lützow trial, building on efforts, as early as 1925, to educate its readers about the problem of recognition in court and the new provisions for psychological experts in cases involving juvenile witnesses.[37] In this regard, *Vorwärts* declared that this trial, in which the witnesses' credibility was so important, would allow an exploration of '… the peculiar psychology of the pubescent and pre-pubescent …'[38] The conservative *Deutsche Allgemeine Zeitung*, also interested in the problem of children's credibility, elaborated on this idea, writing,

> The observer has clearly before their eyes, how easy it would be to lead young people into confusion, to tangle them up in contradictions and even to induce in them false statements. That is one of the core problems of this trial, which particular attention is to be dedicated to.[39]

In intimating the suggestibility of young witnesses and the adverse effects that puberty had on juvenile mental function, both newspapers rehearsed for their readers the discourse of children's dangerousness, taking tentative steps towards establishing their own expertise in witness psychology. None of the publications surveyed, however, featured critiques of the experts, despite their heated courtroom debates and the highly contentious nature of some of their reports. The psychiatrist Otto Mönkemöller (1867–1930), for instance, concluded that a number of the key witnesses were psychopaths, while the neurologist, Siegfried Placzek (1866–1946), claimed not only that young boys, in general, were very reliable witnesses, but that Lützow's main accuser, labelled psychopathic by Mönkemöller, was completely credible.[40] None of the newspapers criticized the presiding judge's use of the psychological evidence either; although this may have been a result of the defendant's eventual acquittal and press approval of this verdict, which only served to underline the idea that juvenile testimony was problematic. This first major engagement with the issues arising from forensic psychology, although lacking in depth and breadth, clearly primed the press for a more substantial analysis of children's credibility and psychological expertise in subsequent trials. This is evident in the 1928 Krantz and Hussmann trials.

In the February 1928 trial of Paul Krantz, a nineteen-year-old who stood accused of killing two of his friends, *Vorwärts* demonstrated a newfound interest in appropriate psychological expertise by discussing the controversial status of the prosecution expert Placzek, while the *Vossische Zeitung* critiqued this expert's unseemly courtroom tussles over young people's testimony with the sexologist Magnus Hirschfeld (1868–1935) in this and other trials.[41] Bolder still, in the 1928 Hussmann trial, in which the adolescent Karl Hussmann stood charged with the sexually motivated murder of his friend, Adolf Daube, the Social Democratic *Danziger Volksstimme* complained that reports on witness credibility during this trial had been prepared by a forensic physician, rather than by psychological experts, like the well-known sexologists and pedagogues employed in the Lützow and Krantz trials.[42] In labelling the *Gerichtsarzt* an amateur, portraying sexologists and pedagogues as the real experts in the field and criticizing the court for not arranging more appropriate expertise, the *Danziger Volksstimme* demonstrated the press' growing confidence in psychological matters; a confidence that would reach its apotheosis in the 1930 Frenzel trial.

Unlike the psychological questions raised by the Lützow trial, which had attracted attention primarily from the socialist and conservative press, those provoked by the Frenzel trial elicited intense interest from newspapers across the political spectrum. Arthur Frenzel, a former mayor and civil servant, stood accused of sexually abusing his teenaged daughters Hilde and Gertrud; the case complicated by the fact Hilde subsequently retracted her claims. As the *Vossische Zeitung* noted, this meant that the entire case hung on the question,

> Did Hildegard tell the truth when she accused or when she retracted? ...If the court should believe the retraction, how the girl came to make the false accusation must be explained. If Hildegard is now telling the truth, Gertrud must be lying and always have lied. Then further, must be clarified, how Gertrud came to raise the false accusation and why she, in contrast to her sister, persisted with it.[43]

Juvenile credibility, specifically that of the two girls, was thus understood by all the newspapers that covered the trial as central to the court's decision as was the lay and professional judges' comprehension of the findings of the psychology of testimony, which the press tended to interpret as saying that children's testimony was *a priori* unreliable. The guilty verdict in the first trial, in spite of the testimony of the sexologist Hirschfeld that young girls often became mentally unbalanced during puberty and that Gertrud was psychopathic, therefore led to strong critiques of the judges, who were accused of being incapable of understanding the complex psychological evidence. The *Danziger Volksstimme* wrote in this regard,

> The general impression is that there has been a misjudgement of the worst kind here. It should not be said that the judges—a small-minded, old fashioned-thinking, old man as presiding judge, an always archly-smiling assessor and two manufacturers—did not want to understand the material. They could not understand the highly complicated case. [44]

Similarly, the *Vossische Zeitung*, concluded, '…not from gross negligence and wilfully, but from inadequate knowledge of sexual-psychological interactions, a faulty judgement has occurred.'[45]

But, while the presiding judge in the first trial was accused of ignorance of forensic psychology, the presiding judge in the appeal, Albert Hellwig (1880–1950), who was both a strong advocate of psychological expertise in the courtroom and the author of a practical guide to its use, was portrayed as a dilettante, too confident in his own knowledge and dictatorial in his exclusion of the press from the courtroom; a decision that newspapers of all political persuasions complained contravened the principle of open justice. Beyond anger at the exclusion of reporters from the trial, complaints about Hellwig were largely a response to his siding with the experts, Siegfried Placzek and Paul Plaut (1894–1960), who declared Gertrud a reliable witness. Commenting on this in the wake of the second guilty verdict, the *Danziger Volksstimme* summed up the attitude of both the socialist and liberal press, writing,

> The tremendous increase of incest trials in Germany is not only a striking symptom of a psychological deficiency of the courts and total lack of appre-

ciation of the juvenile psychology of testimony… The German courts are today totally incapable of trying an incest trial unobjectionably, because again and again they are completely taken in by spiteful youths and of the expert witnesses, [they] intentionally only listen to those, ideally, whose orientation is reactionary.[46]

The reactionary position alluded to here, represented in the Frenzel trial by Placzek and Plaut, was the belief that children's testimony could be reliable and should be assessed on a case by case basis. In the view espoused by the socialist and liberal newspapers, these experts and the judges who believed them naively abetted children in their delusions and helped facilitate miscarriages of justice that ruined the lives of respectable men. For the majority of the press, it was only those experts, like Hirschfeld, Marcuse and Mönkemöller, having trained in fields such as sexology and juvenile psychiatry, which tended to view adolescence as a labile period that adversely impacted on mental health and veracity, who accurately represented the findings of witness psychology. The refusal of the courts to properly appreciate this, was, in the eyes of the socialist and liberal press, indicative of a legal system that was outmoded in its understanding of science and often illiberal and dictatorial in its mediation of justice.

In contrast, the conservative *Deutsche Allgemeine Zeitung* was less ready to read the outcome of the trial as indicative of a legal system ill-equipped to deal with complex psychological evidence. Not only did this newspaper provide features highlighting the complexity of making decisions about children's credibility in sex crimes trials, but praised the court's competency in this area, calling Hellwig one of the country's best criminalists and one of the few psychologically educated jurists.[47] The newspaper suggested, that it was simply the defendant's misfortune, in this case, to be faced with a presiding judge, who was capable of using the experts' reports to form his own opinion about the psychological evidence.[48] Nonetheless, the *Deutsche Allgemeine Zeitung*, although sympathetic to the reasons that Hellwig had excluded the press from this trial, suggested there had been alternatives to such a blanket ban, arguing also that the uncertainty caused by the conflicting expert and witness testimony was sufficient to necessitate the defendant's acquittal.[49] Less wedded to the idea that German courts were antiquated and corrupt institutions that demanded reform than their socialist and liberal competitors, the conservative press provided a slightly different perspective on the meaning of trials in which the questions of children's credibility and psychological expertise were prominent.

While newspapers of all persuasions appeared to agree that the courts must better incorporate psychological expertise and maintain the openness and transparency of justice, they seem to have diverged on the issue of appropriate expertise and judges' ability to understand it. The socialist and liberal press tried hard to persuade their readers that those experts convinced of the labile nature of young people's minds and thus the unreliability of their testimony, most accurately represented the consensus among those who practised forensic psychology. The conservative press, however, suggested that decisions about credibility were more complex and must involve not only a consideration of typological information about the kind of witness being assessed, but a thoroughgoing evaluation of the individual witness' credibility. This divergence raises the question of which group most accurately reflected the state of the field and why press expertise on the meaning and use of forensic psychology may have differed from that promoted by practitioners.

An Accurate Portrayal of Forensic Psychology?

By the time of the Frenzel and Polte trials, much of the Weimar press was espousing its own expertise on forensic psychology, loudly criticizing those experts and judges, who offered opinions favourable to children's testimony. Their insistence, however, that the discipline had established the unreliability of young witnesses and their portrayal of sexologists and pedagogues as the leading authorities in the field, was problematic. As an area of expertise over which a range of disciplines, including psychology, pedagogy, psychiatry, forensic medicine and sexology, competed, consensus was difficult to establish and the nuances of expert debates and courtroom practice were often hard to ascertain. The variety of methodologies used by those who appeared in court as experts on children's credibility, for instance, helps highlight the fact that practitioners were not agreed either on whether children were worse witnesses than adults or the best means of establishing credibility.

Those pedagogues and sexologists praised by the socialist and liberal press for their expertise, relied primarily on typological information, which tended to suggest *a priori* that children's testimony was problematic. Derived from experiments conducted with groups of young people in the first decade of the twentieth century, these typological assessments were supplemented by observations of witness behaviour and performance during trials. Rarely did pedagogues and sexologists conduct in depth and prolonged assessments of individual witnesses, as did those trained in psychiatry and forensic medicine; these experts maintaining that witness typologies must take a back seat to personal observation. Many of the leading voices in forensic psychology during the Weimar period, figures like William Stern, Albert Moll (1862–1939) and Paul Plaut, were highly critical of those expert witnesses, who neglected such individual assessment. Although such methodological differences were not appreciated by the press, they were significant in the attempts of practitioners to establish authority within the field. During the Polte trial, for instance, the *Volksstimme* sang the praises of the sexologist Marcuse, impressed by his lengthy expert report on the typological grounds for dismissing the testimony of at least two of the young female witnesses.[50] In contrast, this same report received a scathing review from Plaut in the discipline's leading journal, *Zeitschrift für Angewandte Psychologie.* Plaut asked whether it should be permissible to decide on a witness' credibility on typological grounds without consideration of that witness' individuality.[51] In addition, he complained that while Marcuse had reached his conclusions about the witnesses on what was known generally about children's mentality, lies and fantasies, he had decided on the defendant's innocence on individual grounds, but without actually examining him.[52] Plaut ended his critique by stressing that given that psychological expertise had only recently been accepted in the courts, reports such as Marcuse's must be openly condemned.[53]

Clearly, lack of consensus around methodology created tensions in the field, but so did differing ideas about the scope of the expert role. Some experts believed their duty was to establish not only whether a witness was credible in general, but whether they were reliable in the case at hand. Others, however, determined not to trespass on judges' prerogative to decide credibility, provided an opinion solely on whether the young witnesses they examined were reliable in general.[54] In the Frenzel trial, for instance, Placzek and Plaut took this latter approach, arguing that in general Gertrud was credible, but not venturing an opinion on whether her accusations against her father were true.[55] Whether the press appreciated this distinction or not, their reports portrayed such experts as uncritically convinced, in defiance of all evidence to the contrary, that children's testimony was reliable.

For the socialist and liberal press, whose principal concern in claiming expertise on forensic psychology appears to have been protecting individual liberty and preventing miscarriages of justice, the nuances and debates within the discipline were best ignored, as these could not be instrumentalized, in the way that the discourse of children's dangerousness could, to push for legal reform. The conservative press, with its acknowledgement of the complexity of the field, came closest to portraying the actual state of forensic psychology in the late 1920s and early 1930s, but this did little to override the impact of the more strident critiques of the socialist and liberal press, which had both positive and negative effects on the discipline. The insistence of the press that Germany's courts must embrace the findings of psychology and make use of experts in cases involving children's testimony was a boon for this emerging field, further embedding them in the legal process. In promoting epistemological stances and methodological approaches criticized by the field's leading practitioners, however, press expertise on forensic psychology ultimately slowed the progress of the discipline towards both consensus and professionalization.

Conclusion

By the early 1930s, Germany's press, once hesitant to comment on such issues, was presenting itself as an expert voice in debates over psychological expertise and the value of children's testimony. Promoting a view of juvenile credibility, which had first been moulded by professionalizing defence lawyers, socialist and liberal newspapers used the popular discourse of children's dangerousness, in order to critique a legal system that they contended still laboured under the illiberal imperial yoke. While newspapers like the *Volksstimme* stated that child abusers should be punished to the full extent of the law, they were simultaneously ill-disposed to believing eye witness and even physical evidence of such crimes, arguing that it was better that the guilty go free than even one innocent man go to prison. What concerned such newspapers, then, were questions of individual liberty and judicial error, rather than child abuse, which they seem to have found difficult to believe happened among the middle and upper classes. Critiques of courtroom procedure and personnel in cases involving children's testimony such as the Lützow, Frenzel and Polte trials were used by the press, as this chapter has shown, to push for legal reform, which was intended to ensure greater use of scientific expertise in the courts and better control of dictatorial and illiberal judges.

Adding yet another voice to a field riven by conflict over epistemological and methodological issues, it is clear that the expertise espoused by the Weimar press in sex crimes trials impacted on public discourse about forensic psychology and affected the ability of its practitioners to establish their own authority in the field. The story of the Weimar press as expert in sex crimes trials thus provides a compelling example of just how important the expertise of the press, an institution outside the disciplinary communities that actually practise forensic science, can be in the acceptance and public understanding of such science; sometimes to the detriment of the professional ambitions of its practitioners.

Notes

1. 'Betrachtungen über einen Sittlichkeitsprozess. Kinderaussagen und ihre Glaubwürdigkeit—Wissenschaft und Laientum', *Volksstimme*, 12 November 1930, p. 11.
2. This point was reiterated in nearly all of the newspaper's reports on this case, including the following: 'Sittliche Verfehlungen eines Lehrers in Güsen?' *Volksstimme*, 9 November 1930, p. 4; 'Güsener Sittlichkeitsprozess in zweiter Instanz', *Volksstimme*, 29 January 1931, p. 10; 'Freispruch im Güsener Sittlichkeitsprozess', *Volksstimme*, 1 February 1931, p. 11; 'Nach dem Güsener Sittlichkeitsprozess', *Volksstimme*, 7 March 1931, p. 9.

3. 'Betrachtungen', p. 11.

4. 'Betrachtungen', p. 11.

5. 'Der Güsener Lehrer verurteilt', *Volksstimme*, 11 November 1930, p. 13.

6. 'Güsener Sittlichkeitsprozess', p. 10; 'Freispruch', p. 11.

7. M. Marcuse, 'Über die Glaubwürdigkeit von sexueller Beschuldigungen durch Kinder und Jugendliche. Zwei Gutachten', *Zeitschrift für Sexualwissenschaft und Sexualpolitik*, 1931, 17(8): 463–486.

8. 'Freispruch', p. 11; 'Nach dem Güsener Sittlichkeitsprozess', p. 9.

9. For a case study of this trial, see H. Wolffram, *Forensic Psychology in Germany: Witnessing Crime, 1880 to 1939*, New York: Palgrave Macmillan, 2018.

10. 'Nach dem Güsener Sittlichkeitsprozess', p. 9.

11. B. Kerchner, 'Unbescholtene Bürger' und 'gefährliche Mädchen' um die Jahrhundertwende. Was der Fall Sternberg für die aktuelle Debatte zum sexuellen Mißbrauch an Kindern bedeutet', *Historische Anthropologie: Kultur–Gesellschaft–Alltag*, 1998, 6(1): 1–32, pp. 18–19.

12. 'Betrachtungen', p. 11.

13. This was particularly evident in cases like that of Langanki, an incest case that occurred in a working-class neighbourhood of Berlin, where the press stressed the role of the 'milieu.' 'Blutschande Prozess wieder augenommen', *Volksstimme*, 3 November 1929, p. 11; 'Ist der Schuhmacher Schuldig?', *Vorwärts*, 2 November 1929, p. 3; 'Langanke-Milieu' *Vorwärts*, 4 November 1929, p. 3; 'Die entscheidende Frage', *Vossische Zeitung*, 2 November 1929, p. 6.

14. B. Kerchner, "Kinderlügen'? Zur Kulturgeschichte des sexuellem Missbrauchs', in U. Finger-Trescher and H. Krebs (eds.), *Mißhandlung, Vernachlässigung und sexuelle Gewält in Erzeihungsverhältnissen*, Gießen: Psychosozial, 2000, pp. 15–41; G. Jeske, *Die gerichtliche und soziale Medizin in Berlin von 1930 bis 1954 unter Victor Müller-Heß*, Unpublished PhD thesis, Free University Berlin, 2008, pp. 124–125.

15. M. Steller, 'Kinderschutz durch forensische Aussagepsychologie—von William Stern zu Udo Undeutsch', *Monatsschrift für Kriminologie und Strafrechtsreform*, 1997, 80(5): 274–282, p. 276.

16. A. Mülberger, 'Karle Marbe und die Anwendung der Psychologie im Rechtswesen vor dem ersten Weltkrieg', in M. Schmoeckel (ed.), *Psychologie als Argument in der juristischen Literatur des Kaiserreichs*, Baden-Baden: Nomos, 2009, 133–152, p. 136.

17. For an early example of a pedagogue's work in this field as well as an admission that teachers were often the target of children's accusations, see

O.H. Michel, *Die Zeugnisfähigkeit der Kinder vor Gericht: Ein Beitrag zur Aussagepsychologie*, Langensalza: Hermann Beyer & Söhne, 1907, p. v.

18. Wolffram, *Forensic Psychology in Germany*.
19. B. Hett, 'The 'Captain of Kopenick' and the transformation of German criminal justice, 1891–1914', *Central European History*, 2003, 36(1): 1–43, pp. 5, 10–11.
20. R. Heinemann, *Das Kind als Person: William Stern als Wegbereiter der Kinder- und Jugendforschung 1900 bis 1933*, Bad Helbrunn: Verlag Julius Klinkhardt, 2016, p. 311.
21. B. Hett, *Crossing Hitler: The Man Who put the Nazis on the Witness Stand*, London: Pier 9, 2009, pp. 123–125; H. Grunwald, *Courtroom to Revolutionary Stage: Performance and Ideology in Weimar Political Trials*, Oxford: Oxford University Press, 2012, pp. 180–182; D. Siemens, "Vom Leben getötet'. Die Gerichtsreportage in der liberal-demokratischen Presse im Berlin der 1920er Jahre', in W. Hardtwig (ed.), *Ordnungen in der Krise: Zur politischen Kulturgeschichte Deutschlands 1900–1933*, Munich: R. Oldenbourg Verlag, 2007, pp. 327–356.
22. Hett, *Crossing Hitler*, pp. 123–125; Grunwald, *Courtroom*, pp. 180–182.
23. Hett, *Crossing Hitler*, p. 124; Grunwald, *Courtroom*, p. 181.
24. Hett, *Crossing Hitler*, p. 124.
25. On press engagement in crime reporting during the Weimar years, see R.F. Bowling, *Expertise and Sensational Reportage in Weimar Berlin*, Unpublished PhD thesis, University of Michigan, 2012, p. 38; Siemens, 'Vom Leben getötet', pp. 327–356.
26. Bowling, *Expertise and Sensational Reportage*, p. 38.
27. Ibid.
28. Ibid., pp. 5, 21, 26.
29. 'Sittliche Verfehlungen', p. 4.
30. Ibid.
31. Ibid.
32. 'Nach dem Güsener Sittlichkeitsprozess', p. 9.
33. Ibid.
34. For a book-length exploration of this trial, see P. Dudek, *'Liebevolle Züchtigung': Ein Mißbrauch der Autorität im Namen der Reformpädagogik*, Bad Heilbrunn: Nomos, 2012.
35. 'Der Verteidiger v. Lützow', *Deutsche Allgemeine Zeitung*, 5 June 1926, p. 3.

36. Siemens, 'Vom Leben getötet', pp. 330–331; 'Prozeß von Lützow', *Vossische Zeitung*, 26 February 1926, p. 5; 'Gegen die Prügelpädagogen', *Vossische Zeitung*, 25 February 1926, p. 7; 'Lützows Trommelfeuer', *Vossische Zeitung*, 2 March 1926, p. 5.

37. 'Das Wiederkennen vor Gericht: Ein Problem der Aussagepsychologie', *Vorwärts*, 12 September 1925, p. 6; 'Vernehmung Jugendlicher in Strafsachen', *Vorwärts*, 2 March 1927, p. 3.

38. 'Die Prügelstrafe', *Vorwärts*, 20 February 1926, p. 6.

39. 'Die Zeugen im Prozeß Lützow', *Deutsche Allgemeine Zeitung*, 26 February 1926, p. 3.

40. 'Seltsame Dinge im Lützow-Prozeß', *Danziger Volksstimme*, 27 May 1926, p. 5; 'Der Lützow-Prozeß: Drei weitere Sachverständigegutachten', *Vorwärts*, 19 May 1926, p. 6; 'Der Lützow-Prozeß: Die letzten Gutachten der Sachverständigen', *Vorwärts*, 27 May 1926, p. 6; 'Die Sachverständigen im Lützow-Prozeß', *Deutsche Allgemeine Zeitung*, 19 May 1926, p. 3; 'Sachverständige gegen Lützow', *Deutsche Allgemeine Zeitung*, 27 May 1926, p. 3; 'Der Prozeß Lützow', *Deutsche Allgemeine Zeitung*, 30 May 1926, p. 3.

41. On the Krantz trial, see H. Sack, *Moderne Jugend vor Gericht: Sensationsprozesse, 'Sexualtragödien' und die Krise der Jugend in der Weimarer Republik*, Bielefeld: Transcript Verlag, 2016; 'Neue Beweisanträge im Krantz-Prozess', *Vorwärts*, 11 February 1928; 'Die Tragödie der Jugendlichen', *Vossische Zeitung*, 11 February 1928, pp. 5–6; 'Krise im Krantz-Prozeß', *Vossishe Zeitung*, 11 February 1928, p. 4.

42. For more detail of this case, see, E. Bischoff and D. Siemens, 'Class, youth, and sexuality in the construction of the *Lustmörder*: The 1928 murder trial of Karl Hussmann', in R.F. Wetzell (ed.), *Crime and Criminal Justice in Modern Germany*, New York and Oxford: Berghahn, 2014, 207–225; 'Was wird der Staatsanwalt tun?' *Danziger Volksstimme*, 27 October 1928, p. 5.

43. 'Die Töchter und ihr Vater', *Vossische Zeitung*, 23 May 1930, p. 5.

44. 'Frenzel verurteilt!' *Vorwärts*, 29 May 1930, p. 6.

45. 'Zuchthaus-Urteil gegen Frenzel', *Vossische Zeitung*, 29 May 1930, p. 2.

46. 'Revision im Frenzel-Prozeß', *Danziger Volksstimme*, 3 December 1930, p. 5.

47. H. Pollnow, 'Die Ausagen von Kindern und Jugendlichen', *Deutsche Allgemeine Zeitung*, 23 November 1930, p. 6.

48. 'Gertrud Frenzels Aussagen für glaubwürdig erachtet', *Deutsche Allgemeine Zeitung*, 2 December 1930, p. 3.

49. 'Gertrud Frenzels Aussagen', p. 3.
50. 'Betrachtungen', p. 11; 'Nach dem Güsener Sittlichkeitsprozess', p. 9.
51. P. Plaut 'Beiträge zur forensischen Psychologie, II', *Zeitschrift für angewandte Psychologie*, 1931, 39: 535–550, pp. 544–545.
52. Ibid., p. 545.
53. Ibid., p. 546.
54. S. Placzek, 'Gutachten', *Zeitschrift für Kinderforschung*, 1932, 39: 387–417, pp. 404–405.
55. P. Plaut, 'Gutachten', *Zeitschrift für Kinderforschung*, 1932, 39: 418–439, p. 418; Placzek, 'Gutachten', pp. 391–392, 404.

Newspapers

Berliner Volks-Zeitung
Danziger Volksstimme
Deutsche Allgemeine Zeitung
Volksstimme
Vorwärts
Vossische Zeitung

Bibliography

Bischoff, E. and Siemens, D., 'Class, youth, and sexuality in the construction of the *Lüstmörder*: The 1928 Murder Trial of Karl Hussmann', in R.F. Wetzell (ed.), *Crime and Criminal Justice in Modern Germany*, New York and Oxford: Berghahn, 2014, 207–225.
Bowling, R.F., *Expertise and Sensational Reportage in Weimar Berlin*, Unpublished PhD thesis, University of Michigan, 2012.
Dudek, P., *Liebevolle Züchtigung: ein Mißbrauch der Autorität im Namen der Reformpädagogik*, Bad Heilbrunn: Klinkhardt, 2012.
Grunwald, H., *Courtroom to Revolutionary Stage: Performance and Ideology in Weimar Political Trials*, Oxford: Oxford University Press, 2012.
Heinemann, R., *Das Kind als Person: William Stern als Wegbereiter der Kinder- und Jugendforschung von 1900 bis 1933*, Kempten: Julius Klinkhardt, 2016.
Hett, B., 'The 'Captain of Kopenick' and the transformation of German criminal justice, 1891–1914', *Central European History*, 2003, 36(1): 1–43.

Hett, B., *Crossing Hitler: The Man who put the Nazis on the Witness Stand*, London: Pier 9, 2009.

Jeske, G., *Die gerichtliche und soziale Medizin in Berlin von 1930 bis 1954 unter Müller-Heß*, Unpublished PhD thesis, Free University of Berlin, 2008.

Kerchner, B., 'Kinderlügen? Zur Kulturgeschicte des sexuellen Mißbrauchs', in U. Finger-Trescher and H. Krebs (eds.), *Misshandlung, Vernachlässigung und sexuelle Gewalt in Erziehungsverhältnissen*, Giessen: Psychosozial, 2000, 15–41.

Kerchner, B., 'Unbescholtene Bürger' und 'gefährliche Mädchen' um die Jahrhundertwende. Was der Fall Sternberg für die aktuelle Debatte zum sexuellen Mißbrauch an Kindern bedeutet', *Historische Anthropologie: Kultur–Gesellschaft–Alltag*, 1998, 6(1): 1–32.

Marcuse, M., 'Über die Glaubwürdigkeit von sexueller Beschuldigungen durch Kinder und Jugendliche. Zwei Gutachten', *Zeitschrift für Sexualwissenschaft und Sexualpolitik*, 1931, 17(8): 463–486.

Michel, O.H., *Die Zeugnisfähigkeit der Kinder vor Gericht: Ein Beitrag zur Aussagepsychologie*, Langensalza: Hermann Beyer & Söhne, 1907.

Mülberger, A., 'Karl Marbe und die Anwendung der Psychologie im Rechtswesen vor dem ersten Weltkrieg', in M. Schmoeckel (ed.), *Psychologie als Argument in der juristischen Literatur des Kaiserreichs*, Baden-Baden: Nomos, 2009, 133–152.

Placzek, S., 'Gutachten', *Zeitschrift für Kinderforschung*, 1932, 39: 387–417.

Plaut, P., 'Beiträge zur forensischen Psychologie, II', *Zeitschrift für angewandte Psychologie*, 1931, 39: 535–550.

Plaut, P., 'Gutachten', *Zeitschrift für Kinderforschung*, 1932, 39: 418–439.

Sack, H., *Moderne Jugend vor Gericht: Sensationsprozesse, 'Sexualtragödien' und die Krise der Jugend in der Weimarer Republik*, Bielefeld: Transkript, 2016.

Siemens, D., "Vom Leben getötet'. Die Gerichtsreportage in der liberal-demokratischen Presse im Berlin der 1920er Jahre', in W. Hardtwig (ed.), *Ordnungen in der Krise: Zur politischen Kulturgeschichte Deutschlands 1900–1933*, Munich: Oldenbourg Verlag, 2007, 327–356.

Steller, M., 'Kinderschutz durch forensische Aussagepsychologie—von William Stern zu Udo Undeutsch', *Monatsschrift für Kriminologie und Strafrechtsreform*, 1997, 80(5): 274–282.

Wolffram, H., *Forensic Psychology in Germany: Witnessing Crime, 1880 to 1939*, New York: Palgrave Macmillan, 2018.

12

Murder Cases, Trunks and the Entanglement of Ethics: The Preservation and Display of Scenes of Crime Material

Angela Sutton-Vane

Introduction

The aim of this chapter is to examine contemporary evidential residue from historic murder cases and to pose that such material survives because it is protean: when a domestic utensil (a trunk, a suitcase or a chef's knife) is drawn into a murder it changes meaning; when it is then retained indefinitely as an artefact or *objet curieux* it creates moral and legal dilemmas and demands a different level of attention. Research will pivot around four historic murders which occurred between 1924 and 1934 in the South East of England and which were all connected by one object: the bodies of the victims were stored in trunks with three of the murders dubbed by the press 'trunk murders.' Referring to material culture[1] and, in particular, to the work of Janet Hoskins around object biographies[2] one trunk has been identified as an exemplar and its life cycle will be traced as it moves through entanglements of social ties, space, time and

A. Sutton-Vane (✉)
Open University, Milton Keynes, UK

© The Author(s) 2020
A. Adam (ed.), *Crime and the Construction of Forensic Objectivity from 1850*, Palgrave Histories of Policing, Punishment and Justice,
https://doi.org/10.1007/978-3-030-28837-2_12

meaning. The chapter will conclude by asking how the unplanned survival of the trunk as a kind of accidental tourist presents contemporary ethical challenges.

An overwhelming quantity of material is available about the four trunk murders, but in order to provide some context a brief overview of each case has been given below. The first of the four victims was Emily Beilby Kaye who was murdered on either 14 or 15 April 1924 by her lover, Patrick Herbert Mahon, at a holiday bungalow known as 'The Officer's House' on 'The Crumbles' in Eastbourne. The term 'lover' is used figuratively because Mahon was a married man, a serial womanizer with a history of violence and extorting money from women. Having killed Kaye he dismembered her body, storing parts in her trunk at the bungalow and left the murder weapon along with blood-soaked clothing in a Gladstone bag at Waterloo train station's left-luggage office. The second victim was Minnie Alice Bonati who was murdered on 4 May 1927 by John Robinson in his second floor office at 86 Rochester Row, London. He also dismembered her body leaving it in a trunk at Charing Cross station's left-luggage office. It is difficult to form a narrative around the third victim or the first 'Brighton trunk murder': the remains of a woman were found in a trunk at Brighton train station's left-luggage office on 17 June 1934 and in a suitcase at Kings Cross station on the following day. Despite an intensive investigation to identify the woman and establish a motive the case remains unsolved. It was, however, during the search for the missing woman that the body of Violet Saunders was discovered not far from the station at 52 Kemp Street. Violet, Violette Saunders or Kaye was the fourth victim and was believed to have been murdered by her partner and pimp, Cecil Lois England (also known as Toni Mancini or Jack Notyre) in Brighton on 10 May 1934.[3] England stowed her body in a large trunk in his rented room and this became known as the second 'Brighton trunk murder.'

In their book *Murder and the Making of English CSI* Ian Burney and Neil Pemberton describe murder investigations as 'flash moments casting bright light on discrete moments'[4] but they also pose that the over-riding narrative of crime scene investigation is not a linear story but 'networks of fields and labs, regimes of expertise and objectivity, incommunicable knowledge, matter out of place, boundary objects and spatial production.'⁵ Although these murders happened across different planes they nevertheless appropriate significant aspects from each other and, although not serial murders, they have been clumped together retrospectively and culturally as a serial. Drawing together these complex, interlinking relationships around the criminal investigations, geographies of transient spaces, the upheaval of the interwar period, around gender, poverty, people and physical evidence will illuminate how material culture can be used to understand firstly why the trunk survived and secondly what it represents.

All four murders were gender specific and featured the brutalization of women by men. Saunders and Kaye were both murdered by their partners England and Mahon respectively; Mahon and Robinson were to use the defense of accidental killing which suggested that it was somehow a 'miscalibration of domestic violence.'⁶ As if the hearth, the heart of the English home, became implicated in these acts both presented a surprisingly similar story of an argument turning into a struggle with the victim falling backward and hitting her head against the most innocuous of furnishings, a fireplace or fender (for Robinson) or a coal scuttle by the fireplace (for Mahon). In the privacy of an isolated holiday cottage, a second floor office and an unknown location Robinson, Mahon and the unidentified murderer carried out acts of 'defensive mutilations' in that the motive was to assist in hiding or moving the body, getting rid of evidence or making identification of the victim more difficult.⁷ They meticulously dissected or destroyed the corpses with the apparent conviction that this was a normative state; a state reflected by the mass murderer John Christie: 'I left her there in the bedroom. After that, I believe I had a cup of tea and went to bed.'⁸ These were not acts committed in blind panic as Mahon and Robinson wished their audiences to believe; Kaye's uterus (which would have held her unborn child) and her head and neck (which would have shown the cause of death) were never found; nor were the head and hands of the unknown woman. England's method was different; he simply concealed Saunders' body in a trunk within the domestic setting of his Brighton bedsit where it sat for over two months, covered in a cloth and used as a spare seat for guests; the noxious smell and leaking fluids he somehow explained away.

Transience, Left-Luggage and Trunks

The four murders all occurred during the twenty-year interwar period of 1918 to 1939; in fact more precisely during the ten years of the second half of this period. It was an era defined at the start by the slow recovery from the Great War and the Spanish flu pandemic which was believed to have killed around 228,000 British citizens and, toward the end, by the Great Depression of the 1930s when output of heavy industry fell by a third and registered unemployed reached three and a half million. Demobilized and frequently traumatized or disabled men were returning to civilian life looking for work, welfare or housing and certainly Robinson had been in the Territorial Army posted to Egypt. In her work *British Boarding Houses in Interwar Women's Literature* Terri Mulholland writes that, for women in particular, it was a period 'defined by its contradictions': increasing independence and greater opportunities outside the home (for some) contrasted with a dominant ideology which maintained that 'a woman's place was firmly within the familial structure.'[9] During the war there had been ample work for single women but when the troops were demobilized in 1918 they found that they were expected to step back and approximately 750,000 were made redundant; for those who were able to remain in work many commercial companies still required them to resign if they wished to marry.[10] Three of the four women killed were unmarried and in their late thirties or early forties and, again, putting this into context this would not have been considered unusual given that over 700,000 British men had lost their lives.

Transience was a significant theme of the period and, it seemed, a time of missing women or a time when it became apparent that records for this phenomenon had not been collated. During the search for Bonati the Metropolitan Police were clearly surprised by the number of women who had been reported to them as missing[11] and, by January 1935, the joint investigations of the first 'Brighton Trunk murder' between the Metropolitan Police and East Sussex Constabulary revealed a list of over 2000 missing women, although many were subsequently traced.[12] Kaye was approximately three months' pregnant when she was murdered, the unknown woman around five months' pregnant and one of the unsubstantiated causes of her death was that it was as a result of a failed backstreet abortion. The intensive month-long combing of left-luggage offices during the first 'Brighton trunk murder' investigation revealed the potential extent to which trunks and left-luggage offices were being used as places for the disposal of child corpses: on 20 June 1934 the body of a female baby was found at Brighton station left-luggage wrapped in newspaper, placed face down in a 'wicker fish-basket' and concealed in an old leather bag[13] and on 4 July the badly decomposed body of a baby girl aged about six or seven months was discovered in a trunk at Piccadilly Circus.[14]

All four women could be described as being in transient and vulnerable states, although on first impressions Kaye appeared to be in a position of stability as a middle-class and independent woman from a respected Mancunian family. The premature deaths of her parents and some of her siblings had, however, required her to work from a young age and at thirty-eight she moved to London to seek work. Here, as a single woman she was obliged to stay in private hotels or hostels, a subject itself which was sparking fierce debate in that such accommodation was considered unsuitable for women 'encouraging transience and discouraging domesticity.'[15] Kaye's smart travelling trunk, monogrammed with her initials, could be viewed as a representation of her transience and some of the contents used as exhibits in court were later published in newspapers: 'One by one, pretty-coloured hats, coats and skirts, a tortoiseshell comb, even a string of beads, were held up by Superintendent Sinclair to be recognized. The roughly-folded clothes and the little trinkets dear to the woman's heart, seem to tell of Miss Kaye's tragedy more poignantly than legal documents or the spoken word.'[16] As a kind of *ecphrastic* list these very personal things have been frozen very publicly in time.

What is evident through newspaper reports of Robinson's trial at the Old Bailey is the emergence of a sub-narrative for Minnie Bonati as a troubled and near-destitute woman whose marriage had failed and who struggled with alcoholism and mental health issues. She was in and out of work as a live-in or daily cook at a time just before the start of the Great Depression when an increasing number of women were migrating to London in search of employment in domestic service. Despite advances in women's suffrage and the introduction of National Insurance in 1911 many sectors, including servants, were initially excluded and for these workers, in times of hardship, the old Poor Law system[17] still remained their main source of welfare. Although none of the contemporary newspapers referred to it, Bonati was almost certainly supplementing her wages with prostitution[18] and poverty along with lack of access to welfare was clearly evident on the day of her murder on 4 May 1927 when 'dead broke'[19] she visited the offices of Mr. James Shand, the Chelsea Relieving Officer.[20]

In opening the defence at the trial of Cecil Lois England for the murder of Violette Saunders in 1934 Norman Birkett made no attempt to normalize their lives describing them as: 'a class of men and women belonging to an underworld that makes the mind reel.'[21] Saunders, then known as Kaye, had been a music hall dancer since her teens but by the time she met England in London in 1933 she was a convicted prostitute. Agreeing to be his 'breadwinner' they had moved to Brighton where they lived in a string of shabby bedsits and small flats. On the day of her murder Saunders, fuelled by drugs and alcohol, had publicly argued with England at the Skylark Café where he worked as a waiter. Her work was drying up, she was angered by his apparent grooming of a young waitress and she was certainly vulnerable and isolated; not only was England her pimp, but her live-in partner and possibly her drug supplier.[22]

The very fact that the last of the four victims, the unidentified woman, has never been named nor her killer prosecuted would suggest that her absent state was not noted because it was normal.

Transience is a state of being but it also has a clearly defined geography and culture around places of arrival and departure and railway stations have come to epitomize in-between or non-spaces: 'a necessary connective towards a somewhere else—an experience better measured in (waiting) time than in space.'[23] Both Robinson and the unknown murderer deposited trunks containing the dismembered remains of their victims at mainline train station's left-luggage offices, along with Mahon who deposited the murder weapon in a Gladstone bag at Waterloo.

There may be no clear psychological motive as to why they did this, but there were potentially a number of pragmatic reasons for doing so. Anonymity would have been key: at the time of the murders depositors of luggage seemed to have been issued with a simple, numbered and time-stamped ticket with a tear-off section which was attached to the suitcase; the concept of checking luggage was only introduced after the

IRA bombing campaigns of 1939.[24] During the interwar period car own-
ership, which could have discretely transported a body anywhere (and
was used by Dr Buck Ruxton in 1935) was still way beyond the average
person's reach and was compounded, certainly for Robinson in his second floor office on the busy Rochester Row, by the lack of access to a
private garden or outbuildings (afforded to John Christie at 10 Rillington
Place); the opportunities for disposing of a body were clearly limited.
Robinson would have banked on the proximity of a city-centre train station and the normality it afforded of transporting a heavy trunk to it by
taxi and the use of porters to assist in moving it to the left-luggage office.

Burney and Pemberton write that culturally crime scene investigations
are regarded as the opening act of a multistage drama, one that 'proceeds in
an ordered fashion, first to forensic laboratories, in which the crime scene
objects are analyzed, and ultimately to the court-room where the evidentiary status is decided.'[25] And yet the things which become entangled in
that 'flash moment' were present well before the act of murder and continued to be present after the courtroom and were simply, briefly, drawn into
a parallel narrative. Luggage has been described as 'the physical embodiment of travel and dislocation'[26] but trunks especially have acquired an
additional cultural patina of antiquity in addition to a place in the history
of travel. Often called 'steamer trunks' and distinguished by their flat or
slightly curved tops, these trunks were built for longer journeys mostly by
sea, longer absences and for an era when porters and servants were plentiful. The late nineteenth century, however, marked a pivotal point in transportation with the beginning of mass tourism and of travel for travel's sake
and by the 1920s the new tourists wanted suitcases. It was, perhaps, no
coincidence that it was around this time that the trunk entered the murder
narrative. Although they were becoming increasingly obsolete items gathering dust in attics or sold on to secondhand luggage dealers, they were still
implanted in the psyche of the public as a relatively inconspicuous item of
travel. And yet, with their large dimensions (generally about 14 inches tall
to accommodate steamship luggage regulations) and strength (to with-
stand the battering of a ship's hold) they were easily obtainable and transformed into inexpensive items of storage. It could be argued that the
decline of the trunk murder by the early 1930s coincided with the moment
that the trunk, due to its antiquity or obsolescence, became noticeable.

The press obsession with the trunk murders has ensured that detailed descriptions or images of them have been preserved: Kaye's trunk was described as brown fibre marked with the initials 'E.B.K.' on the lid and it was to appear later in a police photograph employed as a kind of butcher's slab on which her remains were displayed outside the bungalow.[27] Struggling to identify the body of the woman left at Brighton and Kings Cross stations the police turned to the trunk as the key witness and released detailed descriptions to the press along with a photograph: it was a small cabin trunk described one paper,[28] a 'cheap, common type, of plywood and canvas, largely used by holiday makers,'[29] described another, covered in painted canvas, strengthened with four cane bands and fitted with brass corners and two brass locks. The trunk containing the body of Bonati, however, had a particularly rich biography attached to it.

The *Hastings and St Leonards Observer* described Mr Frank Austin as 'a middle-aged, married man' who had been living in Hastings for many years[30] but he had, at one time, been the chief high diver for Barnum and Bailey, an American circus. At some point, probably whilst working in the States he owned a large black trunk, 31 inches in length, 32 inches in depth and 19 inches wide. Touring, Mr Austin not only needed something of good quality but, as chief high diver, something to reflect his status and it was a beautifully crafted thing covered in hand-stitched glossy black American leather with black iron locks, leather straps and a leather handle at one end. Possibly during his touring days Mr Austin had painted the initials 'I.F.A.' in white on the lid and also an initial 'A' on one end and, later, perhaps during his move to Hastings, a cardboard ticket had been tied to the trunk reading 'F. Austin; to St Lenards' [sic]. At some point Mr Austin disposed of the trunk because it was acquired by Mr G.H. Ward who ran the Brixton Trunk Store in South London and who described it to the police as an 'antique, somewhat obsolete sort of trunk.'[31] On the morning of Friday, 6 May 1927, the day after the murder of Bonati, Robinson travelled to Brixton and purchased the secondhand trunk from Mr Ward for 12 shillings and 6 pence. He first carried it on his back and then caught a bus from Kennington Church to his second floor office at No 86 Rochester Row. At around midday Mr Gush, a solicitor with offices on the ground floor, noticed the trunk sitting in the entrance hall and at this point it contained the body of Bonati as Robinson had gone to hail a cab to take him to Charing Cross station. At the station he found a porter who took him and the trunk to the cloakroom and left-luggage office. Robinson did not return for the trunk, however, and with suspicions raised when he was observed crumpling up and discarding the cloakroom ticket as he left the station, the trunk was identified and on Sunday 8th moved into an adjoining room. On Monday when another trunk was placed next to it an 'offensive smell' was noted so on the following day the decision was taken by station staff to open it. The *Daily Herald* reported that they 'hacked it apart' so it would have been significantly damaged in the process[32] and one of the station staff described to the paper what they found: 'It was a revolting sight [...] One of the men gave way. We saw a number of brown paper parcels, and realised at once that they contained human remains. We could see that in one was the head of a woman.'[33]

It was not until 1934 that police investigators developed the bureaucratic regime for documenting the handling, transportation or storage of evidence from crime scene, to laboratory to courtroom, protocols that now underwrite what is known as 'continuity of evidence,'[34] so there were probably little in the way of records to support the next stage of the trunk's narrative. However, from press reports its movements can be followed: on the same day that the trunk was opened at Charing Cross, 10 May, Detective Inspector Steele from Bow Street Police Station delivered it and the body of Bonati to Westminster Mortuary. Here Chief Inspector George Cornish of the Metropolitan Police noted in his statement that the trunk had been left in the back yard whilst doctors Bright, Weir and Rose completed the post-mortem; here it was also photographed. The press then reported each subsequent public appearance with interest: three days later it was an exhibit during Bonati's inquest and on 1 and 8 June it was carried into Westminster Magistrate's Court. Its last public appearance, for the time being, was as a court exhibit on 11 July 1927 at The Old Bailey when the *Portsmouth Herald* reported: 'Among the exhibits in court were the grim black trunk [...]'[35] It was carried in by two police officers and placed on the solicitor's table in front of the dock for Mr William Frank Isted, a cloakroom attendant at Charing Cross, to identify.

The trunk had now transmuted a number of times: from a utilitarian and domestic item for travel, to a secondhand and somewhat obsolete commodity, to a sarcophagus; to forensic evidence containing body parts and fluids and to a legal and documented exhibit appearing in court. From the moment its discovery at Charing Cross left-luggage office was reported in the press it also took on a mantel of notoriety and became part of something wider, a cult.

The Cult of the Trunk

After the trials of Robinson, Mahon and England although the four trunks disappeared from view their legacy continued. It has been mentioned earlier in the chapter that the murders of Bonati, Saunders and the unknown woman were dubbed by the press 'trunk murders' and they went on to discover further acts to report such as the 'Riviera trunk mystery' of 1936[36] and the murder of sixteen-year-old Irene Hart in the same year whose body was found in a tin trunk at her home.[37] Trunk murders go back in time; in 1831 the torso of Celia Bashford was found in a trunk at Preston Park in Brighton and they were also not unique to the UK. In the USA the 1909 'Chinatown trunk mystery' and the 'Great trunk mystery' of 1871 both occurred in New York and in 1931 a double trunk murder was committed by Winnie Ruth Judd. In France there were *le mystere de la malle sanglante*: in 1907 a couple murdered a wealthy Swedish woman in Monte Carlo, cut up and transported her body in a trunk to Marseilles and in 1929 the body of Mr Golchtin was found in a trunk in the baggage room at Lille railway station.

The three trunks in the English murders gathered literary fame in both fictional and factual writings. Four years after the case *The Trial of Patrick Mahon* was published in 1928 as part of the 'Famous trials series'[38] and in 1935 Hutchinson published *Great Unsolved Crimes* which featured the first 'Brighton Trunk murder.'[39] On his retirement in 1934 Detective Inspector Savage from the Metropolitan Police published his memoirs *Savage of Scotland Yard* in which he wrote in detail about the murder of Kaye and his part in the case[40]; following suit a year later George Cornish who led the Robinson investigation also published his memoirs.[41]

Younger readers were not excluded with *The Mystery of the Brass Bound Trunk* published in 1940,[42] and in the cinemas *The Trunk Mystery*[43] and *The Silent Passenger*[44] both appeared in 1935. The myth persisted: for example, the murder of Kaye was featured in biographies of Sir Bernard Spilsbury who was another linking factor between all four cases[45]; *The Brighton Trunk Murders* was published in 2008[46] and the murder of Saunders by England was included in the 2005 publication *Sussex Murders*.[47]

What Does the Trunk Want?

Such a question reflects Frederick Douglas' 1865 antislavery speech 'What the black man wants' which subsequently became a question 'What *does* the black man want?'[48] It is a question since posed as a springboard for numbers of theses around inanimate things; in material culture Chris Gosden asked 'What do objects want?'[49] and in art history W.J.T. Mitchell 'What do pictures want?'[50] It is a useful question to pose at this point in that it turns the emphasis away from the murders, the victims, the press, the researcher and the reader and provides the trunk with agency.[51]

The Charing Cross trunk has moved as a time traveller through space and meaning and out of the four trunks it alone seems to have survived. At some point after 1927 it entered the Metropolitan Police's Crime Museum; how or why it did so is not clear. For a period from 1935 the museum seems to have moved from its home at New Scotland Yard on Victoria Embankment to the new Forensic Science Laboratory at the Metropolitan Police's Hendon training college. The press were allowed access to the new facility and to the rebranded Exhibits Room and 'Here' they reported 'is the trunk in which Robinson concealed the body of his victim after murdering her in the vicinity of Victoria Station.'[52] Surely, briefed by the police, they presented the contents of the room as private teaching aids not for public consumption: 'The very fact that it so difficult to obtain the privilege of a visit proves that it is not kept up merely for historical or sensational ends. The "Black Museum" […] is kept up entirely for the purpose of instructing detectives in the ways and methods of criminals.'[53] Around 20 years later, however, in 1951 the trunk re-emerged as something of a radio celebrity in episode forty-seven of *The Black Museum* and at this point it most definitely was not interpreted as an educational tool. Orson Welles, as the narrator, introduced each radio programme with: 'The Black Museum; a repository of death, a reportorial of violence. Here in a grim, stone structure on the Thames which houses Scotland Yard is a warehouse of homicide where everyday objects [...] are touched by murder.'[54] Period music and dramatization aside, the series was an early example of the use of material culture based around the object biographies of items supposedly randomly picked by Welles from the museum store as he walked its gloomy aisles: 'Now this old-fashioned trunk is a familiar object; brass-bound, well made in its previous-generation kind of way; perhaps you have one like it in the attic or the store room? Perhaps you travelled with it at one time—even checked it into the luggage room'[55] and so the drama of the Charing Cross murder unfolded.

What the trunk wants is not an easy question to answer because it remains a silent surviving witness and also because it isn't entirely clear what its owners, the Metropolitan Police, want. Early on the collection of ex-trial exhibits and prisoner property was clearly named a 'museum'[56] with the press dubbing it the 'Black Museum' and yet, the force has also rigidly adhered to the fact that this is a teaching resource and not a public amenity. In doing so they have created an eternal dichotomy which has caused them nothing but trouble in terms of issues around access, or lack of and ethics. They did open the collection for private tours and if the description of Bonati's great-nephew, who was finally allowed to visit the Crime Museum with his mother as part of a group in 2003, was a true account the methods they employed were ill-considered and misguided:

> The director of the museum soon appeared, a retired police officer with a slightly flamboyant attitude and style about him, he wore a rather garish tie and shirt which seemed to suggest he was somewhat of a performer, someone who would not be shy about his views [...] Our guide proceeded to tell us not to touch anything as these relics had not been cleaned and were still dangerous, he swung a blood stained samurai sword over his head to illustrate his point [...] He was now standing next to a bath and cooker [...] and started to explain how this knife was used by Dennis Nilsen to cut

away the flesh from his victims, the morbid showman was showing no signs of waning. I was conscious that I did not want to see this kind of approach used with my family history. Thankfully he did not mention the trunk and artefacts from my relatives case and passed them by, showing us the display privately as the group looked around.[57]

The clearly fraught issues of interpreting such material were evident in 2015 when, after sixty years away from the limelight, the trunk re-emerged. In partnership with the Metropolitan Police and the Mayor's Office for Policing and Crime, The Museum of London hosted an exhibition of carefully selected items from the Crime Museum.[58] Given the mixed messages around the aims and purposes of the collection it was an exceptionally difficult exhibition to curate and required the high level of expertise that the Museum of London were able to provide. Their solution was to turn back to a *Wellesian* concept of object biographies and material culture with twenty-four individual 'cases of cases' couched between the bookends of a historical background to the collection and a seating area for reflection. With its lid discretely closed the Charing Cross trunk was displayed in a case called 'John Robinson,' next to 'Patrick Mahon,' alongside other pieces of gathered evidence from the murder scene: a waste paper basket, a bloodied match found at Rochester Row and the knife used to dismember Bonati's body. Time travel had not been its friend; it was battered, missing its straps and locks with delaminating edges (Fig. 12.1).

When objects collected as legal evidence find their way into a museum or as part of a display they slip gear into the discipline of museum studies

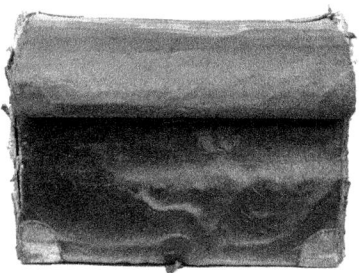

Fig. 12.1 The Charing Cross trunk at the Crime Museum in 2015

or museology and as artefacts the expectations, guidance and ethics attached to them alter radically. Fundamentally they become subject to the sensibilities of a viewing public with clear ideals and this was evident back in 1934 during the reportage of the 'Brighton trunk murders' when Haymarket Amusements Limited exhibited the car belonging to Al Capone: 'Are there not other ways of making money in England than by exhibiting American murderers' cars? You might as well take a trunk from Brighton and exhibit it. Was it for the educational benefit of the British working classes that they should see a car belonging to a murderer?'[59] What the trunk may literally want is recognition that it was designed simply as a utilitarian object which had been misappropriated and redefined and this was acknowledged by the Head of Programmes at the Museum of London: 'We thought a lot about what it meant to put these objects on public display—objects with an earlier history, whether always intended as weapons or with more benign domestic purposes; that became tools in, and then evidence of, a crime; that were transformed again into teaching items within the Metropolitan Police; and that we were now using in yet another new way.'[60] The reactions that the trunk evokes through its unexpected relationship with the museum viewer are far more complex and attempts were clearly made to carefully 'curate' the visitor experience away from the realms of dark tourism[61] and simply gawping into cabinets of curiosities. This connection between the object and emotional responses is key, a point raised by the *Illustrated Police News* during the display of Kaye's personal things in court which they described as being more poignant than legal documents.

Conclusion

In most cases records are all that are left, and after the files have been archived and the press turn away the impacts of the crime continues to reach far and deep into the families of both the victim, the offender and more often than not into the wider community of which they were a part. In *After Homicide* Paul Rock writes that the voices of the victims: '[…] have been silenced through death or neglect, and in their place we are supplied with analyses of secondary accounts in police files and newspapers and of primary accounts tendered at trial.'[62] In an era of a desire for memorialization of spaces, for example, where sites of car accident deaths become roadside shrines, there are no remnants of the physical place for the trunk murders. As with 10 Rillington Place or 25 Cromwell Street, following intense public interest not only was the 'Officer's House' in Eastbourne demolished, but the entire Crumbles was redeveloped as Sovereign Harbour; Kemp Street in Brighton was renumbered and 86 Rochester Row has been swallowed up by a modern office block. Perhaps it should be acknowledged that this absence of physical landmarks may have resulted in the Charing Cross trunk (along with other forensic evidence) representing something more, a solitary tangible memory of the victim; a scenario reflected with sensitivity in 2015 when the Wellcome Collection listened to and remembered the unheard voices of the victims through the use of remembrance art in their *Forensics* exhibition.[63] What was, for example, the reason behind the visit of Bonati's niece and great-nephew to the Crime Museum?

The majority of guidelines or research around the ethics of museum displays concentrate on archaeological human remains or occasionally on the criminal body. For example, Shane McCorristine is clear about the ethical needs of the skull of a criminal: 'Whenever human body parts are put in a glass case and displayed for public view people should be provided with context and extensively informed about what they see. The gaze is never innocent and human remains acquire new meanings as they pass through the hands of different practitioners, custodians, and collectors.'[64] Although surviving criminal evidence rarely consists of the entire body, it may include tissue, hair samples or bodily fluids and it is the fact that these may be attached to, or associated with, on the one hand mundane, everyday objects and on the other with violent crime that makes them particularly difficult to interpret.

As a result of advances in evidence storage and protocols,[65] in forensic science and following a raft of legislation such as the Human Tissue Act 2004, the Data Protection Act 1998 or the Police and Criminal Evidence Act (PACE) 1984, it will actually become increasingly rare for such scenes of crime evidence to enter the public domain and arguments around the ethics of displaying such material will become largely self-closing. Fundamentally, evidence collected by legal or scientific experts is safest in their hands as forensic evidence and whether such material should in the future be preserved and made accessible for a wider audience is another debate. However, for objects that have informally or accidentally slipped through the pre-legislative net and remain in police museums and collections it is clearly important to avoid a repetition of the experiences of Bonati's great-nephew and, returning to the trunk, to recognize its needs as a multifaceted, complex and emotive object.

Notes

1. Material culture refers to the physical objects, resources and spaces that people use to define their culture.
2. J. Hoskins, *Biographical Objects: How Things Tell the Stories of People's Lives*, London and New York: Routledge, 1998.
3. Believed because England was found not guilty, though later in 1976 he confessed to her murder in a *News of the World* interview.
4. I. Burney and N. Pemberton, *Murder and the Making of English CSI*, John Hopkins University Press, 2016, p. 3.
5. Ibid., p. 7.
6. S. D'Cruze, S. Walklate and S. Pegg, *Murder: Social and Historical Approaches to Understanding Murder and Murderers*, Devon: Willan, 2006, p. 105.
7. H. Häkkänen-Nyholm et al., 'Homicides with mutilation of the victim's body', *Journal of Forensic Sciences*, 54(4): 2009, 933–937.
8. C. Quigley, *The Corpse: A History*, Kindle (ed.), McFarland & Company, 2005, location 2820–2823, Citing R. Jackson and F. Camps, *Famous Case Histories of the Celebrated Pathologist*, London: Hart-Davis, MacGibbon, 1975, p. 77.
9. T. Mulholland, *British Boarding houses in Interwar Women's Literature: Alternative Domestic Spaces*, Routledge, 2017, p. 3.
10. R. Wall. '"Surplus women": A legacy of World War One?' *World War I Centenary: Continuations and Beginnings* (website), University of Oxford, http://ww1centenary.oucs.ox.ac.uk/unconventionalsoldiers/%E2%80%98surplus-women%E2%80%99-a-legacy-of-world-war-one/.
11. 'Her identity: Trunk victim wife of Italian waiter', *Western Daily Press*, Bristol, 13 May 1927, 6.30 a.m. ed., Back page.

12. 'Trunk crime No. 1 unsolved', *Illustrated Police News*, London, 28 February 1935, 3.
13. 'Another body found in Brighton cloakroom: Trunk mystery deepens', *The Midland Daily Telegraph*, Warwickshire, 20 June 1934, Last ed., front page.
14. 'Baby in trunk at station', *Daily Herald*, London, 5 July 1934, 11.
15. Mulholland, *British Boarding Houses*, p. 2.
16. 'The bungalow crime: Amazing statement said to have been made by accused', *Illustrated Police News*, London, 29 May 1924, p. 3.
17. The Poor Law system was only finally abolished in 1948 with the introduction of the modern welfare state and the passing of the National Assistance Act.
18. For example, G. Nicholls, *Avenues of the Human Spirit*, Hampshire: John Hunt Publishing Limited, 2011, p. 64.
19. 'Clue to "Jim the chauffeur"', *Daily Herald*, London, 20 May 1927, Late London ed., p. 5.
20. The 1834 Poor Law Amendment Act introduced a new national system of poor relief based on administrative areas called Poor Law Unions. Each Union employed a Relieving Officer to evaluate applications for medical or poor relief and to authorize emergency relief or entry to the workhouse.
21. W.H. Johnson, *Sussex Murders* (True Crime History Series), Stroud: The History Press, 2011, p. 124.
22. S. Slater, 'Prostitutes and popular history: Notes on the "underworld"', *Crime, History & Societies*, 2009, 13(1): 25–48. The author writes about the isolation of prostitutes and their dependency on their pimps: many were forced to move frequently and because of their work lost touch with family and friends.
23. A. Wollensak and B. Terry, 'Transient spaces', Generative Art Conference, held at Politecnico University, Milan, 2005.
24. In which bombs were exploded on the London Underground and in left-luggage offices at Kings Cross and Victoria railway stations.
25. Burney and Pemberton, *Murder*, p. 2.
26. J. Schlör, 'Means of transport and storage: Suitcases and other containers for the memory of migration and displacement', *Journal of Jewish Culture and History*, 2014, 15(1–2): 76–92.
27. Album of six photographs, 15–19 July 1924. SPA 2/37/34. *Criminal conviction: R v Patrick Herbert Mahon*, collection of Sussex Police Authority. East Sussex Record Office, Brighton.

28. Cabin trunks were flatter versions of steamer trunks designed to fit under beds or seats in steamer cabins or train compartments.

29. 'Pencilled word clue in trunk murder', *Sunderland Daily Echo and Shipping Gazette*, 19 June 1934, six o'clock ed., Front page.

30. 'Link with trunk murder: Label addressed to "St Lenards"', *Hastings and St Leonards Observer*, Sussex, 14 May 1927, p. 2.

31. 'The trunk mystery: First steps of police investigation', *Belfast News-Letter*, County Antrim, 12 May 1927, p. 7.

32. 'Woman's body found in trunk', *Daily Herald*, London, 11 May 1927, Late London ed., Front page.

33. Ibid.

34. Burney and Pemberton, *Murder*, p. 76.

35. 'Women at the Old Bailey: Trunk murder trial', *Evening News and Southern Daily Mail*, Portsmouth, 11 July 1927, p. 5.

36. 'The Riviera trunk mystery', *Dundee Courier and Advertiser*, Angus, Scotland, 6 January 1936, 2nd ed., p. 7.

37. 'The trunk murderer executed at Armley Gaol', *Illustrated Police News*, London, 18 February 1937, p. 9.

38. G. Dilnot (ed.), *The Trial of Patrick Herbert Mahon* (Famous Trials Series), London: Geoffrey Bles, 1928.

39. A.J. Alan et al., *Great Unsolved Crimes*, London: Hutchinson & Co., 1935, pp. 342–351.

40. P. Savage, *Savage of Scotland Yard: The Thrilling Autobiography of Ex-superintendent Percy Savage of the C.I.D.*, London: Hutchinson & Co. Ltd., 1934.

41. G.W. Cornish, *Cornish of the 'Yard': His Reminiscences and Cases*, London: John Lane and The Bodley Head, 1935.

42. C. Keene, *The Mystery of the Brass Bound Trunk* (Nancy Drew Mystery Stories), Grosset & Dunlap, 1940.

43. J. Conway, 'The trunk mystery', Metro-Goldwyn-Mayer, 1935, Film.

44. R. Denham, 'The silent passenger', Associated British Film Distributors, 1935, Film.

45. D.G. Browne and E.V. Tullett, *Bernard Spilsbury: His Life and Cases*, Penguin Books, 1955, pp. 143–160.

46. D. Rowland, *The Brighton Trunk Murders*, East Sussex: Finsbury Publishing, 2008.

47. Johnson, *Sussex Murders*, pp. 115–130.

48. 'What does the black man want?' was asked by Frantz Fanon in the introduction to his 1952 publication, *Black Skin, White Masks*.

49. C. Gosden, 'What do objects want?', *Journal of Archaeological Method and Theory*, 2005, 12(3): 193–211.
50. W.J.T. Mitchell, *What Do Pictures Want?: The Lives and Loves of Images*, 2nd ed., University of Chicago Press, 2005.
51. In material culture agency is an action or intervention producing a particular effect.
52. 'Where notorious criminals' secrets are revealed', *Lancashire Daily Post*, Lancashire, 12 August 1935, 4.
53. Ibid.
54. H. Towers, 'Episode 47: The trunk', in *The Black Museum*, Narrated by Orson Welles: Radio Luxembourg, 1952.
55. Ibid.
56. The International Council of Museums defines a museum as a 'non-profit, permanent institution in the service of society and its development, open to the public, which acquires, conserves, researches, communicates and exhibits the tangible and intangible heritage of humanity and its environment for the purposes of education, study and enjoyment.' http://archives.icom.museum/definition.html.
57. Nicholls, *Avenues*, p. 63.
58. J. Keily and J. Hoffbrand (curators), 'The Crime Museum uncovered: Inside Scotland Yard's special collection', Exhibition hosted by The Museum of London, 9 October 2015 to 10 April 2016.
59. 'Al Capone's car', *Northern Daily Mail*, Durham, 17 July 1934, West Hartlepool six o'clock ed., p. 2.
60. A. Day, 'Crime Museum uncovered: The complex ethics and expectations', *Museum ID* (website), http://museum-id.com/crime-museum-uncovered-the-complex-ethics-and-expectations-by-annette-day/.
61. Dark tourism has been defined as tourism involving travel to places historically associated with death and tragedy.
62. P. Rock, *After Homicide: Practical and Political Responses to Bereavement*, Clarendon Studies in Criminology, New York: Oxford University Press, 1998, p. 25.
63. L. Shanahan (curator), 'Forensics: The anatomy of crime', Exhibition held by the Wellcome Collection, London, 26 February to 21 June 2015.
64. S. McCorristine, 'The dark value of criminal bodies: Context, consent and the disturbing sale of John Parker's skull', *Journal of Conservation and Museum Studies*, 2015, 13(1): 1–7.

65. Police forces such as Merseyside and Thames Valley now publish property and evidence management policies: https://www.merseyside.police.
uk/media/12798/property-evidence-mgt-policy-procedure-2016-
06-23.pdf and https://www.thamesvalley.police.uk/SysSiteAssets/foi-
media/thames-valley-police/policies/policy%2D%2D-property-man-
agement-evidential.pdf.

Bibliography

Alan, A.J., Armstrong, A., Armstrong, M., Beresford, J.D. and Berkeley, A., *Great Unsolved Crimes*, London: Hutchinson & Co., 1935.
Browne, D.G. and Tullett, E.V., *Bernard Spilsbury: His Life and Cases*, Penguin Books, 1955.
Burney, I. and Pemberton, N., *Murder and the Making of English CSI*, John Hopkins University Press, 2016.
Cornish, G.W., *Cornish of the 'Yard': His Reminiscences and Cases*, London: John Lane and The Bodley Head, 1935.
D'Cruze, S., Walklate, S. and Pegg, S., *Murder: Social and Historical Approaches to Understanding Murder and Murderers*, Devon: Willan, 2006.
Day, A., 'Crime Museum uncovered: The complex ethics and expectations', *Museum ID* (website), http://museum-id.com/crime-museum-uncovered-the-complex-ethics-and-expectations-by-annette-day/
Dilnot, G. (ed.), *The Trial of Patrick Herbert Mahon* (Famous Trials Series), London: Geoffrey Bles, 1928.
Gosden, C., 'What do objects want?', *Journal of Archaeological Method and Theory*, 2005, 12(3): 193–211.
Häkkänen-Nyholm, H., Weizmann-Henelius, G., Salenius, S., Lindberg, N. and Repo-Tiihonen, E., 'Homicides with mutilation of the victim's body', *Journal of Forensic Sciences*, 2009, 54(4): 933–937.
Hoskins, J., *Biographical Objects: How Things Tell the Stories of People's Lives*, London and New York: Routledge, 1998.
Johnson, W.H., *Sussex Murders* (True Crime History Series), Stroud: The History Press, 2011.
Keene, C., *The Mystery of the Brass Bound Trunk* (Nancy Drew Mystery Stories), Grosset & Dunlap, 1940.
McCorristine, S., 'The dark value of criminal bodies: Context, consent and the disturbing sale of John Parker's skull', *Journal of Conservation and Museum Studies*, 2015, 13(1): 1–7.

Mitchell, W.J.T., *What Do Pictures Want?: The Lives and Loves of Images*, 2nd ed., University of Chicago Press, 2005.

Mulholland, T., *British Boarding Houses in Interwar Women's Literature: Alternative Domestic Spaces*, Routledge, 2017.

Nicholls, G., *Avenues of the Human Spirit*, Hampshire: John Hunt Publishing Limited, 2011.

Quigley, C., *The Corpse: A History*, Kindle (ed.), McFarland & Company, 2005.

Rock, P., *After Homicide: Practical and Political Responses to Bereavement* (Clarendon Studies in Criminology), New York: Oxford University Press, 1998.

Rowland, D., *The Brighton Trunk Murders*, East Sussex: Finsbury Publishing, 2008.

Savage, P., *Savage of Scotland Yard: The Thrilling Autobiography of Ex-superintendent Percy Savage of the C.I.D*, London: Hutchinson & Co. Ltd., 1934.

Schlör, J., 'Means of transport and storage: Suitcases and other containers for the memory of migration and displacement', *Journal of Jewish Culture and History*, 2014, 15(1–2): 76–92.

Slater, S., 'Prostitutes and popular history: Notes on the "underworld"', *Crime, History & Societies*, 2009, 13(1): 25–48.

Wall, R., '"Surplus women": A legacy of World War One?' *World War I Centenary: Continuations and Beginnings*, University of Oxford, http://ww1centenary. oucs.ox.ac.uk/unconventionalsoldiers/%E2%80%98surplus-women%E2%80%99-a-legacy-of-world-war-one/, Accessed 24 September 2018.

Wollensak, A. and Terry, B., 'Transient spaces', Generative Art Conference, held at Politecnico University, Milan, 2005.

Exhibitions, Film and Radio

Conway, J. 'The trunk mystery', Metro-Goldwyn-Mayer, 1935. Film.

Denham, R., 'The silent passenger', Associated British Film Distributors, 1935. Film.

Keily, J. and Hoffbrand, J. (curators), 'The Crime Museum uncovered: Inside Scotland Yard's special collection', Exhibition hosted by The Museum of London, 9 October 2015 to 10 April 2016.

Shanahan, L. (curator), 'Forensics: The anatomy of crime', Exhibition held by the Wellcome Collection, London, 26 February to 21 June 2015.

Towers, H., 'Episode 47: The trunk', In *The Black Museum*. Narrated by Orson Welles: Radio Luxembourg, 1952. Radio broadcast.

Archive

Album of six photographs, 15–19 July 1924. SPA 2/37/34. Criminal conviction: R v Patrick Herbert Mahon, collection of Sussex Police Authority. East Sussex Record Office, Brighton.

Newspapers

'Al Capone's car', *Northern Daily Mail*, Durham, 17 July 1934, West Hartlepool six o'clock ed., 2.

'Another body found in Brighton cloakroom: Trunk mystery deepens', *The Midland Daily Telegraph* (Warwickshire), 20 June 1934, Last ed., front page.

'Baby in trunk at station', *Daily Herald*, London, 5 July 1934, 11.

'The bungalow crime: Amazing statement said to have been made by accused', *Illustrated Police News*, London, 29 May 1924, 3.

'Clue to "Jim the chauffeur"', *Daily Herald*, London, 20 May 1927, Late London ed., 5.

'Her identity: Trunk victim wife of Italian waiter', *Western Daily Press*, Bristol, 13 May 1927, 6.30 a.m. ed., back page.

'Link with trunk murder: Label addressed to "St Lenards"', *Hastings and St Leonards Observer*, Sussex, 14 May 1927, 2.

'Pencilled word clue in trunk murder', *Sunderland Daily Echo and Shipping Gazette*, 19 June 1934, six o'clock ed., front page.

'The Riviera trunk mystery', *Dundee Courier and Advertiser*, Angus, Scotland, 6 January 1936, 2nd ed., 7.

'Trunk crime No. 1 unsolved', *Illustrated Police News*, London, 28 February 1935, 3.

'The trunk murderer executed at Armley Gaol', *Illustrated Police News*, London, 18 February 1937, 9.

'The trunk mystery: First steps of police investigation', *Belfast News-Letter*, County Antrim, 12 May 1927, 7.

'Where notorious criminals' secrets are revealed', *Lancashire Daily Post*, Lancashire, 12 August 1935, 4.

'Woman's body found in trunk', *Daily Herald*, London, 11 May 1927, Late London ed., front page.

'Women at the Old Bailey: Trunk murder trial', *Evening News and Southern Daily Mail*, Portsmouth, 11 July 1927, 5.

Index[1]

A

Accidental tourist, 280
Administrative objectivity, 76, 83
Adversarial legal system, 2
Aitken, Elizabeth Henrietta,
          137–138
Allanson, Mr, 189, 195
Angus, William, 141
Animal cases, 196
Anxiety, 233, 235, 237, 238, 241,
          243, 248
Appeal, 83, 226, 258, 265
Appearance, 10, 52, 143, 144,
          167, 168, 170, 196, 201,
          215, 224, 233, 234,
          236–241, 245, 247–249,
          258, 287
    physiognomy, 239, 240

Approved school, 69, 71, 73, 74, 77,
          92n29
    'List D' school, 74
Aropoff, Cyril, 22
Arsenic, 196, 198, 199, 203, 204
    See also Poison
Austin, Frank, 286
Autopsy
    See also Post-mortem

B

Baker, Arthur Reginald, 241
Barberi, Maria, 245, 246
Baxandall, Michael, 21
Bayesian Approach/Reasoning, 8,
          100–106, 109, 113, 114,
          119n27

---

[1] Note: Page numbers followed by 'n' refer to notes.

© The Author(s) 2020   **303**
A. Adam (ed.), *Crime and the Construction of Forensic Objectivity from 1850*, Palgrave
Histories of Policing, Punishment and Justice,
https://doi.org/10.1007/978-3-030-28837-2

Beagrie, George, 84
Belgium, 101
Bellocq, E.J., 21
Berlin, 262
Berliner Volks-Zeitung, 265
Bertillon, Alphonse, 19, 21
Bias, 105, 110–112, 117
    confirmation bias, 112, 113
Biggar, 69–89, 222
    Town Council, 70, 72–74
Birkett, Norman, 284
Bishop Auckland, 199, 203
Bite-mark, 7, 8, 69, 70, 76, 78–89
Blair, Eliza, 142
Blench, Thomas, 20
Blood, 25, 33, 53, 54, 60, 77, 107,
    109, 126, 136, 137,
    167–169, 173, 178, 179,
    194, 201, 202, 216, 217,
    219–221, 290
    blood-grouping, 76
Boat-hook, 78
Bodies, 11, 12n15, 17–34, 52–55,
    69, 76–81, 84, 86–89, 126,
    128, 130, 134–136, 138,
    140–143, 145, 146,
    147n10, 151n65, 152n75,
    162, 167–171, 174, 175,
    178, 179, 191, 194, 196,
    202–204, 212–219,
    221–224, 236, 239–243,
    248, 279–281, 283,
    285–289, 291, 293
Bolton, 24
Bonati, Minnie Alice, 280, 282–284,
    286–288, 290, 291, 293, 294
Brandt, Bill, 22
Brighton, 280–284, 286, 288, 292,
    293

Britain, 21, 22, 71, 84, 146, 193,
    197, 212
    See also UK
Brophy, Mary, 245
Bullas, Thompson, 196
Burg, 263
Butler, DI Osborne, 79, 80, 83, 84,
    88
Byron, Emma 'Kitty, 241, 245–247

C

Camera technology, 17, 20, 23, 24
    Kodachrome, 32
    Leica camera, 20 (*see also*
        Photography)
    Thornton Pickard Ruby Reflex
        camera, 20
Canine, 81, 82, 84, 88
Canning, Elizabeth, 47
Capital punishment, 212
Capone, Al, 292
Cardiff, 31
Carlisle, 211
Carter, Miranda, 24
Cartier-Bresson, Henri, 24
Casebook, 189, 191–194, 197, 198,
    201, 204, 205
Case notes, 200, 216
Casswell, J.D., 33
Certainty, 7, 8, 70, 99, 100, 102,
    105, 109
Chain of custody, 76, 203
    continuity of evidence, 287
Chantrelle, Elizabeth, 135
Chemical analysis, 189, 195, 199,
    203
Chemist, 191, 193
Child abuse, 265, 273

Children's lies, 259
Christie, John, 281
Christison, Robert, 129
Cignarale, Chiara, 238, 242
Class, 5, 7, 22, 24, 59, 60, 133, 146,
    165, 166, 235, 236, 238,
    240, 246, 249, 273, 292
  middle class, 236, 238, 243, 246,
    258, 259, 283
  working class, 292
Cornish, Chief Inspector George,
    287, 288
Coroner, 9, 167, 190, 195, 197, 199,
    203, 242
Corporal punishment, 266
Cotton, Charles Edward, 203
Cotton, Mary Ann, 192, 203
County Durham, 197, 203, 204
Courtroom, 2, 3, 7, 18, 27, 33, 34,
    43–61, 85, 86, 127, 144,
    149n24, 217, 237, 243,
    246, 260–262, 266–268,
    270, 273, 285, 287
Coventry, 211
Credibility, 10, 104, 105, 257–267,
    269–272
  juvenile, 264, 268, 272
Crime, 2, 3, 127, 128, 130, 146,
    163, 191, 241, 292
  crime history, 2, 3, 5
  history, 1
  scenes, 2, 5, 6, 8–10, 17, 19–21,
    44, 48–50, 52, 55, 56, 60,
    77, 101, 106, 114, 117,
    140, 162, 163, 165, 166,
    168, 170, 173, 174, 177,
    181, 280, 285
    model, 8, 106–108, 110–117,
    119n23

Crime Scene Investigation (CSI), 50,
    52
  CSI effect, 49, 60
Crime scene report, 8, 100, 106,
    109, 114
Crime scene technician, 8, 99–101,
    106, 108–117, 119n23,
    119n27
Criminal anthropology
  born criminal, 234–237, 239
    hereditary degeneracy, 236
  female born criminal, 234, 236,
    246 (*see also* Appearance;
    Lombroso, Cesare)
Criminal investigation, 8, 70,
    125–147, 176, 198, 199,
    281
Criminal justice, 3
Crippen, Hawley Harvey, 10
Crown Office, 214, 222
Crumbles bungalow, 7, 50, 52, 280,
    286, 293
Culpable homicide, 225, 226

D

Daily Mirror, 17, 30, 43, 45, 47
Daly, Mary, 241, 248, 249
Danziger Volksstimme, 265, 267,
    268
Darwin, Charles, 175
Daston, Lorraine, 1, 100, 103, 105,
    116
Database, 102
Data Protection Act 1998, 293
Dean, Thomas, 199
Dease, William, 193
Death sentence, 242
Defence lawyers, 260, 261, 264, 272

Dental model, 75, 76, 80–88
    acrylic resin, 76, 80, 86
    copper, 86
    dental impressions, 69, 79–84,
        88, 89 (*see also* Miniatures/
        models)
    overlay transparencies, 81, 83, 86
    plaster, 76, 79, 80, 86
Detection, 165, 170, 174, 176, 181
    See also Police
Deutsche Allgemeine Zeitung, 266,
    269
Director of Public Prosecutions
    (DPP), 25, 31, 53
DNA, 4, 7, 102, 105
Docherty, Margaret, 162, 163, 165,
    166, 169, 174, 177, 179,
    181
Documentary, 7, 17–34, 86, 145,
    177
Documentary modernism, 21–22, 34
Documentary realism, 32
Dodsworth, John, 196
Dolls' houses/dollhouses, 44, 48, 49
Domestic crime, 6, 24, 27, 281
Donnan, John, 219, 220
Dooley, Catherine, 239, 246, 247
Dooley, John, 247
Dudson, Charles, 212
Dumfries, 9, 211, 219–221, 225,
    226
    Crichton Royal Institution, 225
Duncan, Andrew, 193
Dundee, 136

E
Eastbourne, 53, 293
Easton, Sergeant John, 20

Edinburgh, 9, 84, 91n18, 125,
    127–130, 132–140, 146,
    147, 152n84, 193, 214,
    216, 219, 220, 222, 225
    Bangour Hospital, 225
    Medical School, 132
    New Town, 130
    Old Town, 135
    Police Commission, 129, 139
    Royal College of Surgeons, 132
    Royal Infirmary, 135
    Town Council, 129–130
    University, 84, 133, 220, 225
Egypt, 221, 282
Emotions, 7, 10, 17, 18, 27, 29,
    233, 237, 243–248
Endpoint anchoring, 108
England, 3, 10, 18, 44, 48, 70,
    94n74, 101, 130, 139, 193,
    203, 217, 279
    Northern England, 6, 191
England, Cecil Lois, 280, 281, 284, 288
Epistemology, 3
Ethics, 6, 10, 11, 290, 292, 293
    See also Moral/morality
Ethnicity, 236, 238, 249
Evans, Charles, 28
Evans, Ethel, 28
Evans, Walker, 24
Evatt, Edward Pratt, 142
Evidence, 10, 19, 48, 56, 69, 76–78,
    83, 85, 86, 102, 126, 144,
    145, 162, 167, 176–178,
    181, 216, 217, 220, 226,
    249, 281, 288, 291, 293
    admissibility, 83
    circumstantial evidence, 88
    detailed traces, 107
    'science of proof', 180

Exhumation, 203, 219, 222, 223
Experiment, 73, 74, 88, 189, 191,
   194, 260, 271
Expert, 5, 8–10, 44, 55, 79, 80, 88,
   89, 100, 101, 103, 126,
   127, 129, 142, 144, 146,
   147, 190–192, 197, 204,
   205, 213, 217, 219, 221,
   222, 224, 257–273
   psychological, 260, 264
Expertise, 5, 6, 9, 179–181, 185n66,
   191, 195, 197, 203–205,
   211–226, 260–268,
   270–273, 280, 291
   psychological, 258, 264, 267
   See also Expert
Expert witnesses, 2, 3, 8–11, 56, 69,
   70, 84, 87–89, 128, 133,
   152n84, 180, 203, 204,
   212, 225, 258, 265, 269,
   271
   See also Witness

F

Fact, 2, 17, 25, 56, 84, 110, 112,
   113, 115, 116, 138, 179,
   185n66, 194, 218, 236,
   240, 241, 246–248, 259,
   261, 267, 270, 290
Farr, Samuel, 193
Femininity/Feminine, 234, 236,
   243, 244, 246, 249, 250
Fingerprints, 21, 81, 85, 103, 115,
   175
First impulse, 107, 110
Fitzakerly, Jessie M., 194, 202
Forensic dentist, 79, 80
   See also Forensic odontology

Forensic knowledge, 190
Forensic laboratory, 4, 8, 101, 104,
   106, 285
   See also Laboratory
Forensic medicine, 3, 78, 80, 128,
   145, 146, 152n83,
   192–197, 215, 216, 222,
   224, 228n39, 270, 271
Forensic objectivity, 2–11, 17, 70,
   76, 99–118
Forensic odontology, 7, 70, 78, 89
Forensic pathologist, 5
Forensic practice, 8, 9, 204, 205
Forensic psychology, 10, 260, 262,
   265, 266, 268, 270–273
Forensic science, 4, 101, 175, 176,
   180, 192, 262, 273, 293
Forensic scientist, 99, 102, 103
   See also Forensic specialists
Forensic specialists, 222, 224, 260,
   261, 267
Forensic technique, 9, 70, 85, 127,
   181, 190
   analogy, 85 (*see also* Forensic
   science)
Foster, Campbell, 204
Foucault, Michel, 4
Frenzel, Arthur, 259, 267
   See also Trial
Furness, John, 80, 82

G

Gainford, Co. Durham, 199
Galashiels, 142
Galison, Peter, 1, 100, 103, 105, 116
Galton, Francis, 21
Garland, David, 4
Gender, 5–7, 235, 236, 281

Germany, 2, 31, 259, 261, 268, 272
  German justice system, 258, 265
  Weimar Republic, 259, 261, 262,
    265
Gibbons, Elizabeth, 244
Gillespie, William, 172
Glaister, John Jr., 224
Glaister, John Sr., 215, 216, 218
Glasgow, 78, 215
  Glasgow Dental Hospital, 79, 80
  University, 78, 224
Glasgow Police, 78, 79
  Glasgow Police Identification
    Bureau, 79, 88
Glover, George, 130
Glover, Robert Mortimer, 193
Goole, 196
Gorringe murder, 80
Gothenburg, 101
Grant, Lord, 87
Great Depression (1930s), 282, 283
Great War, 282
Grierson, John, 17, 22
Guy, William, 192
Guy's Hospital, 179

H
Hall, John Fallows, 20
Hanging, 248
Harrisson, Tom, 24
Hart, Judith, 72–74, 91n21, 91n25
Harvey, Warren, 76, 79–82
Hastings, 286
Hay, Gordon, 70, 73, 74, 77, 78,
    81–84
Hellwig, Albert, 268, 269
Henderson, David Kennedy, 203, 225
Hepple, PC John, 171

Hertfordshire, 197
Hirschfeld, Magnus, 267–269
Hirst, Brooke and Hirst, 196
History of the present, 4
Hogg, Phoebe, 240
Hogg, William, 240
Hollingsworth, Dr, 194–195
Holmfirth, 201
Huddersfield, 190
Human Tissue Act 2004, 293
Hunter, Gordon, 219, 220
Hussmann, Karl, 267

I
Impartiality, 2, 104, 110, 111
Imrie, James, 78, 86, 87
Incest, 24, 144, 258, 259, 268, 269,
    274n13
Injury, 194
Inquest, 178, 180
IRA (Irish Republican Army), 285
Ireland, 2, 10, 101, 233–250
Italian, 238, 239, 245
  'Italianness,' 238

J
Juvenile delinquency, 71

K
Kaye, Emily Beilby, 45, 51, 54, 55,
    57, 58, 64n44, 280–284,
    286, 288, 289, 292
Kellett, Richard, 201
Kerr, Douglas, 216
Kilbrandon, Lord, 71
  Kilbrandon Report, 71

Kinane, Charles, 144
King, William, 138
Kirriemuir, 136
Krantz, Paul, 267

L
Laboratory, 7, 8, 56, 99–101, 103,
      105, 106, 109, 110,
      114–118, 119n22, 119n27,
      214, 221, 287
   'lab thinking,' 114 (see also
      Forensic laboratory)
Labourer, 165
Laird, Ronald, 80
Lanark, 72
Lancashire, 18, 25
Latour, Bruno, 105
   'black box', 213
Lavater, Johann, 239
Lee, Frances Glessner, 50
Leeds, 189, 190, 193, 195–197,
      202–204
   Hospital for Women and
      Children, 191
   Leeds General Infirmary, 190
   Leeds Musical Festival
      Committee, 191
   Leeds Sanitary Aid Society, 191
   Leeds School of Medicine, 191,
      197
   University
      Brotherton Library, 193
Left-luggage office, 280, 283–285,
      287, 288, 295n24
Legal reform, 262, 272, 273
Lewes Court, 45
Likelihood ratio, 102, 104, 118n8
Lincolnshire, 197

Linlithgow, 138
Lipmann, Otto, 260
Liston, Robert, 179
Littlejohn, Henry Duncan, 12n15,
      125, 126, 128–147,
      149n24, 152n84
Littlejohn, Henry Harvey, 222, 223
Loaningdale, 69–74, 77, 78, 82, 88,
      89, 91n25, 92n29
   Loaningdale School Management
      Board, 70, 72
Lombroso, Cesare, 10, 236, 239, 246
   born criminal (see also
      Appearance)
London, 7, 17, 19, 20, 22, 25, 27,
      30, 54, 59, 80, 82, 163,
      164, 179, 192, 193,
      233–250, 280, 283, 284,
      286
   Brixton, 50
   Charing Cross, 280, 287–291,
      293
   Guy's Hospital, 192
   Kennington Church, 286
   Kilburn, 27
   King's College, 192
   Kings Cross, 280, 286
   Museum of London, 291, 292
   Piccadilly Circus, 283
   Royal College of Surgeons, 179
      Member of the Royal College
      of Surgeons (MRCS), 190
   Shepherd's Bush, 27
   Society of Apothecaries, 190, 193
   Stepney, 18, 23
   Westminster Magistrate's Court,
      287
London School of Economics, 71,
      72

Lorant, Stefan, 31
Lützow, Freiherr Kurt von, 265

M
Maclagan, Andrew, 141
Maclagan, Douglas, 135
Madge, Charles, 24
Magdeburg, 257, 263, 264
Mahon, Patrick, 45, 46, 50, 52–54,
    56–59, 64n43, 64n44, 280,
    281, 284, 288, 291
Male, G.E., 193
Malmö, 101
Manchester, 283
Manchester City Police, 20
    Manchester Police Museum, 21
Marbe, Karl, 260
Marcuse, Max, 258, 263, 264, 269,
    271
Marshall, Dr, 222, 223
Martin, Harry, 20
Masculine/masculinity, 236
Mass Observation (MO), 17, 22, 24
Match, 7, 8, 48, 80–82, 84, 99, 100,
    102, 103, 109
Mayne, Roger, 22
McAlister, William, 225
Mcilwaine, Isabella, 246
McPhee, Torquil, 84
McQue, Ann, 126, 127, 140
Mechanical objectivity, 104, 105,
    109
Medical jurisprudence, 127, 129,
    130, 132, 133, 142,
    145–146, 155n123, 179
Medicine, 8, 18, 128, 190–197,
    207n17, 271
Medico-legal practice, 9, 127, 129,
    147, 189, 192, 203, 204, 214

Melbourne, 135
Metropolitan Police, 20, 25,
    33, 57, 58, 164, 165, 282,
    287–292
    Bow Street Police Station, 287
    Detective Branch, 165
    Metropolitan Police Crime
        Museum/The Black
        Museum, 49, 50, 289–291
    Metropolitan Police Laboratory,
        20, 289 (*see also* Police)
    Scotland Yard, 49, 52, 53, 179,
        290
Mexico City, 19
Microscope, 201
Middlesbrough, 171
Millan, Bruce, 72–74, 91n25
Miniatures/models, 3, 7, 43, 44, 75,
    86
Model railways/trains, 48
Moll, Albert, 271
Monck, Margaret, 22
Mönkemöller, Otto, 266, 269
Montreal, 242
Moral/Morality, 59, 104, 236, 238,
    239, 243, 244, 247, 248,
    257, 258, 279
Mortuary, 78, 79, 81, 88, 128, 135,
    136, 167, 213, 287
Muir, John Maxwell, 211, 212, 219,
    225, 226
Muir, Lena, 211, 212, 219–222,
    224–226
Mullins, Rev. Joseph, 19
Muncie, DCS William, 75, 77–79
Murder, 2, 5, 7, 18, 19, 24, 43–61,
    70–75, 77, 112, 125, 139,
    162, 173, 191, 194, 197,
    201, 203, 220, 233–250,
    262, 279–294

Murderess, 10, 192, 233–250
  born murderess, 242
Murray, Inspector, 201
Murray, William Henry, 143

N
National Archives, 50, 163, 164
National Forensic Centre (NFC),
    100–103, 106, 116, 118n5,
    119n22
National Insurance, 283
Netherlands, 101
Newcastle upon Tyne, 6, 9, 163,
    165, 173, 190, 193
  Newcastle upon Tyne Police, 163,
    165, 166, 170, 173, 179,
    181
    Westgate Road Police Station,
    171
  Watch Committee, 164, 165,
    171
  West Walls, 167, 172, 178, 180
New Journalism, 234, 235, 237
New Orleans, 21
New York City, 19, 21, 233–250,
    288
New Zealand, 101
Nilsen, Dennis, 290
Nineteenth century, 2–4, 6, 8,
    9, 18, 47, 48, 51, 86,
    127–129, 132, 134,
    135, 137, 145–147,
    152n83, 162, 163, 166,
    172, 175, 180, 181,
    190–192, 204, 205,
    206n13, 217, 235–237,
    260, 285
Northern Ireland, 79
Northumberland, 165

O
Object biography, 279, 290, 291
Objectivity, 2, 3, 11
  See also Forensic objectivity
Old Bailey, 48, 283, 287
Old Bailey Proceedings, 48, 49, 51,
    64n46

P
Paine, Clemence, 23
Paris, 135
Parker, George, 49
Pathologist, 78–80
Paton, DS Jack, 79, 88
Peacock, Linda, 69, 73, 77, 78, 80
Pearcey, Mary Eleanor, 240, 241,
    243, 244, 250n6
Pearson, Elizabeth, 192, 199
Pearson, Sarah Anne, 242
Pearson, William, 49
Peattie, Jessie, 140
Peel, Robert, 163, 164
  'Peel's Principles', 164, 173
Performativity, 243
Perjury, 216, 217
Perth, 144
Petition, 226
Pevensey, 53
Pharmacologist, 193
Photography, 5–7, 17–22, 24,
    30–34, 60, 82, 85, 86
  Bartlane method, 30
  black and white film, 22, 31–33,
    84, 86, 88
  crime scene photography, 3, 6,
    18, 20–22, 24, 27, 29–34,
    44, 61n3, 76, 79, 85, 86
  culture of construction, 86
  photographic aesthetics, 21, 22

Physiognomy, 241
Picasso, Pablo, 32
Picture Post, 17, 30, 31
Place, Martha, 239
Place, William, 240
Placzek, Siegfried, 266, 268
Plaut, Paul, 268, 271
Poison, 141, 142, 196, 203, 217,
    247
    Marsh test, 198
    nitrate of potash, 142
    poisoning, 190, 196–198, 203,
        205
    Reinsch test, 198, 199
Poland, 101
Police, 5, 9, 17, 44, 69, 70, 74, 81,
    101, 125, 127, 134, 139,
    140, 146, 162, 163, 165,
    172, 190, 194–196, 203,
    212, 215, 245, 286, 287
    Association of Chief Police
        Officers of England and
        Wales, 33
    Chief Constable, 173
    'new police', 163, 164, 171
    police investigation, 181, 182n4
    policing, 5, 8, 75, 128, 163, 204
        guidance, 173, 174
    Royal Irish Constabulary, 164
    scientific policing, 175–177, 180,
        181
    Transport Police, 164
Police and Criminal Evidence Act
    (PACE) 1984, 293
Police surgeon, 8, 78, 79, 125–147,
    168, 169, 177, 179, 180,
    185n60, 212, 214, 216, 219
    United Kingdom of Police
        Surgeons' Association, 134

Polte, Erich, 257–259
Poor Law, 283
Post-mortem, 9, 78, 79, 88, 127–128,
    130, 134–137, 140,
    152n76, 167, 179, 195,
    197, 204, 211–226, 287
    post-mortem report, 78, 212,
        213, 218, 222–224
Potsdam, 258
Precognition, 126, 127, 139, 140,
    142, 147
Presiding judge, 257, 263, 266, 268
Press, 5, 10, 17, 18, 21, 24, 43–46,
    51, 70, 72, 74, 129, 130,
    147, 195, 233, 234,
    237–241, 243–247, 249,
    250n6, 259, 261, 262,
    265–273, 274n13, 275n25,
    279, 286–290, 292
    critique, 261
    media reportage, 189, 190
    Weimar press, 262, 270, 273
Pre-trial proceedings, 264
Probability, 7, 8, 82, 102, 105
Procurator Fiscal, 127, 143, 214
Professional fees, 197
Professional networks, 3, 6, 145,
    147, 203, 204, 214
Proposition, 102, 106–109, 112,
    113, 115, 118n8
Psychiatry, 192, 225
Psychologists, 260
Psychology, 260, 262, 265
Public health, 128
    medical officer of health, 128, 132
    public hygiene, 236
    sanitary reform, 128
Public inquiry, 73
Purdie, Louisa, 134

R

Race, 7, 236, 238
Railway/Trains, 55, 80, 189,
    197, 203, 280, 284–287,
    296n28
Rape, 112, 137–139, 142, 145, 146,
    152n84
Rayne, Septimus William, 179
Recidivism, 73
Redemption arc, 248
Reid, George Davison, 22
Reid, William, 134
Representation, 3, 4, 6, 7, 19, 44,
    51, 52, 55, 56, 60, 75,
    86–88, 142, 233–250, 262,
    283
Respectable/respectability, 60, 126,
    242, 243, 249, 258, 259,
    269
Rigor mortis, 215
Road network, 197
Robinson, John, 280–289, 291
Roebuck, Marsh, 201
Ross, Margaret, 138
Russell, Lord William, 48
Ruxton, Buck, 285

S

Sabbage, John, 165
Sanderson, Fred, 25
Saunders, George, 84
Saunders, Violette/Violet, 280, 281,
    284, 288, 289
Savage, Chief Inspector Percy, 53,
    54, 288
Scattergood, Oliver, 195
Scattergood, Thomas, 9, 189–205
Science, 191

Scotland, 3, 6–9, 70–72, 74, 76, 81,
    83, 88, 89, 94n74, 125–147,
    211, 212, 214, 215
Scottish legal system, 9, 70, 83
    corroboration, 214, 221
    High Court of Justiciary, 129,
        132, 144
    sheriff, 214
    warrant, 83
Scottish Office, 70–72
Secretary of State for Scotland,
    71–73, 226
Social Work Department, 70, 72
Scott, Sub-Inspector Thomas, 168
Seddon, Maria, 242
Segall, Judge, 264
Selkirk, 129
Sexologist, 258, 271
Sexology, 270
Sexual assault, 259
Shelah, Police Constable Edward, 50,
    53, 55, 57–60
Shoe mark, 102
Shropshire, 18, 28, 197
Simpson, Keith, 79–88
Sisal string, 77
Smith, Sydney A., 12n15, 216, 217,
    220–224
Spain, 101
Spanish flu pandemic, 282
Spectroscope, 201
Spender, Humphrey, 18, 22–24, 26,
    30
Spilsbury, Bernard, 56, 289
Stables, James, 134
Standardization, 103–105, 111, 114,
    116
Statistics, 8, 109
    See also Probability

Steele, Detective Inspector, 287
Steen, Mary Ann, 25
Stephens, John, 164
Stephenson, James Henry, 201
Stern, William, 260, 271
Stockholm, 101
Strychnine, 195, 196, 198, 200
    See also Poison
Subjectivity, 104, 110, 117
Suicide, 242
Sutherland, Halliday, 133, 145
Svensson, Arne, 32
Sweden, 2, 7, 101, 106
Sydney, 19

T
Tacit knowledge, 75
Tate, PC William, 166
Taylor, Alfred Swaine, 192, 197
Taylor, Detective Inspector Joseph, 28
Taylor, Joseph, 248
Taylor, Louisa Jane, 247
Territorial Army, 282
Testimony, 257, 261, 262
Therapeutic regime, 71, 74, 88, 89
Torphichen, 138
Town Council, 164
Toxicologist, 9, 141, 189, 190, 197
Toxicology, 191–193, 198, 204, 205
Traill, Thomas Stewart, 129
Transience, 283, 284
Tregellis, Mary Ann, 247
Trial, 10, 70, 73–77, 83, 85, 87,
    144, 145, 163, 176, 177,
    180, 203, 237, 241–243,
    245–247, 249, 257, 283
  Frenzel trial, 258
  Polte trial, 263

psychological, 259
sex crimes, 258, 261, 262, 265
transcript, 75
Trunk, 47, 54, 279–294
  steamer trunk, 285
Trunk murder, 11, 279, 280, 282,
    285, 286, 288, 292, 293
Twentieth century, 3, 6, 9, 217, 218,
    237, 260
Twenty-first century, 8

U
UK, 2–4, 9, 10, 70, 89, 191, 288
University, 146, 219
Upright citizens ('unbescholtene
    Bürger'), 259
USA, 2, 4, 10, 22, 213, 239, 240,
    286, 288

V
Vass, George, 162, 163, 177, 180
Violence, 234
Volksstimme, 257–259, 263–265,
    271, 273

W
Wales, 44, 48, 70, 94n74, 193, 203
Walker, Elizabeth Smith, 140
Walker, John, 138
Walker, William, 140
Watson, Sergeant Thomas, 167
Webster, John, 56
Weegee, *see* New York City
Weir, Walter, 78, 87
Wellcome Collection Forensics
    Exhibition, 131, 293

Welles, Orson, 290
West Riding Police Force, 201, 204
Wilson, Harold, 72
Witness, 7, 10, 19, 32, 43, 44, 46–48,
    55–57, 59, 76, 77, 79, 82,
    84, 86, 115, 127, 132, 133,
    135, 142, 144, 162, 163,
    167, 169–172, 177, 180,
    181, 185n65, 190, 204, 213,
    214, 216, 218, 221, 223,
    224, 241, 257–262,
    264–272, 286, 290
  virtual witness, 3, 10, 86–87, 213

Women's suffrage, 283
Wounds, 217, 219, 220, 222
Wyllie, Andrew, 225

Y

York Railway Museum, 49
Yorkshire, 6, 9, 196, 197
Yorkshire College, 191, 194, 197

Z

Zossen, 265

Printed by Printforce, the Netherlands